D0951997

DREYER'S ENGLISH

DREYER'S ENGLISH

An Utterly Correct Guide to Clarity and Style

BENJAMIN DREYER

RANDOM HOUSE

NEW YORK

Published in the United States by Random House,
an imprint and division of Penguin Random House LLC,
New York.

RANDOM HOUSE and the HOUSE colophon are
registered trademarks of Penguin Random House LLC.

A brief portion of this work was originally published by
The Toast (the-toast.net) in "Shirley Jackson and Me"
on August 4, 2015.
The backgrounds of the title and part-title pages are
from *Webster's Third New International Dictionary
of the English Language,* Unabridged (Springfield, Mass.:
Merriam-Webster, 1981) and are used here
by permission of the publisher.

LIBRARY OF CONGRESS CATALOGING-IN-PUBLICATION DATA
Names: Dreyer, Benjamin, author.
Title: Dreyer's English : an utterly correct guide to clarity and style /
Benjamin Dreyer.
Description: First edition. | New York : Random House, [2019] | Includes
bibliographical references and index.
Identifiers: LCCN 2018027979 | ISBN 9780812995701 | ISBN 9780812995718 (ebook)
Subjects: LCSH: Authorship—Technique.
Classification: LCC PN145 .D74 2019 | DDC 808.02—dc23
LC record available at https://lccn.loc.gov/2018027979

Printed in the United States of America on acid-free paper

randomhousebooks.com

6 8 9 7 5

Book design by Carole Lowenstein

For my parents, Diana and Stanley

For Robert

MARTHA. So? He's a biologist. Good for him. Biology's even better. It's less . . . abstruse.

GEORGE. Abstract.

MARTHA. ABSTRUSE! In the sense of recondite. (Sticks her tongue out at GEORGE) Don't you tell me words.

—Edward Albee, *Who's Afraid of Virginia Woolf?*

CONTENTS

INTRODUCTION

By Way of Introduction

I am a copy editor. After a piece of writing has been, likely through numerous drafts, developed and revised by the writer and by the person I tend to call the *editor* editor and deemed essentially finished and complete, my job is to lay my hands on that piece of writing and make it . . . better. Cleaner. Clearer. More efficient. Not to rewrite it, not to bully and flatten it into some notion of Correct Prose, whatever that might be, but to burnish and polish it and make it the best possible version of itself that it can be—to make it read even more like itself than it did when I got to work on it. That is, if I've done my job correctly.

On the most basic level, professional-grade copyediting entails making certain that everything on a page ends up spelled properly. (The genius writer who somehow can't spell is a mythical beast, but everyone mistypes things.) And to remind you of what you already likely know, spellcheck and autocorrect are marvelous accomplices—I never type without one or the other turned on—but they won't always get you to the word you meant to use. Copyediting also involves shaking loose and rearranging punctuation—I sometimes feel as if I spend half my life prying up commas and the other half tacking them down someplace else—and keeping an eye open for dropped words ("He went to store") and repeated words ("He went to the the store") and other glitches that can take root during writing and revision. There are also the rudiments of grammar to be minded, certainly—applied more formally for some writing, less formally for other writing.

Beyond this is where copyediting can elevate itself from what sounds like something a passably sophisticated piece of software should be able to accomplish—it can't, not for style, not for grammar (even if it thinks it can), and not even for spelling (more on spelling, much more on spelling, later)—to a true craft. On a good day, it achieves something between a really thorough teeth cleaning—as a writer once described it to me—and a whiz-bang magic act.

☙

Which reminds me of a story.

A number of years ago I was invited to a party at the home of a novelist whose book I'd worked on. It was a blazingly hot summer afternoon, and there were perhaps more people in attendance than the little walled-in garden of this swank Upper East Side townhouse could comfortably accommodate.

As the novelist's husband was a legendary theater and film director,[*] there were in attendance more than a few noteworthy actors and actresses, so while sweating profusely I was also getting in a lot of happy gawking.

My hostess thoughtfully introduced me to one actress in particular, one of those wonderfully grand theatrical types who seem, onstage, to be eight feet tall and who turn out, more often than not, to be quite compact, as this one was, and surprisingly lovely and delicate-looking for a woman who'd

---

[*] It's not name-dropping if I don't drop the name, right?

made her reputation playing, for lack of a better word, dragons.

It seemed that the actress had written a book.

"I've written a book," she informed me. A memoir, as it turned out. "And I must tell you that when I was sent the copyedited manuscript and saw it all covered with scrawls and symbols, I was quite alarmed. 'No!' I exclaimed. 'You don't understand!'"

By this time she'd taken hold of my wrist, and though her grip was light, I didn't dare to find out what would happen if I attempted to extricate myself from it.

"But as I continued to study what my copy editor had done," she went on, in a whisper that might easily have reached a theater's uppermost seats had she wanted it to, "I began to understand." She leaned in close, staring holes into my skull, and I was hopelessly enthralled. "'Tell me more,' I said."

Pause for effect.

"Copy editors," she intoned, and I can still hear every crisp consonant and orotund vowel, all these years later, "are like priests, safeguarding their faith."

Now, *that's* a benediction.*

꩜

I wandered into my job nearly three decades ago—a lot of people wandered into careers in those days; you could just sort of *do things*—after a few too many years post-university waiting on tables and bartending, attending revival-house double features, and otherwise faffing about. I had no idea what I wanted to be when I grew up, which is a problem when you've already grown up, but thanks to the intercession of a writer friend and a leap of faith on the part of his production editor—that's the person in a publishing house who squires a book through the copyediting and proofreading process—

---

* Oh, OK. The actress is Zoe Caldwell and the book in question is a charming, svelte little memoir called *I Will Be Cleopatra*. Seek it out.

I found myself doing freelance proofreading work: an assignment here and an assignment there until, after a while, I was taking on this sort of work full-time.

Now, proofreading—because that's your entrée into the business, especially if you have no experience whatsoever—is a basic and mechanical process, and my first jobs were simply to ensure that everything on the copyedited manuscript pages (you kept that stack to your left) had made its way properly onto the accompanying typeset pages (you kept that stack on the right). Mind you, we're even further back in the paper era than in the garden-party story, so what I was reading on the manuscript pages included not only the writer's original typing but layers of rewriting and revision in two sets of handwriting—the writer's own and the copy editor's—to say nothing of the copyeditorial directives indicated by those mysterious scrawls and symbols. Proofreading requires a good deal of attention and concentration, but it's all very binary, very yes/no: Something is right or something is wrong, and if it's wrong you're expected to notice it and, by way of yet more scrawling, repair it. It's like endlessly working on one of those spot-the-difference picture puzzles in an especially satanic issue of *Highlights for Children*.

As I dutifully worked away, I became increasingly fascinated by what I observed on the manuscript pages, a kind of conversation in dueling colored pencils between the writer and the copy editor. Because often—almost invariably—the copy editor had gone well beyond fixing misspellings, rearranging punctuation, and attending to errant subject-verb agreement and was digging deeper, more thoughtfully, and considerably more subjectively into the writer's prose: deleting words a sentence might live without, adding a word here or there in one that was perhaps too tightly constructed for its own good, reordering a paragraph so that it built its case more strongly, calling out the overuse of a writer's pet adjectives or adverbs. The copy editor might also suggest that a bit of prose was clumsy ("AU: AWK?" would be jotted in the margin)* or that a turn of phrase was stale and shopworn ("AU: CLICHÉ?"). Occasionally, if the copy editor had determined that the same point had been made one too many times, or was simply too obvious to be made at all, an entire sentence might simply be crossed out, and the note in the margin would read—saucily, I thought—"AU: WE KNOW."

That isn't to say that every suggestion a copy editor made was embraced by the writer. Though changes were often tacitly accepted simply by being left in place—or an author would indicate assent by crossing out the question mark in the circled "OK?" the copy editor had jotted in the margin— occasionally a correction or revision was itself crossed out, a row of percussive dots was penciled in underneath the original text, and the word "STET"—that's Latin, I learned, for "let it stand," a.k.a. "keep your hands to yourself"—would be marked alongside the revised, then unrevised text, occasionally accompanied by an exclamation point, also occasionally accompanied by a choice word or two of dissent.†

And that's how I learned to copyedit: by observing copyediting, how it was done and how writers responded to it, by taking note of the sorts of flaws, ranging from more or less inarguable errors of grammar to more or less arguable missteps of style and taste, and how copy editors addressed them. (More or less, more or less: Truly, I'm not hedge sitting. There are fewer absolutes in writing than you might think. More on that soon, and repeatedly.)

* "AU" is "author," and one needed to specify this because on occasion one was marginally addressing the "COMP," that is to say the compositor, or typesetter.

† "Can you give an example?" my own editor requested while we were working over this passage. Well, let's see. There was that one writer who, in overriding a copy editor's attempt to repair one of his (I must point out for the historical record) godawful sentences, sniffily noted "It's called style" in the margin. And the one who, in response to a perfectly demure piece of editorial advice, scrawled in what was either red crayon or blood, "WRITE YOUR OWN FUCKING BOOK."

Copyediting is a knack. It requires a good ear for how language sounds and a good eye for how it manifests itself on the page; it demands an ability to listen to what writers are attempting to do and, hopefully and helpfully, the means to augment it. One can, and certainly should, study the subject, if one is to do this sort of work professionally. Lord knows the world does not lack for books about grammar and word usage. But I do think that it's a craft whose knowledge can only be built on some mysterious predisposition. (The one thing I know that most copy editors have in common is that they were all early readers and spent much of their childhoods with their noses pressed into books.) As one of my colleagues once described it: You're attempting to burrow into the brains of your writers and do for, to, and with their prose what they themselves might have done for, to, and with it had they not already looked at each damn sentence 657 times.

∾

Which brings me, somewhat circuitously, to you, dear reader—I've always wanted to say that, "dear reader," and now, having said it, I promise never to say it again—and why we're here.

We're all of us writers: We write term papers and office memos, letters to teachers and product reviews, journals and blog entries, appeals to politicians. Some of us write books. All of us write emails.* And, at least as I've observed it, we all want to do it better: We want to make our points more clearly, more elegantly; we want our writing to be appreciated, to be more effective; we want—to be quite honest—to make fewer mistakes.

As I said, I've been doing this sort of work for a long time now, and my favorite thing about it is still the pleasure of assisting writers and conversing with them on the page, even if

---

* We also, many of us, text and tweet, and these activities have spawned their own rules, all of which lie outside the realm of this book.

the page now tends to be not paper on my desk but a Word file on my screen.

This book, then, is the next conversation. It's my chance to share with you, for your own use, some of what I do, from the nuts-and-bolts stuff that even skilled writers stumble over to some of the fancy little tricks I've come across or devised that can make even skilled writing better.

Or perhaps you're simply interested in what one more person has to say about the series comma.

Let's get started.

No. Wait. Before we get started:

The reason this book is not called *The Last Style Manual You'll Ever Need,* or something equally ghastly, is because it's not. No single stylebook can ever tell you everything you want to know about writing—no two stylebooks, I might add, can ever agree on everything you want to know about writing—and in setting out to write this book, I settled on my own ground rules: that I would write about the issues I most often run across while copyediting and how I attempt to address them, about topics where I thought I truly had something to add to the conversation, and about curiosities and arcana that interested or simply amused me. And that I would not attempt to replicate the guidance of the exhaustive books that still and always will sit, and be constantly referred to, on my own desk.* And, I should add, that I would remember, at least every now and then, to own up to my own specific tastes and noteworthy eccentricities and allow that just because I think

---

* For the record: *Words into Type,* a splendid volume that long ago went out of print but copies of which are easily found online, and *The Chicago Manual of Style,* whose edicts I don't always agree with but whose definitive bossiness is, in its way, comforting. I also commend to you *Merriam-Webster's Dictionary of English Usage,* and of course—I mean, *of course*—you need to own a dictionary: Get yourself a copy of *Merriam-Webster's Collegiate Dictionary*—in its eleventh edition, as of this writing. Whenever in this book I refer to the big fat stylebooks, these are the books I'm talking about.

something is good and proper and nifty you don't necessarily have to.

Though you should.

So, then, in the spirit of selective and idiosyncratic and, I hope, useful advice:

Let's get started.

PART I

The Stuff in the Front

CHAPTER 1

The Life-Changing Magic
of Tidying Up
(Your Prose)

Hᴇʀᴇ'ꜱ ʏᴏᴜʀ ꜰɪʀꜱᴛ ᴄʜᴀʟʟᴇɴɢᴇ:
Go a week without writing

- very
- rather
- really
- quite
- in fact

And you can toss in—or, that is, toss out—"just" (not in the sense of "righteous" but in the sense of "merely") and "so" (in the "extremely" sense, though as conjunctions go it's pretty disposable too).

Oh yes: "pretty." As in "pretty tedious." Or "pretty pedantic." Go ahead and kill that particular darling.

And "of course." That's right out. And "surely." And "that said."

And "actually"? Feel free to go the rest of your life without another "actually."*

If you can last a week without writing any of what I've come to think of as the Wan Intensifiers and Throat Clearers—I wouldn't ask you to go a week without *saying* them; that would render most people, especially British people, mute—you will at the end of that week be a considerably better writer than you were at the beginning.

CLARIFICATION NO. 1

Well, OK, go ahead and write them—I don't want you tripping over your own pencil every time you compose a sentence—but, having written them, go back and dispose of them. Every single one. No, don't leave that last one intact just because it looks cute and helpless. And if you feel that what's left is somehow missing something, figure out a better, stronger, more effective way to make your point.

CLARIFICATION NO. 2

Before you get all overwrought and but-but-but, I'm not saying never use them†—go count the "very"s in this book. I'm merely asking you to skip them for a week. A single measly little week. Now, as a show of good faith, and to demonstrate that even the most self-indulgent of us can and should every now and then summon up a little fortitude, I hereby pledge that this is the last time you'll see the word "actually" in this book.

For your own part, if you can abstain from these twelve terms for a week, and if you read not a single additional word of this book—if you don't so much as peek at the next page—I'll be content.

---

* "Actually" has been a weakness of mine my entire life, speaking and writing, and I realized that it was contagious the first time I heard my two-year-old nephew declare, "Actually, I like peas."

† Except for "actually," because, seriously, it serves no purpose I can think of except to irritate.

Well, no.

But it sounded good.

CHAPTER 2

Rules and Nonrules

I HAVE NOTHING AGAINST RULES. They're indispensable when playing Monopoly or gin rummy, and their observance can go a long way toward improving a ride on the subway. The rule of law? Big fan.

The English language, though, is not so easily ruled and regulated. It developed without codification, sucking up new constructions and vocabulary every time some foreigner set foot on the British Isles—to say nothing of the mischief we Americans have wreaked on it these last few centuries—and continues to evolve anarchically. It has, to my great dismay, no enforceable laws, much less someone to enforce the laws it doesn't have.*

Certain prose rules are essentially inarguable—that a sentence's subject and its verb should agree in number, for instance. Or that in a "not only x but y" construction, the x and

---

* That the French have had for centuries an *académie* that keeps a sharp and controlling eye on their language is why it's easier for a modern French speaker to read and understand Molière than it is for a modern English speaker to read and understand Shakespeare.

the y must be parallel elements. (More on this in Chapter 6: A Little Grammar Is a Dangerous Thing.) Why? I suppose because they're firmly entrenched, because no one cares to argue with them, and because they aid us in using our words to their preeminent purpose: to communicate clearly with our readers. Let's call these reasons the Four C's, shall we? Convention. Consensus. Clarity. Comprehension.

Also simply because, I swear to you, a well-constructed sentence sounds better. Literally sounds better. One of the best ways to determine whether your prose is well-constructed is to read it aloud. A sentence that can't be readily voiced is a sentence that likely needs to be rewritten.

A good sentence, I find myself saying frequently, is one that the reader can follow from beginning to end, no matter how long it is, without having to double back in confusion because the writer misused or omitted a key piece of punctuation, chose a vague or misleading pronoun, or in some other way engaged in inadvertent misdirection. (If you *want* to puzzle your reader, that's your own business.)

As much as I like a good rule, I'm an enthusiastic subscriber to the notion of "rules are meant to be broken"—once you've learned them, I hasten to add.

But let's, right now, attend to a few of what I think of as the Great Nonrules of the English Language. You've encountered all of these; likely you were taught them in school. I'd like you to free yourself of them. They're not helping you; all they're doing is clogging your brain and inciting you to look self-consciously over your own shoulder as you write, which is as psychically painful as it is physically impossible. And once you've done that, once you've gotten rid of them, hopefully* you can put your attention on vastly more important things.

---

* Oh, yes indeed. I'll meet you in Chapter 9: Peeves and Crotchets.

Why are they nonrules? So far as I'm concerned, because they're largely unhelpful, pointlessly constricting, feckless, and useless. Also because they're generally of dubious origin: devised out of thin air, then passed on till they've gained respectable solidity and, ultimately, have ossified. Language experts far more expert than I have, over the years, done their best to debunk them, yet these made-up strictures refuse to go away and have proven more durable than Keith Richards and Mick Jagger. Put together. Part of the problem, I must add, is that some of them were made up by ostensible and presumably well-meaning language experts in the first place, so getting rid of them can be a bit like trying to get a dog to stop chasing its own tail.

I'll dispatch these reasonably succinctly, with the hope that you'll trust that I've done my homework and will be happy to see them go. I'm mindful of Gertrude Stein's characterization of Ezra Pound as "a village explainer, excellent if you were a village, but if you were not, not," and no one wants to be that guy. Also, if you persist in insisting that these nonrules are real and valid and to be hewed to, all the expert citations in the world won't, I know through experience, change your mind one tiny little bit.

An admission: Quite a lot of what I do as a copy editor is to help writers avoid being carped at, fairly or—and this is the part that hurts—unfairly, by People Who Think They Know Better and Write Aggrieved Emails to Publishing Houses. Thus I tend to be a bit conservative about flouting rules that may be a bit dubious in their origin but, observed, ain't hurting nobody. And though the nonrules below are particularly arrant nonsense, I warn you that, in breaking them, you'll have a certain percentage of the reading and online-commenting populace up your fundament to tell you you're subliterate. Go ahead and break them anyway. It's fun, and I'll back you up.

THE BIG THREE

1. Never Begin a Sentence with "And" or "But."

No, *do* begin a sentence with "And" or "But," if it strikes your fancy to do so. Great writers do it all the time. As do even not necessarily great writers, like the person who has, so far in this book, done it a few times and intends to do it a lot more.

But soft, as they used to say, here comes a caveat:

An "And" or a "But" (or a "For" or an "Or" or a "However" or a "Because," to cite four other sentence starters one is often warned against) is not always the strongest beginning for a sentence, and making a relentless habit of using any of them palls quickly. You may find that you don't need that "And" at all. You may find that your "And" or "But" sentence might easily attach to its predecessor sentence with either a comma or a semicolon. Take a good look, and give it a good think.*

Let's test an example or two.

> Francie, of course, became an outsider shunned by all because of her stench. But she had become accustomed to being lonely.
> Francie, of course, became an outsider shunned by all because of her stench, but she had become accustomed to being lonely.

Which do you think Betty Smith, the author of *A Tree Grows in Brooklyn*, chose? The former, as it happens. Had I been Smith's copy editor, I might well have suggested the second, to make one coherent, connected thought out of two unnecessarily separated ones. Perhaps she'd have agreed, or

---

*As a copy editor, I'm always on my guard for monotonous repetition, whether it's of a pet word—all writers have pet words—or a pet sentence construction. Two sentences in a single paragraph beginning with the same introductory term, especially "But," are usually one sentence too many.

perhaps she'd have preferred the text as she'd written it, hearing it in her head as a solemn knell. Authors do often prefer their text the way they've written it.*

Here's another, in two flavors:

> In the hospital he should be safe, for Major Callendar
>   would protect him, but the Major had not come,
>   and now things were worse than ever.
> In the hospital he should be safe, for Major Callendar
>   would protect him. But the Major had not come,
>   and now things were worse than ever.

This is E. M. Forster, in *A Passage to India*, and I suspect you'll not be surprised to learn that version 2 is his. For one thing, version 1's a bit long. More important, version 2, with that definitive period, more effectively conveys, I'd say, the sense of dashed expectations, the reversal of fortune.

These are the choices that writers make, and that copy editors observe, and this is how you build a book.

One thing to add: Writers who are not so adept at linking their sentences habitually toss in a "But" or a "However" to create the illusion that a second thought contradicts a first thought when it doesn't do any such thing. It doesn't work, and I'm on to you.

2. Never Split an Infinitive.

To cite the most famous split infinitive of our era—and everyone cites this bit from the original *Star Trek* TV series, so zero points to me for originality—"To boldly go where no man has gone before."†

---

*It's not, I admit, entirely fair of me to present two isolated sentences and make a ruling about them. In copyediting, one is listening to the text not sentence by sentence but paragraph by paragraph and page by page, for a larger sense of sweep and rhythm.

†Latterly and laudably rewritten to "To boldly go where no one has gone before." Relatedly, on some not too distant page I'll touch briefly on the mess of

There's much more—*much more*—one could say on the subject, but I don't want to write about the nineteenth-century textual critic Henry Alford any more than you want to read about the nineteenth-century textual critic Henry Alford, so let's leave it at this: A split infinitive, as we generally understand the term, is a "to [verb]" construction with an adverb stuck in the middle of it. In the *Star Trek* example, then, an unsplit infinitive version would be "Boldly to go where no man has gone before" or "To go boldly where no man has gone before." If either of those sounds better to you, be my guest. To me they sound as if they were translated from the Vulcan.

Otherwise, let's skip right to Raymond Chandler. Again, as with the *Star Trek* phrase, everyone loves to cite Chandler on this subject, but it's for a God damn [*sic*] good reason. Chandler sent this note to the editor of *The Atlantic Monthly* in response to the copyediting of an article he'd written:

> By the way, would you convey my compliments to the purist who reads your proofs and tell him or her that I write in a sort of broken-down patois which is something like the way a Swiss waiter talks, and that when I split an infinitive, God damn it, I split it so it will stay split.

Over and out.

3. Never End a Sentence with a Preposition.

This is the rule that invariably (and wearily) leads to a rehash of the celebrated remark by Winston Churchill that Winston Churchill, in reality, neither said nor wrote:

"This is the kind of arrant pedantry up with which I will not put."

Let me say this about this: Ending a sentence with a prepo-

---

sexism and poor prose construction that is the plaque we humans left on the Moon back in 1969.

sition (*as, at, by, for, from, of,* etc.*) isn't always such a hot idea, mostly because a sentence should, when it can, aim for a powerful finale and not simply dribble off like an old man's unhappy micturition. A sentence that meanders its way to a prepositional finish is often, I find, weaker than it ought to or could be.

What did you do that for?

is passable, but

Why did you do that?

has some snap to it.

But to tie a sentence into a strangling knot to avoid a prepositional conclusion is unhelpful and unnatural, and it's something no good writer should attempt and no eager reader should have to contend with.

If you follow me.

The Celebrated
Ending-a-Sentence-with-a-Preposition Story

Two women are seated side by side at a posh dinner party, one a matron of the sort played in the old Marx Brothers movies by Margaret Dumont, except frostier, the other an easygoing southern gal, let's say, for the sake of the visuals, wearing a very pink and very ruffled evening gown.

Southern Gal, amiably, to Frosty Matron: So where y'all from?

Frosty Matron, no doubt giving Southern Gal a once-over through a lorgnette: I'm from a place where people don't end their sentences with prepositions.

Southern Gal, sweetly, after a moment's consideration: OK. So where y'all from, bitch?

---

* Were you taught not to use "etc." and to either spell it out as "et cetera" or to use "and so on" or something in that vein? So was I. Oh well.

THE LESSER SEVEN

I'm sure there are many more secondary nonrules than these seven, but these are the ones I'm most often asked about (or challenged on), so:

1. Contractions Aren't Allowed in Formal Writing.

This may be a fine rule to observe if you want to sound as if you learned English on your native Mars, but there's not a goshdarn thing wrong with "don't," "can't," "wouldn't," and all the rest of them that people naturally use, and without them many a piece of writing would turn out stilted and wooden. The likes of "I'd've" and "should've" are perhaps a bit too loosey-goosey outside casual prose, but generally speaking: Contractions are why God invented the apostrophe, so make good use of both.

Speaking of "should've":

The Flannery O'Connor Flowchart

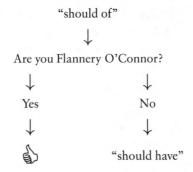

The correct construction is "should have" (also "could have," "would have," etc.). If you are not Flannery O'Connor, or Zora Neale Hurston, or William Faulkner, and you wish to convey the particular sound of a particular character's speech—and I warn you up front, more on it later, about the dangers of phonetic dialogue—please avail yourself of "should've," "could've," "would've," and so forth. They sound precisely the same, no one will yell at you, and we'll all be a lot happier.

2. The Passive Voice Is to Be Avoided.

A sentence written in the passive voice is one whose subject would, in a sentence constructed in the active voice, be its object. That is:

> Active Voice: The clown terrified the children.
> Passive Voice: The children were terrified by the clown.

In a sentence written in the passive voice, the thing that is acted upon is frontloaded, and the thing doing the acting comes at the end. In either case, we can easily agree that clowns are terrifying.

Often, in a sentence constructed in the passive voice, the actor is omitted entirely. Sometimes this is done in an attempt to call attention to a problem without laying blame ("The refrigerator door was left open") and sometimes, in weasel-like fashion, to avoid taking responsibility: "Mistakes were made," for instance, which, uttered on various occasions by various Bushes, may well be the motto of that political dynasty.

Here's a nifty trick that copy editors like to pass among themselves that comes in handy when you're assessing your own writing:

If you can append "by zombies" to the end of a sentence (or, yes, "by the clown"), you've indeed written a sentence in the passive voice.

All this said, there's nothing wrong with sentences constructed in the passive voice—you're simply choosing where you want to put the sentence's emphasis—and I see nothing objectionable in, say,

> The floors were swept, the beds made, the rooms aired out.

Since the point of interest is the cleanness of the house and not the identity of the cleaner.

But many a sentence can be improved by putting its true protagonist at the beginning, so that's something to be considered.*

It's also a good thing to know what the passive voice is—particularly if you're about to rail against the passive voice.

"A car rammed into counter-protesters during a violent white nationalist rally," for example, is a sentence that may legitimately be criticized for neglecting to point out that someone was at the wheel of said car; in this case, though, the avoidance of explicit agency is a moral failure, not a grammatical one.

3. Sentence Fragments. They're Bad.

I give you one of my favorite novel openers of all time, that of Charles Dickens's *Bleak House:*

> London. Michaelmas Term lately over, and the Lord Chancellor sitting in Lincoln's Inn Hall. Implacable November weather. As much mud in the streets as if the waters had but newly retired from the face of the earth, and it would not be wonderful to meet a Megalosaurus, forty feet long or so, waddling like an elephantine lizard up Holborn Hill. Smoke lowering down from chimney-pots, making a soft black drizzle, with flakes of soot in it as big as full-grown snow-flakes—gone into mourning, one might imagine, for the death of the sun. Dogs, undistinguishable in mire. Horses, scarcely better; splashed to their very blinkers. Foot passengers, jostling one another's umbrellas in a general infection of ill-temper, and losing their foot-hold at street-corners, where tens of thousands of other foot passengers have been slipping and sliding since the day broke (if this day ever broke), adding new deposits to the crust upon crust of mud, sticking at those

* By zombies.

points tenaciously to the pavement, and accumulating at compound interest.

Fog everywhere. Fog up the river, where it flows among green aits and meadows; fog down the river, where it rolls defiled among the tiers of shipping, and the waterside pollutions of a great (and dirty) city. Fog on the Essex marshes, fog on the Kentish heights. Fog creeping into the cabooses of collier-brigs; fog lying out on the yards, and hovering in the rigging of great ships; fog drooping on the gunwales of barges and small boats. Fog in the eyes and throats of ancient Greenwich pensioners, wheezing by the firesides of their wards; fog in the stem and bowl of the afternoon pipe of the wrathful skipper, down in his close cabin; fog cruelly pinching the toes and fingers of his shivering little 'prentice boy on deck. Chance people on the bridges peeping over the parapets into a nether sky of fog, with fog all round them, as if they were up in a balloon, and hanging in the misty clouds.*

A, Isn't that great? Don't you want to run off and read the whole novel now? Do! I'll wait here for three months. B, Please count up that excerpt's complete sentences, and let me know when you get beyond zero.†

You may not be Charles Dickens, but a well-wielded sen-

---

*After failed attempts to read *Oliver Twist* and *Great Expectations*—doubtless failed because it was easier, and quicker, to watch the movies—I picked up *Bleak House*, about which I knew nothing, and was immediately and utterly enthralled, starting with Dickens's dinosaur shout-out. It always struck me as weirdly out of place in this most Victorian of novels, but as a Dickens specialist eventually pointed out to me, Dickens always had his eye on what the public found fascinating at that precise second and, showman that he was, made good use of it. Which is why one should not be surprised—though almost everyone I know who's read *Bleak House* remarks on their utter WTF delight when they first got to it—at the eventual appearance in the novel of an instance of—spoiler alert—*spontaneous human combustion*. I mean, wow.

† One might, I suppose, argue that the second half of the bit beginning "As much mud" constitutes a complete and freestanding sentence. I'm not in the mood to make that argument, but you feel free.

tence fragment (or, as here, a passel of them) can be a delight-
ful thing.

That said, do wield your fragments with a purpose, and
mindfully. I lately find them, particularly in fiction, too often
used to establish a sort of hairy, sweaty, unbathed masculine
narrative voice, and what they end up sounding like is asthma.

4. A Person Must Be a "Who."

I don't know why violation of this nonrule flips some people
out, but it does, and they can get loudly cranky about it.

So just as loudly, for the people up there in the cheap seats:
A person can be a "that."

When Ira Gershwin wrote the lyrics of the song "The Man
That Got Away," he knew precisely what he was doing. The
man that got away, the teachers that attended the conference,
the whoevers that whatevered.

A thing, by the bye, can also be a "who," as in "an idea
whose time has come," because you certainly don't want to be
writing "an idea the time of which has come," or worse.
(Though worse might not exist.)

5. "None" Is Singular and, Dammit, Only Singular.

If you can find fault with the sentence "None of us are going
to the party," you have an ear better attuned to the English
language than mine.*

"None" can certainly be used singularly, if that which is to
be emphasized is a collection of discrete individuals: "None
of the suspects, it seems, is guilty of the crime." But if you
mean to emphasize the feelings, or actions, or inactions, of a
group *as a group,* none of us copy editors are going to stop
you from doing that.

---

* Or the ears of people with such flavorful names as H. W. Fowler, Wilson
Follett, and Roy H. Copperud, among others.

6. *"Whether" Must Never Be Accompanied by "Or Not."*

In many sentences, particularly those in which the word "whether" is being used as a straight-up "if," no "or not" is called for.

> Not only do I not care what you think, I don't care
> *whether* you think.

But see as well:

> Whether or not you like movie musicals, I'm sure
> you'll love *Singin' in the Rain*.

Try deleting the "or not" from that sentence and see what happens.

That's the whole thing: If you can delete the "or not" from a "whether or not" and your sentence continues to make sense, then go ahead and delete it. If not, not.

7. *Never Introduce a List with "Like."*

"Great writers of the twentieth century like Edith Wharton, Theodore Dreiser, and William Faulkner . . ."

Screech of brakes as a squad car of grammar police pulls that burgeoning sentence to the side of the road and demands that "like" be replaced with "such as."

I confess to some guilt here, as, like many of us, I had it drummed into my head that inclusive lists should be introduced exclusively with "such as," and that to commence such a list with "like" suggests comparison. By that logic, in the example above, Wharton, Dreiser, and Faulkner may be *like* great twentieth-century writers but are not *themselves* great twentieth-century writers.

But who could possibly read such a sentence and think such a thing?

And that's often the problem, isn't it? In writing and in so many things: that we accept things we're taught without thinking about them at all.

This particular nonrule, I eventually learned and you may be pleased to note, sprung up[*] only as recently as the mid-twentieth century, and it has little foundation in anything other than crotchet.

That said, there's nothing wrong with the slightly more grand-sounding "such as." But feel free to like "like."

[*] Hold on there, People Who Think They Know Better and Write Aggrieved Emails to Publishing Houses. "Sprung" rather than "sprang" is perfectly correct. Look it up.

CHAPTER 3

67 Assorted Things to Do (and Not to Do) with Punctuation

Dogmatizing about punctuation is exactly as foolish as dogmatizing about any other form of communication with the reader. All such forms depend on the kind of thing one is doing and the kind of effect one intends to produce.

—HENRY JAMES

IF WORDS ARE THE FLESH, MUSCLE, AND BONE OF PROSE, punctuation is the breath. In support of the words you've carefully selected, punctuation is your best means of conveying to the reader how you mean your writing to be read, how you mean for it to sound. A comma sounds different than a semicolon; parentheses make a different noise than dashes.

Some writers use as many bits of punctuation as they can think of. (The Mr. James quoted above often used so much of it, you'd think he was being paid by the dot and squiggle.) Some use as few as they can get away with.

Some writers use punctuation with impressionistic flair, and as a copy editor I do my best to support that, so long as the result is comprehensible and consistent.* Not all punctuation is discretionary, though. Typing or not typing even so much as a comma—in fact, especially a comma—can convey key information. The more regular and, you'll par-

---

* Not every writer is intent on being immediately comprehensible or in any way consistent, and a good copy editor working with a nascent James Joyce or Gertrude Stein will recognize and honor that. Even under the most regular circumstances, all a copy editor can do is advise; consent or nonconsent is up to the writer.

don the word, conventional your writing, the more, I'd suggest, you use punctuation in a regular and conventional fashion.

A general note: I'll cover here the punctuational issues/problems/knots/dilemmas I've most often encountered—the greatest hits, let's say—and those I think are most interesting. Any given piece of writing is going to present unique challenges—not just in punctuation—and those can be addressed only on a case-by-case basis. I'm also going to skip the kinds of punctuational quandaries that show up so infrequently they still send me scurrying for one of my big fat stylebooks. Which is what big fat stylebooks are for, so do keep yours handy, right next to this relatively slender, potent missive.

Another general note, which also happens to be a cultural one: I've observed over these last few decades that writers of all sorts use increasingly less punctuation. I guess it's part of the common tendency to be in a great big hurry. No harm with that reduction, and I'm sure you'll find some other use for this comma or that hyphen.

PERIODS

1.

Q. Two spaces after a period at the end of a sentence, right?

A. Wrong. I know that back when you were in seventh-grade typing class and pecking away at your Smith Corona Coronet Automatic 12, Mrs. Tegnell taught you to type a double space after a sentence-ending period, but you are no longer in the seventh grade, you are no longer typing on a typewriter, and Mrs. Tegnell is no longer looking over your shoulder. Either break yourself of the habit or, once you've finished writing whatever it is you're writing, do a global search-and-exterminate for double spaces, which will dispose of not only end-of-sentence offenders but those that have crept into your text between words as you cut, copied, pasted, and otherwise revised. If you don't, I will.*

2.

The fashion of punctuating acronyms and initialisms† with periods has, well, gone out of fashion, so one is far less likely nowadays to see F.B.I. than FBI, U.N.E.S.C.O. than UNESCO, etc. Insofar as academic degrees are concerned, I'm less keen on BA, MD, and PhD (rather than B.A., M.D., and Ph.D.), though I'm getting used to them, especially for the sorts of degrees that run to four or more letters, and especially in the service of those learned sorts who festoon their names with multiple degrees,‡ and am happy to save my instinctual squabbling for something else.§

---

* Whence the double space in the first place? There's contention and muddle attached to the subject, but here's an explanation I've appropriated from an online chum that covers as well as anything a subject I'm not particularly interested in in the first place: "In hand type and on typewriters, every character is the same width. A period centered in the type block or on a typewriter key thus makes space between it and the preceding letter, requiring an extra space after. Computer fonts have proportional space, and set the period right up against the preceding letter."

Some older folks I've encountered are furiously insistent about the eternal propriety of sentence-dividing double spaces. Likely they also advocate for the retention of the long *s*, and I wish them much fuccefs. If you're a younger person who's only ever typed on a computer keyboard, odds are good you were not taught the double-space thing, so feel free to slide past this subject altogether with the head-shaking insouciance of your generation.

† An acronym is an abbreviation pronounced as a word—NASA or UNESCO, for instance. The Brits tend to style these sorts of things as Nasa and Unesco and, worst of the worst, Aids, which makes my teeth itch. Once an acronym turns into a common word—likely you've forgotten that "radar" is short for "RAdio Detecting And Ranging" (how could you not forget that?) and that "laser" stands for "Light Amplification by Stimulated Emission of Radiation" (ditto)—one drops the capital letters altogether, as I've just done.

An initialism is an abbreviation pronounced letter by letter—as, say, FBI or CIA.

‡ If you please, please: You are not Dr. Jonas Salk, M.D. You are Dr. Jonas Salk or Jonas Salk, M.D. Have you forgotten what the *D* stands for?

§ By the way, you don't have a bachelors or masters degree; you have a bachelor's or master's degree. Maybe you have both.

3.

Those two-letter state abbreviations that the USPS—which I'm still tempted to style U.S.P.S. but won't—likes to see on envelopes (MA, NY, CA, and the like) do not take periods. They also shouldn't appear anywhere else but on envelopes and packages. In bibliographies and notes sections, and anywhere else you may need to abbreviate a state's name, please stick to the old-fashioned and more attractive Mass., N.Y., Calif., and so on. Or just be a grown-up and write the whole thing out.

4.

Some of us have a hard time dropping the periods from the abbreviation U.S., perhaps simply out of habit, perhaps because US looks to us like the (shouted) objective case of "we." Some of us were also taught to use U.S. (or that other thing) only as an adjective, as in "U.S. foreign policy," and to refer to the country nounwise only full-out as the United States. I persist in that distinction, because . . . because I do.

5.

Feel free to end a sentence shaped like a question that isn't really a question with a period rather than a question mark. It makes a statement, doesn't it.

COMMAS

6.

On arrival at Random House, I was taught that we had no house style. That is, each manuscript got the attentive copyedit it uniquely needed, and copy editors didn't perform any one-size-fits-all-whether-you-like-it-or-not Bed of Procrustes routine, applying this or that particular rule of punctuation, grammar, etc., to every manuscript, regardless of its needs, in the service of some house-proud notion of universal correctness.

Well, that was not entirely true. We did have one house standard, to be applied to each and every manuscript we squired through the process:

THE SERIES COMMA

The series comma is the comma that separates the last two bits in a list of words or phrases before the concluding conjunction "and" or "or" or sometimes even "but," as in:

> apples, pears, oranges, tangerines, tangelos, bananas, and cherries

The "bananas, and" comma. That's the series comma.

Quite possibly you know this comma as the Oxford comma—because, we're told, it's traditionally favored by the editors at Oxford University Press. But as a patriotic American, and also because that attribution verges on urbane legendarianism, I'm loath to perpetuate that story. Or you may be familiar with the term "serial comma," though for me "serial" evokes "killer," so no again.

Whatever you want to call it: Use it. I don't want to belabor the point; neither am I willing to negotiate it. Only godless savages eschew the series comma.

No sentence has ever been harmed by a series comma, and many a sentence has been improved by one.

In a tote-up of grocery items, as above, the series comma ensures that the final two items in a list aren't seen as having a special relationship, aren't seen after a number of singletons as somehow constituting a couple. In a more complicated sentence, the use of the series comma simply makes it clear that once I've made some particularly deft point, deftly said everything I have to say on the subject, and moved on to a final deft point, the reader doesn't trip from the penultimate deft point to the ultimate deft point thinking that it's all one big deft point.

Many journalist types, I've observed, abhor the series comma because they've been trained to abhor it and find its use as maddening as its champions find its nonuse infuriating. Many Brits, including even Oxford Brits, also avoid it. For whatever it's worth to you, everyone I've ever encountered in U.S. book publishing uses it.

One thing, though: Commas can't do everything, not even series commas. There's a sentence, reputed to have shown up in *The Times*,* often schlepped out in defense of the series comma, and though I'm weary of seeing it, I schlep it out myself to point out its weakness as a series-comma defense. So here it is, hopefully for the last time in all our lives, though I doubt it:

> Highlights of his global tour include encounters with Nelson Mandela, an 800-year-old demigod and a dildo collector.

Oh la la, one is intended to merrily note, is Nelson Mandela really an eight-hundred-year-old demigod and a dildo collector?

Oh la la, I note, even if one sets a series comma, as in:

> Highlights of his global tour include encounters with Nelson Mandela, an 800-year-old demigod, and a dildo collector.

Mandela can still be an eight-hundred-year-old demigod.

Some sentences don't need to be repunctuated; they need to be rewritten.†

---

* *The Times* is a U.K. newspaper whose name is not, never has been, and likely never will be *The London Times*. *The New York Times* is an American newspaper that you may refer to, familiarly, as "the *Times*," no matter that it persists in referring to itself, grandly and pushily, as The Times.

† "Highlights of his global tour include encounters with a dildo collector, an 800-year-old demigod, and Nelson Mandela." Was that so hard? And seriously: What sort of global tour was that?

7.

Re the school of "Apply the series comma when it's needed for clarity and not when it's not needed for clarity":

7a. One person's clarity is another person's "Huh?" Writers who profess to adhere to this notion, I find, often apply the series comma precisely where it might be skipped with no loss in clarity and skip it precisely where it's desperately needed.

7b. It uses up fewer brain cells simply to apply the damn thing every time, brain cells that might well be applied in the cure of more serious issues, like grammatical blunders and one's overuse of the word "murmur."

8.

Exception to the rule: An ampersand in a series rather than an "and"—this sort of thing tends to turn up in book or film titles, the names of law firms (and other companies that want to invest themselves with the cachet of law firms), and nowhere else, but it's a thing to know—negates the necessity of a series comma, mostly because the result would be unsightly. Thus, oh, say:

Eats, Shoots & Leaves

and certainly not

Eats, Shoots, & Leaves

which is a bit belt-and-suspenders, don't you think?

9.

You might well, if you're relatively sparing with your commas, write

On Friday she went to school.

or

Last week Laurence visited his mother.

So long as the commaless rendition is clear and under-standable, you're on safe ground.

The longer the introductory bit, the more likely you are to want/need a comma:

> After three days home sick with a stomachache, she returned to school.
> On his way back from a business trip, Laurence visited his mother.

10.

But do avoid crashing proper nouns, as in

> In June Truman's secretary of state flew to Moscow.

Lest you want your reader wondering who June Truman is and what precisely got into her secretary of state.

Or take note of the sentence above I initially composed as beginning, "On arrival at Random House I was informed," which might set you, if only for a millisecond, to speculating about Random House II and Random House III.*

11.

Sometimes a comma makes no sense at all.

> Suddenly, he ran from the room.

Makes it all rather less sudden, doesn't it.

12.

A comma splice is the use of a comma to join two sentences when each can stand on its own—as in, just picking an ex-ample out of more or less thin air:

---

* When Alan Bennett's 1991 play *The Madness of George III* was filmed, we're told, the title was tweaked to *The Madness of King George* so as not to alienate potential attendees—especially ignorant Yanks—who hadn't seen *The Madness of George* and *The Madness of George II*. Though many such too-good-to-be-true stories turn out to be utter malarkey, this one's partly for real.

> She did look helpless, I almost didn't blame him for
> smiling at her that special way.*

As a rule you should avoid comma splicing, though exceptions can be and frequently are made when the individual
sentences are reasonably short and intimately connected:
"He came, he saw, he conquered" or "Your strengths are
your weaknesses, your weaknesses are your strengths." Another exception arises in fiction or fictionlike writing in
which such a splice may be effective in linking closely related
thoughts or expressing hurried action and even a semicolon—
more on the glorious semicolon below—is more pause than
is desired.

Another thin-air example, from Walter Baxter's undeser-
vedly obscure 1951 novel *Look Down in Mercy*:

> He had never noticed [the sunset] before, it seemed
> fantastically beautiful.

As comma splices go, this one's not doing anyone any
harm, and there's no issue here with comprehension, so let's
let it go.

The result of a comma splice is known as—and you may
well recall this term from middle school English class—
a run-on sentence. One may meet a fair number of people
who like to aim that term at any old sentence that happens
to be long and twisty and made up of any number of innu-
merable bits divided by semicolons, dashes, parentheses, and
whatever else the writer may have had on hand. Nay. A long
sentence is a long sentence, it's only a run-on sentence when
it's not punctuated in the standard fashion. Like that one
just now.

---

*Let it be known that on February 2, 2018, when I was supposed to be typ-
ing up this section on comma splices, I was instead reading *The G-String Murders*, a novel by Gypsy Rose Lee, from which these words are taken.

13.

The vocative comma—or the comma of direct address—is the comma separating a bit of speech from the name (or title or other identifier) of the person (or sometimes the thing) being addressed. As commas go, it's not particularly controversial. No one—at least no one I'd care to associate with—would favor

> I'll meet you in the bar Charlie.

over

> I'll meet you in the bar, Charlie.

Right?

And so it goes with "Good afternoon, Mabel," "I live to obey, Your Majesty," "Please don't toss me into the hoosegow, Your Honor," and "I'll get you, my pretty, and your little dog too."

And yet—there's always an "and yet"—while copyediting one frequently runs into the likes of

> And Dad, here's another thing.

or

> But Mom, you said we could go to the movies.[*]

which one invariably corrects to

> And, Dad, here's another thing.

and

> But, Mom, you said we could go to the movies.

Copy editors periodically run into pushback—generally accompanied by a put-out "But my rhythm!"—on that comma, but they should hold firm, and writers should get over themselves. It's just a comma, and it's a proper and meaningful

---

[*] Not to be confused with an utterly correct "But Mom said we could go to the movies."

comma, and no one's pausing in midsentence to take a walk around the block.*

This is as good a place as any, I suppose, to note that honorifics either attached to names or used in place of them should be capped,† as in the aforementioned

I live to obey, Your Majesty.

and

Please don't toss me into the hoosegow, Your Honor.

Similarly, when one is speaking to one's mother or father:

I live to obey, Mom.

and

Please don't toss me into the hoosegow, Dad.

But: A passing casual reference, not in direct address, to one's mom or dad does not require a capital letter.

A bit of copyeditorial controversy tends to pop up when a writer offers something like:

I'm on my way to visit my Aunt Phyllis.

Which many copy editors will attempt to downgrade to:

I'm on my way to visit my aunt Phyllis.

Writers tend to balk at this sort of thing, and I tend to side with them. I myself had an aunt named Phyllis, and so far as I was concerned, her name was Aunt Phyllis. And thus I refer to her, always, as my Aunt Phyllis.‡

---

* The NSA may be reading your emails and texts, but I'm not. If you prefer "Hi John" to "Hi, John," you go right ahead.

† This does not apply to generic references to someone being addressed as "mister," "miss," "sir," or "ma'am," neither does it apply to terms of endearment like "sweetheart," "darling," "cupcake," or "honey" (unless the honey's name is Honey).

‡ Noting, to be sure, that a biographer would refer to, say, "Henry VIII's

On the other hand, I'd be more than happy to refer to "my grandmother Maude," because that is who she was, not what she was called.*

Note, by the way, that I do not refer to "my grandmother, Maude," as I—like everyone else, I suppose—had two grand-mothers.† Though I might well refer to "my maternal grand-mother, Maude." (See "The 'Only' Comma," in Section 16, below.)

14.

We were all thoroughly indoctrinated in grade school to pre-cede or follow dialogue with a comma in constructions like

> Atticus said dryly, "Do not let this inspire you to fur-ther glory, Jeremy."

or

> "Keep your temper," said the Caterpillar.

It should be noted, though, that this rule does not apply in constructions in which dialogue is preceded or followed by some version of the verb "to be" ("is," "are," "was," "were," that lot), as in:

> Lloyd's last words were "That tiger looks highly petta-ble."

or

> "Happy New Year" is a thing one ought to stop saying after January 8.

In each of these cases, the phrase in question is less dia-logue than a noun-in-quote-marks, and thus no comma is called for.

---

aunt Mary Tudor," presuming that Henry was not in the habit of cozily address-ing her as "Aunt Mary Tudor."

* She was called "Nana," if you must know.

† The other was Lillian.

15.

> Will you go to London too?
> Will you go to London, too?

Q. When do I precede a sentence-ending "too" with a comma, and when not?

A. Whichever you choose, the other way will look better.

I spent a great many years periodically revisiting my big fat stylebooks in an attempt to get it into my head how to properly do the "too" thing, and the explanations never sank in. In the examples above, does one of them mean "Will you go to London as well as Paris?" and does one of them mean "Will you as well as your mother go to London?" I haven't the foggiest. So to blazes with it. If you can hear a comma before the "too," feel free to use it. If you can't, feel free to not.

16.

THE "ONLY" COMMA

If a writer writes a sentence like

> He traveled to Pompeii with his daughter Clara.

a copy editor will, if the fact is not already known to the copy editor, query in the margin:

> AU: Only daughter? If so, comma.

Thus the comma I choose to refer to—since I am perpetually confused by the grammar terms "restrictive" and "nonrestrictive" and can never remember which is meant to be which—as the "only" comma.

"Only" commas (except at the very ends of sentences, they travel in pairs) are used to set off nouns that are, indeed, the only one of their kind in the vicinity, as in, say,

> Abraham Lincoln's eldest son, Robert, was born on
> August 1, 1843.

The notion being that as one can have only one eldest son, his name in this sentence is an interesting, noteworthy, yet *inessential* piece of information. Thus if I encounter

Abraham Lincoln's eldest son was born on August 1, 1843.

there can be no question that it's Robert who is being spoken of, rather than the subsequent Edward or Willie or Tad, whether Robert is named or not.

Conversely, in a sentence lacking the unique modifier "eldest," one must be told which son is being spoken of, thus:

Lincoln's son Robert was an eyewitness to the assassination of President Garfield.

Or, say:

George Saunders's book *Lincoln in the Bardo* concerns the death of Abraham Lincoln's son Willie.

Again, it's crucial, not merely interesting, that we know which of Abraham Lincoln's sons is being spoken of, and that the son in question is not Robert, Edward, or Tad.

At the other end of the spectrum, then, be careful not to set an "only" comma where there is no only-ness, as in, say:

The Pulitzer Prize–winning novelist, Edith Wharton, was born in New York City.

Because Mrs. Wharton is merely one of many winners of the Pulitzer, there should be no "only" comma.

---

*Best Illustration of the Necessity
of the "Only" Comma
I've Ever Managed to Rustle Up*

Elizabeth Taylor's second marriage, to Michael Wilding
Elizabeth Taylor's second marriage to Richard Burton

17.

The "only" comma rule is also helpful in differentiating between "that" and "which," if differentiating between "that" and "which" is your bag.

If you're about to offer a piece of information that's crucial to your sentence, offer it up without a comma and with a "that":

> Please fetch me the Bible that's on the table.

Which is to say: Fetch me the Bible that is on the table rather than the Bible that's under the couch or the Bible that's poised picturesquely on the window seat.

If you're offering a piece of information that's perhaps interesting amplification but might well be deleted without harm, offer it up with a comma and a "which":

> Please fetch me the Bible, which is on the table.

One Bible and one Bible only.

The "that" vs. "which" rule is not universally observed, I must note. Some writers find it pushily constricting and choose between the two by ear. I find it helpful and, admiring consistency as I do, apply it consistently.

18.

What goes up must come down, and that which commences with a comma, if it is an interruption, must also end with one, as in:

> Queen Victoria, who by the end of her reign ruled over a good fifth of the world's population, was the longest-reigning monarch in British history till Elizabeth II surpassed her record in 2015.

It's that comma after "population" I'm wanting you to keep a good eye on, because it has a tendency to go missing. It's so frequently omitted in published British prose that for a long time I thought they had some national rule against it. They don't. They're just sloppy.

That concluding comma has a particular tendency to get forgotten in sentences in which a parenthetical has been stuffed, turducken-like, into the interrupting bit, as in:

> Queen Victoria, who by the end of her reign ruled over a good fifth of the world's population (not all of whom were her own relatives, though it often seemed that way), was the longest-reigning monarch in British history till Elizabeth II surpassed her record in 2015.

That error gets past reasonably adept copy editors with a bit too much frequency, so be better than reasonably adept copy editors, please.

COLONS

Colons are not merely introductory but presentational. They say: Here comes something! Think of colons as little trumpet blasts, attention-getting and ear-catching. Also loud. So don't use so many of them that you give your reader a headache.

19.

If what follows a colon is a full sentence, begin that full sentence with a capital letter, which signals to your reader: What's about to commence includes a subject, a verb, the works, and should be read as such.

Post-colon lists of things or fragmentary phrases should begin with a lowercase letter: items on a grocery list, the novels of a particular author, etc.

This differentiation is by no means universally recommended, much less observed, and writers who were trained to commence anything that follows a colon with a lowercase letter (a convention I find puzzling, as if suggesting that a sentence following a colon is somehow not a legitimate sentence) bristle at it, but I consider it a valuable way to signal to readers what flavor of text they're about to read and to avoid sending them scurrying grumpily back to the colon once they realize that what they thought was going to be a sentence isn't one, or that what they thought wasn't going to be a sentence is one.

APOSTROPHES

20.

Before we get to what you do use apostrophes for, let's recount what you don't use them for.

Step back, I'm about to hit the CAPS LOCK key.

DO NOT EVER ATTEMPT TO USE AN APOSTROPHE TO PLURALIZE A WORD.

"NOT EVER" AS IN "NEVER."

You may reapproach.

Directing their disapproval toward miswritten produce signs advertising "banana's" and "potato's" (or "potatoe's" or even "potato'es"), the Brits have dubbed such incorrectly wielded squiggles "greengrocer's apostrophes." In America, where we don't have greengrocers, we should, I'd say, call them something else. The term I was first taught was "idiot apostrophe,"* but that's not really nice, is it.

Let's simply call them errant apostrophes. Which is kind of classy, don't you think?†

In any event, don't use them. Not for bananas, potatoes, bagels, princesses, Trumans, Adamses, Obamas, or whatever else you've got more than one of.

---

* I was recently informed that *Deppenapostroph* ("idiot's apostrophe") is an established term in German, so the fact that I learned "idiot apostrophe" from a native German speaker now makes a bit more sense. The Dutch, I have also been informed, so long as we're mucking about in western Europe, do properly use apostrophes in the formation of some of their plurals, more power to them.

† If there's a less classy word in the English language to describe classiness than "classy," I'd like to know what it is.

For a modest monthly fee I will come to wherever you are, and when, in an attempt to pluralize a word,* you so much as reach for the apostrophe key, I will slap your hand.

21.

The pluralization of abbreviations, too, requires no apostrophes. More than one CD = CDs. More than one ID = IDs. More than one ATM = ATMs. Etc.

22.

To say nothing of dos and don'ts, yeses and nos, etc.†

23.

There's no such word as "their's." Or "your's."

24.

Here comes a major on-the-other-hand, though: *Do* use an apostrophe to pluralize a letter.

One minds one's p's and q's.
One dots one's i's and crosses one's t's.
One brings home on one's report card four B's and
     two C's.‡

25.

I'll wager you're adept at the use of apostrophes for simple possessives:

the dog's toy
Meryl Streep's umpteenth Oscar

---

*Emphasis, I should add, on the word "word." See entry 24, below.

†Some people, finding "nos" as the plural of "no" to be unsightly, opt for "noes." Which is no beauty contest winner either.

‡Some favor omitting the apostrophe when pluralizing capital letters, but I can't say I care for the sight of As for more than one A or Us for more than one letter U. For, I'd say, obvious reasons.

As to common—that is, not proper—nouns ending with an *s*, one doesn't, at least not in recently published text,* encounter the likes of

the boss' office
the princess' tiara

which I find positively spooky-looking, and for most of us, then,

the boss's office
the princess's tiara

is the no-brainer way to go.

Trouble knocks at the door, though, when terminal *s*'s occur at the ends of proper nouns. When the talk turns to, say, the writer of *Great Expectations* and *Our Mutual Friend* or the urban activist and author of *The Death and Life of Great American Cities* or the nemesis of said urban activist and author, how do we style their ownership?

Well, I can certainly tell you how *I* style them:

Charles Dickens's novels
Jane Jacobs's advocacy
Robert Moses's megalomania

Though you may come across much discussion elsewhere regarding the appending or not appending of post-apostrophe *s*'s based on pronunciation,† convention, or what day of the week it is, I think you'll find that, as with the universal appli-

---

*Sometimes I'll read old books as much for the pleasure of their old-fashioned stylistic oddities as for their actual content. We all have to make our own fun.

†I find specious the notion that you should or even could determine whether to 's or not to 's based on pronunciation, given that there's no universal rule for the pronunciation of proper noun possessives, much less for their construction. And if pronunciation guided orthography, we wouldn't have words like "knight," would we.

cation of the series comma, you'll save yourself a lot of thinking time by not thinking about these *s*'s and just applying them.

I'd even urge you to set aside the Traditional Exceptions for Antiquity and/or Being the Son of God and go with:

Socrates's
Aeschylus's
Xerxes's
Jesus's

26.

A warning:

Hasty typing fingers are apt to render the likes of

Jane Jacobs's activism

as

Jane Jacob's activism

As typos go, that sort of thing is perilously easy to commit and to overlook. Be careful.

27.

THE POSSESSIVIZATION OF DONALD TRUMP, JR.
A GRAND GUIGNOL IN ONE ACT

In July 2017 one of our nation's preëminent if perhaps somewhat self-delightedly parochial magazines foisted upon the world this headline:

DONALD TRUMP, JR.,'S LOVE FOR RUSSIAN DIRT

The writer Michael Colton, in an aghast tweet, identified this particular method of rendering a possessive "period-comma-apostrophe bullshit," which may not be the precise technical term for it but which does just fine anyway.

Let me say this about that:

That's not how this works. That's not how any of this works.

If you are a younger or more forward-thinking person, you may already render the names of photocopied offspring commalessly, thus:

Donald Trump Jr.

In which case you've got it easy:

Donald Trump Jr. is a perfidious wretch.

and thus:

Donald Trump Jr.'s perfidy

Old-school construction, though, sets off a "Jr."* with commas, as in:

Donald Trump, Jr., is a perfidious wretch.

When possessivizing such a person, your options are

- that horror noted above, which I'll refrain from repeating
- Donald Trump, Jr.'s perfidy (which is admittedly a little unbalanced)
- Donald Trump, Jr.'s, perfidy (better balanced, and at least not eye-stabbingly ugly)

You choose.†

28.

Let's move on to plural proper noun possessives, over which many tears have been shed, particularly around Christmas-card time.

---

* And, for that matter, a "Sr.," though in truth there's no reason for the original owner of a name, whether he's replicated or not (and it's almost always a he; there are precious few female Sr./Jr. combos), to set himself off as "Sr." He got there first; it's his name.

† Psst. Take the middle option.

First we have to properly construct the plurals themselves. So then:

Harry S. and Bess Truman = the Trumans
John F. and Jacqueline Kennedy = the Kennedys*
Barack H. and Michelle Obama = the Obamas

And, lurching backward to the birth of our republic:

John and Abigail Adams = the Adamses

The pluralization of *s*-ending proper nouns seems to trip up a lot of people, but John and Abigail are the Adamses, as are John Quincy and Louisa, as are Rutherford B. and Lucy the Hayeses, and that seems to be that for *s*-ending presidents, but you get the point.

People who are perfectly content to keep up with the Joneses—and I'll wager the Joneses are good and tired of receiving Christmas cards addressed to "the Jones's"—sometimes balk at the sight of the Adamses, the Hayeses, the Reynoldses, the Dickenses, and the rest, but balk all you like, that's how the game is played.† If it's bothersome to you, you may address your Christmas card to, say, "the Adams family."

As to the possessives, then, a relative piece of cake:

the Trumans' singing daughter
the Adamses' celebrated correspondence
the Dickenses' trainwreck of a marriage

29.

If Jeanette has some pencils and Nelson has some pencils and Jeanette and Nelson are not sharing their pencils, those pencils are:

---

*People do occasionally trip over the pluralization of *y*-ending proper nouns, overextending the usual jelly/jellies, kitty/kitties formula. Nonetheless, JFK and Jackie were resolutely not "the Kennedies."

†This foolproof system doesn't, alas, easily or attractively carry over to non-English *s*-ending names. Even I wouldn't address René and his wife, had he had one and had they been on my Christmas-card list, as "the Descarteses."

Jeanette's and Nelson's pencils

But if Jeanette and Nelson reject individual ownership and pursue a socialist policy of collectivization for the betterment of humankind, those pencils are now:

Jeanette and Nelson's pencils

Well, truly I suppose they're then the people's pencils, but you get the point.

30.

Q. Is it "farmer's market" or "farmers' market" or "farmers market"?

A. I'm presuming there's more than one farmer, so out goes "farmer's market."

As to the other two, is it a market belonging to farmers or a market made up of farmers?

I say the latter, so:

farmers market*

(I'm reasonably, hopefully certain that no one will mistake a farmers market as a market in which one might purchase a farmer.)

31.

Though it has its champions, the style decision to elide a title's *The* in a possessive construction, as in:

Carson McCullers's *Heart Is a Lonely Hunter*

will always make me wrinkle my nose, and it can lead to such eyebrow raisers as

James Joyce's *Dead*

---

* Let's hold to "ladies' room," though, if only for parity with "men's room."

which looks to me like either a shocked headline or a bit of Dublin toilet graffiti.

SEMICOLONS

32.

> I love semicolons like I love pizza; fried pork dump-
> lings; Venice, Italy; and the operas of Puccini.

Why does the sentence above include semicolons?

Because the most basic use of semicolons is to divide the items in a list any of whose individual elements mandate a comma—in this case, Venice, Italy.

Now, I might certainly have avoided semicolons by reordering the elements in the list, thus:

> I love semicolons like I love pizza, fried pork dump-
> lings, the operas of Puccini, and Venice, Italy.

But semicolons are unavoidable when you must write the likes of:

> Lucy's favorite novels are *Raise High the Roof Beam,
> Carpenters; Farewell, My Lovely;* and *One Time,
> One Place.*

Because:

> Lucy's favorite novels are *Raise High the Roof Beam,
> Carpenters, Farewell, My Lovely,* and *One Time,
> One Place.*

Well, how many novels is that, anyway? Three? Five?

Lucy has fascinating taste in novels, I have to say.

But if that were the sum total use of semicolons, they would not invite, from certain writers who should certainly know better, stuffy derision.

For instance:

> Do not use semicolons. They are transvestite her-
> maphrodites representing absolutely nothing. All
> they do is show you've been to college.*

I counter this with a lovely remark by author Lewis
Thomas from *The Medusa and the Snail:*

> The things I like best in T. S. Eliot's poetry, especially in
> the *Four Quartets,* are the semicolons. You cannot hear
> them, but they are there, laying out the connections be-
> tween the images and the ideas. Sometimes you get a
> glimpse of a semicolon coming, a few lines farther on,
> and it is like climbing a steep path through woods and see-
> ing a wooden bench just at a bend in the road ahead, a
> place where you can expect to sit for a moment, catching
> your breath.

I've been known to insist that the only thing one needs to
say in defense of semicolons is that Shirley Jackson liked
them.† In support of that, I've also been known to whip out
this, the opening paragraph of Jackson's masterwork *The
Haunting of Hill House:*

> No live organism can continue for long to exist sanely
> under conditions of absolute reality; even larks and katy-
> dids are supposed, by some, to dream. Hill House, not
> sane, stood by itself against its hills, holding darkness
> within; it had stood so for eighty years and might stand
> for eighty more. Within, walls continued upright, bricks
> met neatly, floors were firm, and doors were sensibly shut;

---

* I've run across the assertion that this statement—it's Kurt Vonnegut's, to
name the name—was meant as a joke; I don't buy it, and even as a joke it's bad.

† More than likely, you read Jackson's short story "The Lottery" in high
school or thereabouts. She's one of the great prose stylists of the twentieth century and, except by the coterie of those of us who idolize her, woefully underappreciated.

silence lay steadily against the wood and stone of Hill House, and whatever walked there, walked alone.*

One paragraph, three semicolons. One might, I suppose, have replaced those semicolons with periods and started each following clause anew, as an independent sentence. The result, though, would have been the unmooring, the disconnection, of these tightly woven, almost claustrophobic ideas, and a paragraph that grabs you by the hand and marches you from beginning to end would have devolved into a collection of plain old sentences.

While we're here, I'd also like to celebrate that paragraph's final comma, perhaps my favorite piece of punctuation in all of literature. One might argue that it's unnecessary—even grammatically uncalled-for—but there it is, the last breath of the paragraph, the author's way of saying, "This is your last chance to set this book down and go do something else, like work in your garden or stroll down the street for an ice cream cone. Because from this point on it's just you, and me, and whatever it is that walks, and walks alone, in Hill House."

I dare you to walk away.

PARENTHESES

33.

A midsentence parenthetical aside (like this one) begins with a lowercase letter and concludes (unless it's a question or even an exclamation!) without terminal punctuation.

When a fragmentary parenthetical aside comes at the very

---

*Rather than cut and paste this paragraph from some handy online source, I typed it out, because doing so gave me a little thrill. Once upon a time, I typed out in full Jackson's short story "The Renegade" to see whether doing so might make me better appreciate how beautifully constructed the story was. It did. It's an exercise you might want to try out on one of your own favorite pieces of writing, if you have the time.

end of a sentence, make sure that the period stays outside the aside (as here).

(Only a freestanding parenthetical aside, like this one, begins with a capital letter and concludes with an appropriate bit of terminal punctuation inside the final parenthesis.)

34.

This is correct:

> Remind me again why I care what this feckless nonentity (and her eerie husband) think about anything.

This is not correct:

> Remind me again why I care what this feckless nonentity (and her eerie husband) thinks about anything.

An "and" is an "and," and the use of parentheses (or commas or dashes) to break up a plural subject for whatever reason does not negate the pluralness of the subject. Now, if instead of writing "and," I'd written "to say nothing of," "as well as," or "not to mention," then I'd have made me a singular subject:

> Remind me again why I care what this feckless nonentity (to say nothing of her eerie husband) thinks about anything.*

35.

TAKES ONE TO KNOW ONE; OR, DO AS I SAY, NOT AS I DO
As a serial abuser of parentheses, I warn you against their overuse, particularly in the conveyance of elbow-nudging joshingness. One too many coy asides and you, in the person

---

* "You may take fire on this one," my copy editor helpfully points out, noting that *Chicago Manual of Style* (and even *Webster's Dictionary of English Usage*) disagree with me. Fire away.

of your writing, will seem like a dandy in a Restoration comedy stepping down to the footlights and curling his hand around his mouth to confidentially address the audience. One rather needs a beauty mark and a peruke to get away with that sort of thing.

36.

A magazine journalist of my acquaintance once confided that he avoided parentheticals because his editor, when looking to cut words in the interests of minimizing the writer's use of precious print real estate, would home in on them and delete, delete, delete.

BRACKETS

37.

Brackets—or square brackets, as they're called by people who call parentheses "round brackets"—serve a limited but crucial purpose.

First: If you find yourself making a parenthetical comment within a parenthetical comment, the enclosed parenthetical comment is set within brackets. But it's extraordinarily unattractive on the page (I try to find a way around it [I mean, truly, do you like the way this looks?], at least whenever I can), so avoid it.

Second: Any time you find yourself interpolating a bit of your own text into quoted material (a helpfully added clarifying first name, for instance, when the original text contained only a surname) or in any other way altering a quotation, you must—and I mean must—enclose your interpolation in brackets.*

---

*Random House books and book covers, I'm proud to point out, are positively festooned with brackets—and, as well, ellipses for deletions—for the tiniest alterations to published reviews, even unto the likes of "[A] great novel . . . about the human condition" when the original review referred to "this great novel that tells us many things about the human condition." Though this sort of

Ah yes, there's an exception, as there always is: If in the context of what you're writing you have need to change, in quoted material, a capital letter at the beginning of a sentence to a lowercase one, or vice versa, you may do that without brackets.

That is, if you're quoting George Bernard Shaw's "Patriotism is, fundamentally, a conviction that a particular country is the best in the world because you were born in it," you're well within your rights to refer to Shaw's observation that "patriotism is, fundamentally, a conviction," etc., etc.

And in the other direction, quoting Shaw's "All government is cruel; for nothing is so cruel as impunity," you're allowed to do this:

> "Nothing is so cruel as impunity," Shaw once commented.

The exception to the exception arises in cases of legal documents and extreme and especially contentious scholarship in which you need to keep your nose utterly clean; then you'll find yourself doing this sort of thing:

> Shaw once wrote that "[a]ll government is cruel."

I can't say it's pretty, but it gets the job done.

39.

[*SIC*] BURNS

Let's take a moment to talk about [*sic*]. *Sic* is Latin for "thus," and one uses it—traditionally in italics, always in brackets—in quoted material to make it clear to your reader that a misspelling or eccentricity or error of fact you're retaining for the sake of authenticity in said quoted material is indeed not your misspelling or eccentricity or error of fact but that of the per-

---

thing drives some of my colleagues batty, I like to think that it quietly conveys integrity.

son you're quoting. As, for instance and strictly speaking, you might do here, in quoting this piece of text I 100 percent made up out of thin air and didn't find on, say, Twitter:

> Their [*sic*] was no Collusion [*sic*] and there was no Obstruction [*sic*].

But seriously now:

If you're quoting a lot of, say, seventeenth-century writing in which there are numerous old-fashioned-isms you wish to retain, you'd do well, somewhere around the beginning of what you're writing, perhaps in an author's note or a footnote, to make it clear that you're quoting your venerable material verbatim. That'll save you a lot of [*sic*]ing, though you might occasionally drop in a [*sic*] for an error or peculiarity whose misreading or misinterpretation might truly be confounding to your reader.

Writers of nonfiction occasionally choose, when they're quoting a good deal of archaic or otherwise peculiar material, to silently correct outmoded spellings or misspellings, irregular capitalization, eccentric or absent punctuation, etc. I'm not a huge fan of this practice—mostly because I think it's not as much fun as retaining all that flavorful weirdness—though I can understand why you might do it in a work of nonfiction that's meant to be popular rather than scholarly. If you're going to do it, again, let the reader know up front. It's only fair.

Do not—not as in never—use [*sic*] as a snide bludgeon to suggest that something you're quoting is dopey. By which I mean the very meaning of the words, not merely their spelling. You may think you're getting in a good shot at a writer whose judgment you find shaky; the only person whose judgment is going to seem shaky, I'd suggest, is you.

It's the prose equivalent of an I'M WITH STUPID T-shirt and just about as charming.

And for pete's sake, if you're an American quoting British writing, or vice versa, please do not do the following, as I once, hand to God, saw in a U.K. newspaper:

. . . which it said had been "a labor [*sic*] of love."

QUOTATION MARKS

When I was a youth growing up in Albertson, Long Island, a virtually undetectable suburb of New York City, my mother would regularly send me off on my Schwinn to the nearby bakery for a rye bread (sliced) or a challah (unsliced) or six rolls for eight cents each (or was it eight rolls for six cents each?) and, on the best days, a box of black-and-whites. (Black-and-white cookies, as gentiles of my acquaintance tend to call them.)

In the bakery, above the rye bread, was a sign that read:

TRY OUR RUGELACH! IT'S THE "BEST!"

I was fascinated. This, as they say in the comic books, is my origin story.

So, then, to break it down for you:

40.

Use roman (straight up and down, that is, like the font this phrase is printed in) type encased in quotation marks for the titles of songs, poems, short stories, and episodes of TV series.* Whereas the titles of music albums,† volumes of poetry, full-length works of fiction and nonfiction, and TV series themselves are styled in aslant italics.

---

*The fact that the plural of "series" is "series" is almost as bothersome as the fact that "read" is the past tense of "read," but "serieses" is, aside from incorrect, ridiculous-looking.

†I find it charmingly odd that the term "album" has persisted to refer to a collection of music, long past the era in which individual records were packaged in sleeved books—which is to say, albums.

"Court and Spark"
Court and Spark

"Song of Myself"
Leaves of Grass

"The Lottery"
The Lottery and Other Stories

"Chuckles Bites the Dust"
The Mary Tyler Moore Show (also known as, simply,
    Mary Tyler Moore)

It's a fairly simple system, then: little things in roman and quotes, bigger things in italics.*

41.

Individual works of art—named paintings and sculptures—are generally set in italics (*The Luncheon on the Grass*), though works whose titles are unofficial (the Victory of Samothrace, for instance) are often styled in roman, without quotation marks.†

42.

One also sets off dialogue with quotation marks, though some writers (E. L. Doctorow, William Gaddis, and Cormac McCarthy come immediately to mind) like to do without, to which I simply say: To pull that off, you have to be awfully good at differentiating between narration and dialogue.

---

*Titles of plays of any length are set in italics, whether they're wee caprices like Edna St. Vincent Millay's *Aria da Capo* or nine-act extravaganzas (with dinner break) like Eugene O'Neill's *Strange Interlude*.

†For more on this, as well as for the complexities of the styling of titles of works of classical music and other more arcane items, I send you off to your big fat stylebooks, which go into this in exhaustive detail.

43.

Once upon a time, what I'd call articulated rumination was often found encased in quotation marks:

"What is to become of me?" Estelle thought.

Though that, over time, gave way to this:

What is to become of me? Estelle thought.

And now, more often than not, you'll simply see:

What is to become of me? Estelle thought.*

That last is best.†

44.

One does not, as in the rugelach example cited above, use quotation marks for emphasis. That is why God invented italics.

Such quotation marks do not, strictly speaking, come under the heading of scare quotes, which are quotation marks used to convey that the writer finds a term too slangish to sit on its own (I have old books in which young people listen not to jazz but to "jazz"; it makes me chortle every time) and/or is sneering at it. Avoid scare quotes. They'll make you look snotty today and, twenty years on, snotty and comically obsolete.‡

---

* To ensure that "What is to become of me?" and "Estelle thought" are not read as two separate thoughts, I'm not opposed to "What is to become of me?, Estelle thought," but I may be the only one so unopposed.

† Six consecutive words set in italics certainly aren't going to bother anyone, but I caution you against setting anything longer than a single sentence that way. For one thing, italics weary the eye; for another, multiple paragraphs of text set in italics suggest a dream sequence, and readers are always keen to skip dream sequences.

‡ Some people—Sylvia Barrett's student Chas. H. Robbins in Bel Kaufman's splendid novel *Up the Down Staircase*, the forty-fifth president of the United States, others—use quotation marks (or, as Chas. called them, "quotion marks") more or less at random. In the writing of an indifferently educated fictional high

45.

Do not use quotation marks after the term "so-called." For instance, I'm not

a so-called "expert" in matters copyeditorial

I'm simply a

so-called expert in matters copyeditorial

The quotation-marking of something following "so-called" is not only redundant but makes a likely already judgmental sentence even more so.

Though I won't object if you feel compelled, as I often do, to use quotation marks after a "known as," particularly if you're introducing a strange or newfangled term. For example, I might refer to

the long-haired, free-loving, peace-marching young
folk known as "hippies"

if, that is, I were writing in 1967.[*]

46.

In referring to a word or words as, indeed, a word or words, some people go with quotation marks and some people prefer italics, as in:

The phrase "the fact that" is to be avoided.

---

school student, that makes for amusing characterization; in the tweets of the so-called leader of the free world, it's not so amusing.

[*] According to the lovely folks at Merriam-Webster, the term "hippie," in the sense of hirsute member of the counterculture, dates back to 1965, which is a skosh later than I might have guessed. One fun thing about dictionaries is that they'll provide a date of introduction into written English for just about any word you can think of. This comes in awfully handy when you're writing period fiction and wish to be era-appropriate, especially in dialogue. Copyediting a novel set during New York's 1863 Draft Riots, I learned that what we now call a hangover—a term that didn't pop up till 1894—was known in those earlier days as, among other things, a "katzenjammer." Note, please, my use of quotation marks just now. I *needed* them.

or

The phrase *the fact that* is to be avoided.

The former is a bit chattier, I think, more evocative of speech, the latter a bit more technical- and textbooky-looking. It's a matter of taste.

47.

An exclamation point or question mark at the end of a sentence ending with a bit of quoted matter goes outside rather than inside the quotation marks if the exclamation point or question mark belongs to the larger sentence rather than to the quoted bit, as in:

As you are not dear to me and we are not friends, please don't ever refer to me as "my dear friend"!

or

Were Oscar Wilde's last words truly "Either that wallpaper goes or I do"?*

What happens when both the quoted material and the surrounding sentence demand emphatic or inquiring punctuation? Does one truly write

You'll be sorry if you ever again say to me, "But you most emphatically are my dear friend!"!

or

Were Oscar Wilde's last words truly "I'm dying, do you seriously think I want to talk about the decor?"?

No, one does not. One makes a choice as to where the ! or the ? might more effectively reside. (In the examples above, I'd

---

* No, they were not.

opt to retain the second exclamation point and the first question mark.) Or one simply rewrites to avoid the collision entirely.

48.

In American English, we reach first for double quotation marks, as I've been doing above all this time. If one finds the need to quote something within quotation marks, one then opts for single quotation marks. As in:

> "I was quite surprised," Jeannine commented, "when Mabel said to me, 'I'm leaving tomorrow for Chicago,' then walked out the door."

Should one find oneself with yet another layer of quoted material, one would then revert to double quote marks, thus:

> "I was quite surprised," Jeannine commented, "when Mabel said to me, 'I've found myself lately listening over and over to the song "Chicago,"' then proceeded to sing it."

Do, though, try to avoid this matryoshka punctuation; it's hard on the eye and on the brain.

Moreover, I caution you generally, re quotes within quotes: It's quite easy to lose track of what you're doing and set double quotes within double quotes. Be wary.

49.

Though semicolons, because they are elusive and enigmatic and they like it that way, are set outside terminal quotation marks, periods and commas—and if I make this point once, I'll make it a thousand times, and trust me, I will—are always set inside.

Always.

HYPHENS

50.

If you turn to p. 719 in your *Merriam-Webster's Collegiate Dictionary,* eleventh edition, you will find, one atop the other:

light-headed
lighthearted

Which tells you pretty much everything you want to know about the use of hyphens, which is to say: It doesn't make much sense, does it.

If you type "lightheaded" (I note that my spellcheck dots have not popped up) or "light-hearted," the hyphen police are surely not going to come after you, and I won't even notice, but:

If you're invested in getting your hyphens correctly sorted out in compound adjectives, verbs, and nouns, and you like being told what to do, just pick up your dictionary and look 'em up. Those listings are *correct.*

51.

That said, you will find—if you've a penchant for noticing these things, professionally or otherwise—that compounds have a tendency, over time, to spit out unnecessary hyphens and close themselves up. Over the course of my career I've seen "light bulb" evolve into "light-bulb" and then into "lightbulb," "baby-sit" give way to "babysit," and—a big one—"Web site" turn into "Web-site," then, happily, "website."*

---

* At Random House, I was happy to help push "website" along—if you're apt to encounter a word dozens of times a day, you'll tend to want to make that word as simple as possible—though I still feel a pang of remorse over my acquiescence to "email"—doesn't "e-mail" look better and, more important, look like what it sounds like? But "email" was happening whether I liked it or not, and, as in so many things, one can be either on the bus or under the bus.

How and why do these changes occur? I'll let you in on a little secret: Because you make them happen. Yes, you, right there. You grow impatient with the looks of, say, "rest room" ("I mean, it's not a room you rest in, is it?"), so you stick a hyphen in it, coexist with "rest-room" for about twenty minutes, then quickly tire of the hyphen and, boom, "restroom." Multiply this times hundreds of compounds, and watch the language whoosh into the future before your very eyes. Then watch the dictionary keep up with you, because that's how it works. As a lexicographer friend once confided over sushi, the dictionary takes its cues from use: If writers don't change things, the dictionary doesn't change things.

If you want your best-seller to be a bestseller, you have to help make that happen. If you want to play videogames rather than video games, go for it.

I hope that makes you feel powerful. It should.

52.

If that revelation didn't make you go all lightheaded, let's hunker down and focus on a few particular points.

For the sake of clarity, we use hyphens to helpfully link up a pair or passel of words preceding and modifying a noun, as in:

first-rate movie
fifth-floor apartment
middle-class morality
nasty-looking restaurant
all-you-can-eat buffet

However, convention (a.k.a. tradition, a.k.a. consensus, a.k.a. it's simply how it's done, so don't argue with it) allows for exceptions in some cases in which a misreading is unlikely, as in, say:

real estate agent
high school students

And though you may, now that you're staring at these constructions, wonder worryingly about the reality of that estate agent or the sobriety of those school students, I'd urge you to stop staring and move on. (Staring at words is always a bad idea. Stare at the word "the" for more than ten seconds and reality begins to recede.)

Generally—yes, exceptions apart, there are always exceptions—one wields a hyphen or hyphens in these before-the-noun (there goes another one) adjectival cases to avoid that momentary unnecessary hesitation we're always trying to spare our readers.

Consider the difference between, say, "a man eating shark" and "a man-eating shark," where the hyphen is crucial in clarifying who is eating whom, and "a cat related drama," which presupposes an articulate cat with a penchant for talking about the theater, and "a cat-related drama," which is what you meant in the first place.

I recall, for instance, my puzzlement upon encountering this sentence:

> Touch averse people who don't want to be hugged are
> not rude.

What on earth, I wondered, are "averse people," and why on earth are you telling me to touch them if they don't want to be hugged, but wait, what—?

Then the light dawned: People who don't like to be touched and who resist your attempts to hug them are not rude. Got it.

Now, mind you, this confusion kicked off and resolved itself in seconds. And I assure you, I'm not shamming; you may possibly have read the sentence correctly on your first attempt, but I was flummoxed. Surely, though, the confusion might have been avoided entirely had the sentence simply read:

> Touch-averse people who don't want to be hugged are
> not rude.

Now, then, as we navigate these migraine-inducing points of trivia, impossible-to-understand differentiations, and inconsistently applied rules, do you wonder why, though I hyphenated "migraine-inducing" and "impossible-to-understand," I left "inconsistently applied" open?

Because compounds formed from an "-ly" adverb and an adjective or participle do not take a hyphen:

inconsistently applied rules
maddeningly irregular punctuation
beautifully arranged sentences
highly paid copy editors

Why?
Because, we're told, the possibility of misreading is slim to nil, so a hyphen is unnecessary.
Or, if you prefer a simpler explanation:
Because.*

53.

Modern style is to merge prefixes and main words (nouns, verbs, adjectives) seamlessly and hyphenlessly, as in:

antiwar
autocorrect
codependent
extracurricular
hyperactive
interdepartmental
intradepartmental
nonnative
outfight
preexisting

---

*Footnote pop quiz: Why, then, would I hyphenate the likes of "scholarly-looking teenagers" or "lovely-smelling flowers"? Because not all "-ly" words are adverbs. Sometimes they're adjectives. Really, I'm sorry.

pseudointellectual
reelect[*]
subpar
unpretentious

I'd suggest that you follow this streamlined style—and I can see some of you gritting your teeth over this already—because to do otherwise will make you look old-fashioned or, worse, rubelike.[†]

But: If you find any given hyphenated compound incomprehensible or too hideous to be borne, it's OK—but choose your battles, please, and make them rare—to hold on to that hyphen.[‡]

54.

There are some exceptions, though.

Aren't there always?

To recreate is to enjoy recreation, but to create something anew is to re-create it. And you may reform a naughty child, but if you are taking that child literally apart and putting it back together, you are re-forming it. You may quit your job by resigning, but a contract, once signed, can certainly be re-signed.

55.

As ye prefix, so shall ye suffix. We tend not to think about whether to append a suffix with a hyphen, because we're quite

---

[*] A certain magazine famously—notoriously, you might say, and I do—would have you set a diaeresis—the double-dot thing you might tend to refer to as an umlaut—in words with repeat vowels, thus: "preëxisting," "reëlect." That certain magazine also refers to adolescents as "teen-agers." If you're going to have a house style, try not to have a house style visible from space.

[†] I'm getting there. Hold on.

[‡] Now it can be told: Though the hyphenless compound "coworker" is widely derided as looking bovine, and thus you'll often see "co-worker," I have as well an allergy—possibly unique—to "coauthor," and thus you'll see co-authors cited on Random House jackets and covers. You may now "people in glass houses shouldn't throw stones" to your collective hearts' content.

used not to: -ing (as in "encroaching"), -ism (as in "Darwin-ism"), -less and -ness (as in "hopelessness"), and all the rest. But if you don't like the looks of, as above, "rubelike"—is it something to do with Russian money? some sort of insidious cube toy?—I'd simply suggest that you find another, suffixless way to say what you're trying to say. OK, suffixwise, I think we're done here.

56.

The age of people's children trips up a lot of people with children.

> My daughter is six years old.
> My six-year-old daughter is off to summer camp.
> My daughter, a six-year-old, is off to summer camp.

One too often encounters "a six-year old girl" or, though it would be correct in a discussion of infant sextuplets who have just celebrated their first birthday, "six year-olds."

57.

You might—or might not—be surprised to learn that many copyeditorial man-hours* have been expended over the decades as to the correct construction of the common vulgarity—and an enchantingly common vulgarity it is—used to describe an act of fellatio. Is it open, is it hyphen-ated, is it closed up?

Close it up. Hyphenated vulgarities are comically dainty.

58.

What, did you think I was afraid to type the word "blowjob"?

---

*I know I'm supposed to prefer and use "person-hours" or "work-hours." I can't, so I don't. Please forgive me.

DASHES

59.

Dashes come in two flavors: em and en. Em dashes (which most people simply refer to as dashes) are so called because they were traditionally the width of a capital *M* in any particular typeface (nowadays they tend to be a touch wider); en dashes are the width of a lowercase *n*.

This is an em dash: —

This, just a touch shorter yet still longer than a hyphen, is an en dash: –

Likely you don't need much advice from me on how to use em dashes, because you all seem to use an awful lot of them.

They're useful for interruption of dialogue, either midsentence from within:

> "Once upon a time—yes, I know you've heard this story before—there lived a princess named Snow White."

or to convey interruption from without:

> "The murderer," she intoned, "is someone in this—"
> A shot rang out.

And they nicely set off a bit of text in standard narration when commas—because that bit of text is rather on the parenthetical side, like this one, but one doesn't want to use parentheses—won't do the trick:

> He packed his bag with all the things he thought he'd need for the weekend—an array of T-shirts, two pairs of socks per day, all the clean underwear he could locate—and made his way to the airport.

According to copyediting tradition—at least copyediting tradition as it was handed down to me—one uses no more than two em dashes in a single sentence, and I think that's good advice—except when it's not.

En dashes are the guild secret of copyediting, and most normal people neither use them nor much know what they are nor even know how to type them.* I'm happy to reveal the secret.

An en dash is used to hold words together instead of your standard hyphen, which usually does the trick just fine, when one is connecting a multiword proper noun to another multiword proper noun or to pretty much anything else. What the heck does that mean? It means this:

a Meryl Streep–Robert De Niro comedy
a New York–to–Chicago flight
a World War II–era plane
a Pulitzer Prize–winning play

Basically, that which you're connecting needs a smidgen more connecting than can be accomplished with a hyphen.

Please note in the second example above that I've used two en dashes rather than an en dash and a hyphen, even though "Chicago" is a single word. Why? Visual balance, that's all. This

a New York–to-Chicago flight

simply looks—to me and now, I hope, to you, forever afterward—a bit lopsided.

I've also seen attempted, in an attempt to style the last example, the use of multiple hyphens, as in:

a Pulitzer-Prize-winning play

---

*On a Mac, you can create an en dash by typing option-hyphen. On an iPhone, if you lean gently on the hyphen key, an en dash will present itself, as well as an em dash and a bullet. On a PC, I believe one types command–3–do the hokey pokey, or some such.

That simply doesn't look very nice, does it.

You don't want to make en dashes do too much heavy lifting, though. They work well visually, but they have their limits insofar as meaning is concerned. The likes of

the ex–prime minister

certainly makes sense and follows the rules, but

the former prime minister

works just as well.

And something like

an anti–air pollution committee

would do better to be set as

an anti-air-pollution committee

or perhaps to be rethought altogether.

En dashes are also used for

page references (pp. 3–21)

sporting game scores (the Yankees clobbered the Mets, 14–2)[*]

court decisions (the Supreme Court upheld the lower court's ruling by a 7–2 vote)

QUESTION MARKS
AND EXCLAMATION POINTS

60.

If—and I'd restrict this bit of advice for more casual prose or the rendering of dialogue—a sentence is constructed like a question but isn't intended to be one, you might consider con-

---

[*] I'd originally written "the Mets clobbered the Yankees," but a friend, reading the text, insisted I switch the teams "FOR REALISM." Shows you how much I know about (no, I'm not going to write "football," because some jokes are too easy, even for me) baseball.

cluding it with a period rather than a question mark. "That's a good idea, don't you think?" means something quite different from "That's a horrible idea, isn't it."

61.

Go light on the exclamation points. When overused, they're bossy, hectoring, and, ultimately, wearying. Some writers recommend that you should use no more than a dozen exclamation points per book; others insist that you should use no more than a dozen exclamation points in a lifetime.

62.

That said, it would be irresponsible not to properly convey with an exclamation mark the excitement of such as "Your hair is on fire!" The person with the burning head might otherwise not believe you. And the likes of "What a lovely day!" with a period rather than a bang, as some people like to call the exclamation point, might seem sarcastic. Or depressed.

63.

No one over the age of ten who is not actively engaged in the writing of a comic book should end any sentence with a double exclamation point or double question mark.

64.

We won't discuss the use of ?! or !? because you'd never do that.*

65.

Neither will we discuss the interrobang, because we're all civilized adults here.

---

* Or you might, and if I were your copy editor I'd try to stop you, and possibly you'd heed me (in which case hoorah) and possibly you'd stick to your guns (and I might wrinkle my nose, but it's your book).

66.

Sentences beginning with "I wonder" are not questions—they're simply pondering declarations—and do not conclude with question marks.

> I wonder who's kissing her now.
> I wonder what the king is doing tonight.
> I wonder, wonder who—who-oo-oo-oo—who wrote
>   the book of love.

67.

Neither are sentences beginning with "Guess who" or "Guess what" questions. If anything, they're imperatives.

> Guess who's coming to dinner.

CHAPTER 4

1, 2, 3, Go

The Treatment of Numbers

G ENERALLY, in nontechnical, nonscientific text, write out numbers from one through one hundred and all numbers beyond that are easily expressed in words—that is, two hundred but 250, eighteen hundred but 1,823. Print periodicals with a desire to conserve space often set the writing-out limit at "nine" or "ten," but if you've got all the room in the world, words are, I'd say, friendlier-looking on the page.

That said—and automatically excepting writing on subjects like finance that are naturally number-heavy and in which just about all numbers will be expressed as numerals—you'll often have to dance around that guideline, taking into account what will or won't be visually pleasing and easily comprehensible to the reader, especially when writing multiple numbers in a single paragraph. I suppose it's an obvious point, but if a style choice follows the rules but results in something that looks awful or makes no sense on the page, rethink it.

A few fine points:

1.

If in any given paragraph (or, to some eyes, on any given page) one particular number mandates the use of numerals, then all *related* uses of numbers should also be styled in numerals. That is, not:

> The farmer lived on seventy-five fertile acres and owned twelve cows, thirty-seven mules, and 126 chickens.

but rather:

> The farmer lived on seventy-five fertile acres and owned 12 cows, 37 mules, and 126 chickens.

The livestock tallies are set in numerals; the acreage, its own thing, can hold on to words. It's a tiny distinction, but it makes for a prettier page, and it makes it easier for the reader to easily compare things meant to be compared, especially when the comparisons run into further paragraphs.

2.

Numerals are generally avoided in dialogue. That is:

> "I bought sixteen apples, eight bottles of sparkling water, and thirty-two cans of soup," said James, improbably.

rather than

> "I bought 16 apples, 8 bottles of sparkling water, and 32 cans of soup," said James, improbably.

Which rather looks as if the next sentence is going to begin, "If James gives Louella half his apples," and we wouldn't want that.

But don't take your avoidance of numerals to extremes. You certainly don't want anything that looks even vaguely like this:

"And then, in nineteen eighty-three," Dave recounted,
   "I drove down Route Sixty-six, pulled in to a Motel
   Six, and stayed overnight in room four-oh-two, all
   for the low, low price of seventeen dollars and
   seventy-five cents, including tax."

2a.

Should a character say "I arrived at four thirty-two" or "I arrived at 4:32"?

Unless you are forensically reconstructing the timeline of a
series of unsolved murders in a quaint village in the Cots-
wolds, a character should, please, simply say "I arrived just
after four-thirty."

And a character might well say "I left at 4:45," and I think
that looks just dandy ("I left at four forty-five," if you absolutely must), but a character might also as well say "I left at a
quarter to five."

3.

It's considered bad form to begin a sentence with a numeral or
numerals.

   NO: 1967 dawned clear and bright.
   BETTER, THOUGH NOT GREAT: Nineteen sixty-seven
      dawned clear and bright.
   BETTER STILL, ALBEIT TAUTOLOGICAL: The year 1967
      dawned clear and bright.
   EVEN BETTER: Recast your sentence so it needn't begin
      with a year. It shouldn't take you but a moment.

4.

When writing of time, I favor, for example:

   five A.M.
   4:32 P.M.

using those pony-size capital letters (affectionately known as small caps*) rather than the horsier A.M./P.M. or the desultory-looking a.m./p.m. (AM/PM and am/pm are out of the question.)

By the bye, the likes of "6 A.M. in the morning" is a redundancy that turns up with great frequency, so I warn you against it.

5.

For years, then:

> 53 B.C.
> A.D. 1654

You will note, please, that B.C. ("before Christ," as I likely don't have to remind you) is always set after the year and A.D. (the Latin "anno Domini," meaning "in the year of the Lord," as I perhaps don't have to remind you but will anyway) before it.

Perhaps you were taught somewhere along the way to use the non-Jesus-oriented B.C.E. (before the Common Era) and C.E. (of the Common Era). If so, note that both B.C.E. and C.E. are set after the year:

> 53 B.C.E.
> 1654 C.E.

I'll note that, at least in my experience, writers still overwhelmingly favor B.C. and A.D., and that B.C.E. and C.E. remain about as popular, at least in the United States, as the metric system.

Just, please, make sure you get everything in the right

---

* In Microsoft Word you can create small caps by either typing the letters in question in lowercase, highlighting them, then hitting Command+Shift+K or, if that's not a thing you can readily remember, typing the letters in question in lowercase, highlighting them, then heading up to the top of your screen and fiddling your way through Format and Font.

place. Should I ever be touring the Moon,* you can be certain that my first order of business will be to take a Sharpie to the plaque that refers to humanity's arrival there in "JULY 1969, A. D."†

HERE MEN FROM THE PLANET EARTH
FIRST SET FOOT UPON THE MOON
JULY 1969, A. D.
WE CAME IN PEACE FOR ALL MANKIND

NEIL A. ARMSTRONG
ASTRONAUT

MICHAEL COLLINS
ASTRONAUT

EDWIN E. ALDRIN, JR.
ASTRONAUT

RICHARD NIXON
PRESIDENT, UNITED STATES OF AMERICA

6.

I refer to the years from 1960 to 1969‡ as the sixties (or, in a pinch, as the '60s) and the streets of Manhattan from Sixtieth through Sixty-ninth as the Sixties. Some people do it the other way around, but let's not fight about it.

Or let's. I win.

7.

If you're writing dates U.S.-style, note the invariable commas on either side of the year, as in:

> Viola Davis was born on August 11, 1965, in St. Matthews, South Carolina.

---

*You may well encounter contradicting style advice on Moon/moon (speaking of our particular one, that is), Sun/sun (ditto), and Earth/earth (the planet, not the dirt thereon). Let your context be your guide.

†There are a few other things wrong with that plaque, but that's a conversation for another day.

‡Be careful not to write "the years from 1960–1969." If you've got a "from," you need a "to."

If you're writing dates the way people just about anywhere else in the world write them, you can save up your commas for some other use:

> Viola Davis was born on 11 August 1965 in St. Matthews, South Carolina.

Note as well that even if the mind may be hearing "August eleventh," one doesn't, in just about any context, write "August 11th." I don't know why; one just doesn't.

8.

The use of 555 phone numbers looks just as silly* on the page as it sounds in movies or on television. A tiny amount of ingenuity dodges the problem.

> "What's your phone number?"
> I jotted it down on a scrap of paper and handed it to her.

9.

Miscellaneously:

- Degrees of temperature ("a balmy 83 degrees") and longitude/latitude (38°41'7.8351", and note the use not only of the degree symbol but of those austere vertical prime marks, not to be confused with stylishly curly quotation marks) are best set in numerals.
- So are biblical references to chapter and verse (Exodus 3:12, for instance).
- Except in dialogue, percentages should be expressed as numerals, though I'd urge you to use the word "percent" rather than the percentage sign—unless what you're writing is hugely about percentages, in

---

*How easy was it not to write a sentence beginning, "555 phone numbers are just as silly-looking"? Quite.

which case feel free to write "95%" rather than "95 percent."

- Particularly numbery things, like ball game scores ("The Yankees were up 11–2") and Supreme Court rulings ("the 7–2 decision in the Dred Scott case"), look best expressed in numerals. Plus they give you the chance to make good use of those excellent en dashes.

10.

Confronted by numbered army divisions, court cases, and works of classical music right down to Mozart and his Köchel catalog, I'm happy to hie myself to one of my big fat stylebooks, and I'm happy here to urge you to hie yourself as well.

11.

A crucial, *crucial* thing about numbers, no matter how they're styled:

They need to be accurate.

As soon as a writer writes the likes of "Here are twelve helpful rules for college graduates heading into the job market," copy editors start counting. You'd be surprised at how many lists of twelve things contain only eleven things. This is an easy thing to overlook, but don't. Otherwise you'll find yourself with a chapter titled "67 Assorted Things to Do (and Not to Do) with Punctuation" that contains only 66 assorted things. Because I skipped no. 38. Did you notice?

CHAPTER 5

Foreign Affairs

1. Standard practice is to set foreign-language words and phrases in italics. If a word or phrase, however foreign-language-derived, is included in the main part of your handy *Merriam-Webster's Collegiate Dictionary,* eleventh edition, it's to be taken as English. If it's tucked into the appendix of foreign-language words and phrases at the back of the book (or is not to be found at all), it's to be taken as not-English.

The following, then, can be taken as English:

bête noire
château
chutzpah
façade
hausfrau
karaoke
mea culpa
ménage à trois
non sequitur
retsina

schadenfreude

weltschmerz*

The following can be taken as not-English:

concordia discors
dum spiro, spero
n'est-ce pas?
und so weiter†

2. Diacritical marks—accent marks, if you prefer—are the little doodads with which many foreign-derived words are festooned, generally above letters (mostly vowels), in certain cases below them (that ç in "façade," for instance), and in certain cases, especially in certain eastern European languages, through them. In written English they're occasionally omitted, and the dictionary will often give you permission to skip them, but sojourning in a chateau can't be nearly as much fun as sojourning in a château, and if you send me your resume rather than your résumé, I'm probably not going to hire you.‡

3. While we're here: If you must write *n'est-ce pas?* (the French equivalent of that pointless American tic "you know?," which the British pronounce "innit"), you must spell it correctly, and unless you're writing in French, I'd suggest you not write it at all.

4. But here's an idea: Let's say you're writing a novel in which the characters shimmy easily between English and, say, Spanish. Consider not setting the Spanish (or what-have-you) in italics. Use of italics emphasizes foreignness. If you mean to suggest easy fluency, use of roman normalizes your text. (I fig-

---

* Though nouns in German are capitalized, I figure that if a common German noun has made its way into standard English, it should be lowercased like any other standard English common noun.

† By which is meant, indeed, "and so on."

‡ Even if you don't, as a rule, favor accent marks, you really must concede, mustn't you, that "resume" for a word pronounced "rezz-ooh-may" doesn't do the trick. And I presume that people who split the difference and spell it "re-sumé" live in Middle Carolina or Central Dakota.

ured this one out a number of years ago, working on a memoir whose generally English-speaking Filipino American characters' speech was punctuated with bits of Tagalog, and I've suggested the technique to many writers since. Writers seem to find it ingenious, and—bonus—it cuts down on italics, which, used in excess, irk the eye.*)

On the other hand, if you're writing a novel about, say, an isolated young Englishwoman living in Paris who is confounded by the customs, the people, and the language, it would certainly make good sense to set all the bits of French she encounters, in narration or dialogue, in the requisite italics. You want that French to feel, every time, strange.

5. Remembering my teenage frustration in reading nineteenth-century fiction that presumed I was fluent in ancient Greek and Latin, I'd urge you to be judicious and thoughtful in dropping swaths of foreign-language material into your text as if (as many writers seem to think) everyone speaks, say, French. Everyone, say, doesn't.

6. No matter how you're styling your foreign-language bits and pieces, foreign-language proper nouns are always set in roman, as, say:

Comédie-Française
Déclaration des Droits de l'Homme et du Citoyen†

---

* If you want readers to skip over a great big swath of your writing, set it in italics, which, over the course of multiple paragraphs, tend to covey Lengthy Interior Monologue or Something Else I Probably Don't Want to Read.

† As this Déclaration is a document not unlike, say, the Declaration of Independence, it does not take the italics it would be entitled to if it were a novel, like *Les Misérables,* or a mega-novel, like *À la recherche du temps perdu.* While we're here: The styling of French titles can be confounding to someone who mostly knows only English, as the French are apt to capitalize only the first word of a title, and the second word of a title if the first word of the title is an article, and maybe some other words if they're as important as that first or second word, and . . . Well, it's a thing. Faced with this styling challenge as a copy editor, I'll tend to nose around online in search of reliable style guidance on a title-by-title basis. Attempting to impose standard American title casing—that is, capitalizing nouns, verbs, adjectives, etc., and lowercasing articles, prepositions, etc.— not only mandates knowing which French words are which but persists in

Galleria degli Uffizi

Schutzstaffel

And though we don't much speak/write of francs and lire anymore, if we are speaking/writing of them, we do not italicize them.

7. You will find yourself using foreign-language-derived abbreviations in notes sections and bibliographies, as, say:

et al.

ibid.

op. cit.

not to mention

etc.

and these are to be set in roman.

Speaking of foreigners, now's as good a time as any for:

HOW NOT TO WRITE LIKE A BRIT

Our cousins across the ocean had their chance running the world and the language. At a certain point—something about a Stamp Act and some toppled tea bags, as I recall—we decided to go our own way and set about building not only our own political system but, with a major assist from the determined Noah Webster, our own language.

I'm as guilty as the next chap of appropriating British* vocabulary as it amuses me, but a little of that goes a long way,

---

looking inauthentic: *À la Recherche du Temps Perdu*. You may also, by the way and by tradition, skip the accent mark on a capital letter, so then *A la recherche,* etc. This, in relative brief, is why I prefer to copyedit in English.

* Now it can be told: That island to the east of Ireland is called Great Britain, or just plain Britain. Great Britain comprises Scotland (up at the top), Wales (down and to the left), and England (the chunk in the middle). Scottish and Welsh people will tolerate being referred to as British, but do not ever mistake them for Englishpeople.

Never, if you know what's good for you, refer to an Irishperson as British. Irishpeople are Irish.

and even I get shirty when it's overdone. Americans do not live in flats; they live in apartments. When a Brit wears a jumper, it's a sweater; when an American wears a jumper, it's one of those invariably unflattering sleeveless smock things (which the Brits might call a pinafore dress). We ride in elevators; they ride in lifts. They pump petrol; we pump gasoline. Our chips come in a bag; their chips are french fries, as in "fish and," and what we call chips they call crisps. We eat zucchini, eggplant, and arugula; they eat courgettes, aubergines, and rocket (and "rocket," you have to admit, is a spectacular term for a salad green). Brits laugh at us for doing math, because they do maths. And on and endlessly on.*

Of course, some words do drift over here and take legitimate root. I recall first encountering the word "twee" back in the 1980s and being unable to find it in my dictionary; now one can't seem to get away from it here, especially in reference to a studiously adorable sort of pop music invariably including ukuleles. And we've found many good uses for "queue," though patriotic Americans still don't queue up; they get in line. (Unless they're New Yorkers of a certain age, in which case they get on line.)

But one can't endlessly appropriate British English just because one is bored with American English. No American can get away with calling a z a "zed," and as much as one may long to drop "cock-up" into a stateside conversation, to do so would make one sound like a—let me check my phrasebook—cockwomble.

Some other assorted usage, spelling, and punctuational points:

England, Scotland, Wales, and, as of this writing, the portion of Ireland politically designated Northern Ireland constitute the United Kingdom of Great Britain and Northern Ireland.

* Much transatlantic hilarity ensues over confusion between U.K. and U.S. uses of, among other words, "pissed," "fanny," and "fag," to say nothing of "pants," but I think we've had enough transatlantic hilarity for the moment.

- In the United States, Random House is publishing a book. In England, Random House are publishing a book. The Brits often (not always, but often) use a plural for a collective noun.

- The Brits think that the word "gotten" is moronic, and they're not shy about telling you so.

- In the United States, save up your *l*'s for better purposes by writing "traveled," "canceled," and "marvelous" rather than "travelled," "cancelled," and "marvellous."

- Avoid the Brit "ou," as in "neighbour," "colour," "harbour," and "labour," in favor of the streamlined American "neighbor," "color," "harbor," and "labor."* (Proper nouns are always to be kept nation-authentic, though. One should no more refer to the U.K. Labour Party as the "Labor Party" than a Brit should refer to the bombing of "Pearl Harbour.")

If you like concordance, you'll be happy to learn that "glamour" is spelled thus on both sides of the Big Water. One occasionally—very rarely—sees "glamor" over here, but it's drably unglamorous, don't you think? And yes, "glamorous" is the proper spelling everywhere. There's no "glamourous."

I will confess that I do like the looks of the Brit "armour" rather than our "armor"—the *u* seems to add a bit of extra metallic clankiness—but one must follow the rules. (Note proper-noun exceptions for the U.S. company that provides us with various cold cuts and meat spreads—in this case Armour is a family name—and the makers of shiny, form-hugging

---

* An engraved—or faux-engraved—invitation requesting the favour of a reply is also apt to inform you that luncheon will be served at twelve-thirty o'clock. Make of that what you will.

sportswear who decided to call themselves Under Armour.)

• The Brit "-re," as in "mitre," "sceptre," "fibre," and "centre," is our "-er," as in "miter," "scepter," "fiber," and "center."

Not that it comes up all that often, but an American can get away with "sepulchre," which truly looks more sepulchral than "sepulcher," and the dictionary will back you up on that.

A real argument starter over here is "theatre," which persisted in the United States long enough that many of our theatrical edifices use it, and, again, proper nouns are to be respected. Most Broadway theaters are Theatres, as in the Shubert Theatre and the St. James Theatre, but be careful not to apply the "-re" spelling where it doesn't belong: Note the correct Lincoln Center Theater, in uptown Manhattan, and the Public Theater, downtown. (I have an exceptionally large bone to pick with *The New York Times,* which persists in imposing its preference for "theater" on edifices and companies not named thus, here and abroad. The paper's constant references to London's "National Theater" are, on so many levels, galling. *That's not its name.*)

Some Americans dig their heels in re "theatre," often insisting that plays are performed in theatres but movies are shown in theaters (no, we don't call them cinemas over here), or that a building is a theater but the theatrical art is the theatre. And to them I say: You know you're doing it because you think that the "-re" spelling is fancier, and I'd like you to stop.

• A Brit will read up on foetuses in the encyclopaedia; an American will read up on fetuses in the encyclopedia. That said, "archaeology" and "aesthetic" are our spellings of choice here.

• Quite in a class by itself is the U.K. "manoeuvre," which always looks to me as if its pronunciation might well be the sound of a cat coughing up a hairball.

• Over there, things are learnt and burnt and spoilt and smelt. Over here, they're learned and burned (unless the next word is "sienna") and spoiled and smelled.*

• Our zero is their nought.

• Please leave "whilst" and "amidst" and especially "amongst" to our cousins; "while" and "amid" and "among" will do you just fine.

• The Brits are more apt to move backwards, forwards, and towards, whereas Americans will tend to move backward, forward, and toward.†

• And on and on: The Brits analyse; we analyze. We inquire; they enquire. They prise; we pry (or, in a pinch, prize). They plough, we plow. They favor "practise" as a verb and "practice" as a noun; we use "practice" for both. They have licences; we have licenses. (Proper-noun respect, to be sure, to the James Bond film *Licence to Kill*.) They vary between "judgement" and "judgment"; we use the latter. . . .

• Oh, but here's my favorite: The preferred U.K. spelling of the color that describes ashes and the eyes of the goddess Athena is "grey." The preferred American

---

* Yes, except for the olfactory observation that concludes "dealt it."

† The s-concluding versions of these words aren't exactly unseen in published American writing, but most American copy editors will shear off those s's, and Bob's your uncle.

spelling is "gray," but try telling that to the writers who will go ballistic if, in copyediting, you attempt to impose that spelling. In all my years of correcting other people's spelling, I don't think I've ever come up against more pushback than on this point. My long-held theory—make of it what you will—is that the spelling "grey" imprints itself on some people who encounter it in beloved classic children's books, and they form an emotional attachment to it.

Or, I don't know, they're just stubborn.*

• Americans, as I mentioned in the punctuation chapter, start off by encasing quoted material in double quotation marks; quoted material *within* quoted material is encased in singles, as in, say:

"Mabel," I said, "whether you spell the word 'armour' or 'armor' is of no consequence to me."

Brits often—but not always—do it the other way around, as in:

'Mabel,' I said, 'whether you spell the word "armor" or "armour" is of no consequence to me.'

The Brits are also apt, I note, to refer to single quotation marks as inverted commas, which I suppose they are, so I won't argue about it.

• The Brits often set periods or commas outside closing quote marks.

U.K.: When it comes to Beatles songs, Queen Elizabeth is particularly fond of 'Eleanor Rigby', but her absolute favourite is 'Drive My Car'.

---

*Buy me a cocktail or two and I'll regale you at length with my admittedly crackpot notion that gray and grey are, push comes to shove, two different colors, the former having a glossy, almost silvery sheen to it, the latter being heavier, duller, and sodden.

U.S.: When it comes to Beatles songs, Queen Elizabeth is particularly fond of "Eleanor Rigby," but her
absolute favorite is "Drive My Car."

If there's anything that Brits despise about American punctuation, it's this. "The song title does not
contain a comma or a period," they'll growl. "Why
are you sticking it inside the quotation marks?" For
some reason, "It's the American way" does not satisfy
them. But it *is* the American way, and though I do see
the logic of the Brit methodology, I'm certainly not
going to be the person who attempts to upend universal stateside practice. Moreover, I find the sight of
those periods and commas hanging outside quotation
marks saddening. To me they look lonely and un-
loved.

• In British books you'll often see feckless little namby-
pamby freestanding excuses for dashes – something
like this – where we interrupt ourselves—definitively—
with real dashes. Ours are better.

CHAPTER 6

A Little Grammar
Is a Dangerous Thing

I'M GOING TO LET YOU IN ON A LITTLE SECRET:
I hate grammar.

Well, OK, not quite true. I don't hate grammar. I hate grammar jargon.

I suspect that I'm not the only person currently reading this page who was not especially well trained, back in school days, in the ins and outs of grammar. When I started out as a copy editor, I realized that most of what I knew about grammar I knew instinctively. That is, I knew how most—certainly not all—of the grammar things worked; I simply didn't know what they were called.

Even now I'd be hard-pressed to tell you what a nominative absolute is, I think that the word "genitive" sounds vaguely smutty, and I certainly don't know, or care to know, how to diagram a sentence.

I hope I'm not shocking you.

But at a certain point I figured that if I was going to be fixing grammar for a living, I might do well to learn a little something about it, and that's precisely what I did: I learned a little something about it. As little as I needed to. I still, at the slightest puzzlement, run back to my big fat stylebooks, and likely always will.

I do believe, though, that if as a writer you know how to do a thing, it's not terribly important that you know what it's called. So in this chapter—covering the grammar stumbles I tend to run into most frequently—I'll do my best to keep the information as simple and applicable as possible and skip the terminology.

1.

Here's one of those grammar rules that infuriate people:

That's it. That's the rule, or at least an example of it: The correct verb in that sentence is not "infuriates" but "infuriate."

I know that you want to match "one" with a singular verb, but in this case . . .

Well, I keep an adhesive tab on p. 355 of my always handy copy of *Words into Type* because, I've found over time, people will simply not believe me as I stand firm on this point, and citing something written in someone else's book tends to shore up one's argument.

So: "The verb in a relative clause agrees with the antecedent of the relative pronoun, which is the nearest noun or pronoun and is often the object of a preposition, as in the phrase *one of those who* [or] *one of the things that.*"

If you're allergic to phrases like "relative clause,"* as I am, you'll simply have to remember this one by some other method. (My method is to, whenever I see the words "one of those" or "one of the," grab my copy of *Words into Type* and reach for that tab attached to p. 355.)

It's worth noting that when the typically impeccable Cole Porter wrote "one of those bells that now and then rings / just

---

* I'd've made a "Mrs. Santa" joke here but for the fact that even *I* have standards.

one of those things," he made a swell rhyme but committed bad grammar.

It's worth noting as well that on at least one recording of "Just One of Those Things," the ferociously impeccable Lena Horne does sing "one of those bells that now and then ring" rather than "rings," correcting the grammar but wrecking the rhyme.

I don't think there's a bit of grammatical copyediting I've ever been more enthusiastically challenged on than this one—the responses range from a simple "Really?" to, from points east, "Well, maybe that's the way it's done in the United States"—so perhaps I'll concede that this is simply one of those rules that exist so that copy editors can confound laypeople.

Yes, I saw what I just did there. And I'd do it again.

2.

Even as I type these words, I'm listening to a wonderful singer whom I saw onstage repeatedly and who I didn't realize had died twenty years ago.

The reports of the imminent death of the word "whom," to paraphrase that which Mark Twain never quite said,[*] are greatly exaggerated, so you'd do well to learn to wield it correctly or, at least and perhaps more important, learn not to wield it incorrectly.[†]

Basic "whom" use shouldn't pose too many challenges. If you can remember to think of "who" as the cousin of "I," "he," "she," and "they" (the thing doing the thing, a.k.a. a subject) and to think of "whom" as the cousin of "me,"

---

[*] What he did quite say—write, in a note, to be accurate—was "James Ross Clemens, a cousin of mine, was seriously ill two or three weeks ago in London, but is well now. The report of my illness grew out of his illness; the report of my death was an exaggeration."

[†] I'm concerned with how you write, not how you speak, so if you're prone to saying "It's me" rather than "It is I" or inquiring "Who do you love?" rather than "Whom do you love?," you're A-OK tops in my book, and in the books of just about anyone else who aspires to speak English like a normal human being.

"him," "her," and "them" (the thing being done to, a.k.a. an object), you're most of the way there.

> The man whom Shirley met for lunch was wearing a
> green carnation in his lapel.

(You'll note that this sentence would work just as well if you deleted the "whom" altogether. Same goes for the sentence about the singer a handful of paragraphs north of here.)

> To whom did you give the shirt off your back?

To say nothing of "to whom it may concern" and *For Whom the Bell Tolls.*

The thing to avoid is, in a moment of genteel panic, using "whom" when what you really want is "who." This sort of error is generally referred to as a hypercorrection, a term I'm not enamored of and that, I've found, confuses people, because the point of a hypercorrection is not that it's super-duper correct but that it's trying so hard to be correct that it collapses into error. But until someone can come up with a better word, we're stuck with it.

"Whom" hypercorrections—and "whomever" hypercorrections, so long as we're here—tend to fall into two camps: the "No, that's a parenthetical phrase" camp and the "Watch out for that verb!" camp.

For the former, let's think of Viola, the heroine of Shakespeare's *Twelfth Night,* and her brother, Sebastian, whom she believes has drowned in a shipwreck.

No. The "she believes" is parenthetical, settable-off-with-commas, or even utterly extractable, leaving you with, then:

> her brother, Sebastian, whom has drowned in a ship-
> wreck

Well, that won't do, now, will it. So then:

> her brother, Sebastian, who she believes has drowned
> in a shipwreck

In this case, your hypercorrection alarm should ring over the likes of "she believes," "he says," "it is thought," etc.

Is there a correct "whom" version of that phrase? Sure, let's try this (though it's a bit of a mouthful):

> her brother, Sebastian, whom, supposedly drowned in a shipwreck, she mourns

The "Watch out for that verb!" hypercorrection occurs when you've got everything cued up perfectly:

> I gave the candy to

and you're so damn sure that the next word is, well, of course, an object-type thing—a "him," a "her," a "them"—that you continue

> I gave the candy to whomever wanted it the most.

And no again. It's that following verb, that "wanted," that itself demands a subject, leading to a correct:

> I gave the candy to whoever wanted it the most.

You can, to be sure, give the candy to whomever you like, and that will be correct too.

Your hypercorrection alarm, in this case, should sound at the sight of a new verb on the horizon, and a lot of the time that verb is going to be an "is," as in:

> I will give the candy to whoever is most deserving.

In grammarese, that's (and we're back to *Words into Type* here) "The relative pronoun is the subject of the following verb, not the object of the preceding preposition or verb."

3.

I wrote a note to myself not only to write about "not only x but y" constructions but to write about "either x or y" constructions.

I wrote a note to myself to write not only about "not only x but y" constructions but about "either x or y" constructions.

I wrote not only a note to myself to write about "not only x but y" constructions but a note to myself to write about "either x or y" constructions.

No, I'm not reaching the "All work and no play makes* Jack a dull boy" stage. The point is simply this:

In "not x but y," "not only x but y," "either x or y," "neither x nor y," and "both x and y" constructions, you must ensure that the x and the y match in their makeup—that is to say, are parallel.

(Many people, I've found, have lodged in their heads the absolute necessity of including an "also" in this construction, not merely "not only x but y" but "not only x but also y." Seems like a waste of a good "also" to me. I *would* include an "also" if I chose to express myself thus: "Not only did I write a note to myself to write about 'not only x but y' constructions; I also wrote a note to myself to write about 'either x or y' constructions." But I don't think I'd choose to express myself thus.)

It's an easy thing to get wrong—I can assure you of that firsthand. It's quite easy to write:

> She achieved success not only through native intelligence but perseverance.

and not give it a second thought. But you do want to get this correct, so:

> She achieved success not only through native intelligence but through perseverance.

---

* Jack Torrance's verb of choice. I'd have gone with "make." Either would be correct. Why? Because Jack chooses, perfectly justifiably, to view "all work and no play" as one big fat collective noun—a notional singular, we might call it, like "law and order" or "peas and carrots"—which means it takes a singular verb. Whereas I prefer, also with perfect justification, to see "all work and no play" as a compound subject requiring a plural verb.

She achieved success through not only native intelligence but perseverance.

Similarly:

NO: I can either attempt to work all afternoon or I can go buy a new shower curtain.

YES: I can either attempt to work all afternoon or go buy a new shower curtain.

ALSO YES: Either I can attempt to work all afternoon or I can go buy a new shower curtain.

Or as I once said to T. S. Eliot, "Tom, it's not 'Not with a bang but a whimper.' It's 'With not a bang but a whimper' or 'Not with a bang but with a whimper.' Let's get it right."
Oh, and this:
In "neither x nor y" constructions, if the x is singular and the y is plural, the verb to follow is plural. If the x is plural and the y is singular, the verb to follow is singular. That is, simply: Take your cue from the y.

Neither the president nor the representatives have the slightest idea what's going on.
Neither the representatives nor the president has the slightest idea what's going on.

4.
Q. Is it "It is I who is late" or "It is I who am late"?
A. It's "I'm late." Why make things more complicated than they need to be?

5.

If someone were trying to kill you, how do you think they'd go about it?
Did reading that sentence—the issue of my morbidity and your potential corpseness aside—hurt your ears and/or offend

your sensibilities? If it didn't, you might well choose to skip the rest of this section and move on to the next. If it did, stick around, because we need to talk.

The use in prose of the singular "they"—that is, the application of the pronoun "they" to an individual human being whose gender is neither specified nor, at the moment, relevant—tends to raise the eyebrows of many of us of a certain age, because at some point in the journey of our lives we were either taught or simply inferred—because we never saw it used in the books and magazines and newspapers we read— that it was incorrect.

What we saw, over and over, was something like this:

> [A] beginning writer . . . worries to think of his immaturity, and wonders how he ever dared to think he had a word worth saying.
> —DOROTHEA BRANDE, *Becoming a Writer* (1934)

The 1934 copy editor might well say that the pronoun "he" is perfectly appropriate in such cases, because *of course* by "he" we simply mean any sort of person at all.

Well, this twenty-first-century copy editor would like to point out that plenty of twenty-first-century people will take umbrage and/or feel excluded, and they'll do it quite rightfully and righteously, and they won't all be women, either.

Low rumblings of dissatisfaction re the ostensibly genderless "he" were vehemently making themselves known in manuscripts I was assigned to work on in the early 1990s, and some writers, I noted, were attempting any number of workarounds.

The most popular, as I recall them:

- The use of "he or she," as in "A student should be able to study whatever he or she likes." Perhaps clumsy, and undoubtedly quickly tiresome, but inoffensive.
- The alternation of "he" and "she," sometimes paragraph by paragraph, sometimes sentence by sentence. As in: "If your child is reluctant to eat vegetables, don't

force him. But neither can you give in to a child's whims, because this may lead her not only to malnutrition but to a belief that she's the master of her own destiny." Well-meaning, yes. Maybe a bit vertigo-inducing.

- Flat-out use of the pronoun "she," from page 1 till page the last.
- The use of the construction "s/he," which, truth and happily to tell, I didn't run across all that often. Because it's hideous.

Yet so apparently deeply felt was the proscription against the singular "they" that only rarely, once-in-a-blue-moon rarely, did I meet up with a writer who reached for it. And I did what any self-respecting copy editor in those days would do: I got rid of it.

But how? How can you dispose of a he-that's-not-a-he without resorting to a they-that's-not-a-they without tying into knots either oneself or someone else's prose?

One easy out was always to grab the opportunity to turn a singular noun into a plural one, thus obviating the need for a singular pronoun: "A student should be able to study whatever he likes" transforms easily into "Students should be able to study whatever they like."

When that wasn't possible, I'd find myself trying to figure out how to get a sentence to work without any pronoun at all. It's not as difficult as you might think—a nip here, a tuck there—and the result, I found, or at least persuaded myself, was often a tighter, leaner, stronger sentence.

But OK, let's get back to the second decade of the twenty-first century, in which lexicographers and other word folk enthusiastically remind us that the pronoun "they" has been used singularly in prose* for centuries, happily provide exam-

---

* I stress "in prose," noting that in speech most of us use the singular "they" relentlessly and without a second thought. Such as in the sentence "Once you've hired a copy editor, please remind them not to allow the singular 'they,' OK?"

ples of that use in Great Works of Literature,* dutifully point out that the proscription against the singular "they" is yet another of those Victorian-era pulled-out-of-relatively-thin-air grammar rules we've been saddled with, and, for the big finale, encouragingly encourage us to embrace the singular "they" as the ultimate in pronoun efficiency. Not a workaround, not a solution to a problem, but simply A Thing That's Been Right There All Along.

The singular "they" is not the wave of the future; it's the wave of the present. I fear I'm too old a dog to embrace it, and faced with a wannabe genderless "he" or singular "they," I'm still apt to pull out my tried-and-true tricks to dispose of it.

A few notes, though, before we move on:

- We mightn't be having this discussion at all if we all spoke, say, French, in which every noun, from *professeur* to *livre* to *bibliothèque* to *pomme* is gendered (respectively *le, le, la, la*), take it or leave it, so what's a stray *il* among *amis* (or *amies*), right?
- Sentences like "Every girl in the sorority should do what they like" or "A boy's best friend is their mother" are daft.†
- I can't help but note that quite a number of prose stylists who loudly advocate using the singular "they" wouldn't be caught dead using it themselves, according to the evidence of their surrounding prose. Make of that what you will.

---

*I think of this as the "Jane Austen Did It So It Must Be OK" school of wordsmithery, but it's not a school I attend. I don't punctuate like Jane Austen; I feel no compunction to otherwise English like Jane Austen. If our infinitely malleable language gains in expansion, invention, and reinvention, it can also, for the sake of precision and clarity, benefit from occasionally having its screws tightened, and not every centuries-old definition need be retained when a word has, over time, accumulated more meanings than are perhaps useful.

†I've yet to see this sort of barbarism in competent finished prose, but as I do encounter it increasingly online, I'm making a preemptive strike against it here.

- You will note as well that nowhere in this book's 300-odd pages do I ever (outside of innocuous sample sentences) use the pronoun "he" or "she" to refer to a person who isn't specifically a he or a she. Neither will you encounter a "he or she."
- Over the years I've found that the hardest nut to crack, pronounwise, is a book on child-rearing, as authors—unless they're specifically writing about twins, and there are more books about raising twins than you might think—will want to individualize your teething baby, your rambunctious toddler, and your tantrum-throwing six-year-old. In these books, the singular "they" is virtually unavoidable. Yet for what it's worth, I note that in one of my prize possessions, a tattered copy of *Vogue's Book of Etiquette,* copyright 1923, the pronoun of choice for a nonspecific infant or child is "it."

A further thought:

When I first drafted this section, I relegated the discussion of the use of pronouns for nonbinary people—people who do not identify as male or female—to a terse footnote acknowledging the relatively recent invention of alternate pronouns (I guess I've encountered the "ze"/"zir" system most frequently, but there are a number of others, which certainly impedes universal adoption) and the increasing use of what one might call a particularly singular "they," blithely declared the matter cultural rather than copyeditorial, and excused myself from discussing it further.

In other words, I cut and ran like hell.

And yet: I now have a colleague whose pronoun of choice is "they," and thus the issue is no longer culturally abstract but face-to-face personal, no longer an issue I'd persuaded myself was none of my business but one of basic human respect I chose—choose—to embrace. (I'm happy to call myself out for stubbornly avoiding the topic till it became personal. One is supposed to be better than that; one often isn't.)

For months after my colleague joined Random House, I dodged the issue—in speech and in email—by referring to said colleague by name and twisting myself into knots, as I have just stiltedly done, to avoid any pronoun other than "you." It didn't take long before I found myself bored with and embarrassed by the exertion, and one day in conversation, when I wasn't even paying attention, the word "they" slipped out of my mouth, and that was the end of that.

6.

Here's a sentence I was recently on the verge of making public:

> I think of the Internet as a real place, as real or realer
> than Des Moines.

If you recognize immediately what's the matter with that sentence, you've already grasped the concept of parallelism. If you haven't—and don't be hard on yourself if you haven't, because you're in the occasional company of just about every writer I've ever encountered—here is the correct version:

> I think of the Internet as a real place, as real as or re-
> aler than Des Moines.

It's all about that third "as." How come? To cite the handy definition in *Words into Type,* "Parallelism is the principle that parts of a sentence that are parallel in meaning should be parallel in construction." In this case, "as real" and "realer than" do not match in construction, as you'll note if, in my original sentence, you flip them around:

> I think of the Internet as a real place, realer than or as
> real Des Moines.

Sentences lacking parallelism are direly easy to construct. Here's another:

> A mother's responsibilities are to cook, clean, and the raising of the children.

Which should correctly be:

> A father's responsibilities are to cook, to clean, and to raise the children.

Everything's nice and matchy-matchy now.

There's something bracingly attractive about a sentence that brims with parallelism:

> He was not beholden to, responsible for, or in any other way interested in the rule of law.

7.

At some point in your life, perhaps now, it may occur to you that the phrase "aren't I" is a grammatical trainwreck. You can, at that point, either spend the rest of your life saying "am I not?" or "amn't I?" or embrace yet another of those oddball constructions that sneak into the English language and achieve widespread acceptance, all the while giggling to themselves at having gotten away with something.

8.

> Flipping restlessly through the channels, John Huston's *The Treasure of the Sierra Madre* was playing on TCM.

Huston, we have a problem.

Improperly attaching itself to the sentence's subject—that is, "John Huston's *The Treasure of the Sierra Madre*"—we in the copyediting business call that introductory bit (that is, "Flipping restlessly through the channels") a dangler.

This particular flavor of dangler is called in full a dangling participle, but not all danglers are participles, and anyway, using the term "dangling participle" mandates that you remember what a participle is. "Dangling modifier"—sometimes one runs into the term "misattached modifier" or "misplaced modifier"—makes for a better overall designation, but "dangler" is easier and quicker, so let's just stick with that. Whatever we're calling them, danglers are, I'd say, the most common error committed in otherwise competent prose and by far the most egregious type of error that regularly makes it to print. Authors write them, copy editors overlook them, proofreaders speed past them. It's not a good look.

Essentially, a sentence's introductory bit and its main bit need to fuse correctly. Or, as I like to think of it, they need to talk to each other. If a sentence begins "Flipping restlessly through the channels," then the sentence's subject—more than likely, its very next word—has to tell us who's holding the remote. It might be "I," it might be "he," it might be "Cecilia," but it's certainly not "John Huston's *The Treasure of the Sierra Madre*."

> Strolling through the park, the weather was beautiful.
> *Nope.*
> The weather was beautiful as we strolled through the park. *Yup.*

> Arriving at the garage, my car was nowhere to be found. *Nah.*
> When I arrived at the garage, my car was nowhere to be found. *Yeah.*

Perhaps these sorts of errors seem obvious to you—particularly since we're talking about them here and staring at them—but, as I said, they can slip right past you if you're not paying attention.

For instance, please hop back up a few paragraphs and

take another look at the sentence that begins "Improperly attaching itself."

Yeah. Dangler.

Here's the opening sentence of Norman Mailer's 1991 novel *Harlot's Ghost:*

> On a late-winter evening in 1983, while driving
> through fog along the Maine coast, recollections of
> old campfires began to drift into the March mist,
> and I thought of the . . . Algonquin tribe who dwelt
> near Bangor a thousand years ago.

Now, unless it's the recollections driving through the fog, this sentence has a problem.

How to fix it? Easy:

> On a late-winter evening in 1983, as I drove through
> fog along the Maine coast, recollections of old
> campfires began to drift into the March mist, etc.,
> etc., etc.

The narrator is now driving, the recollections are now drifting, and all is right with the world.

At the time of publication, after the dangler was pointed out, Mailer defended it. "The dangling modifier . . . was my decision, repeated several times over several months, to keep the sentence intact. I like the rhythm as it stands. I could not find a better one by fixing the sentence grammatically. For that matter, the meaning is clear. . . . Dangling participles can offend a few readers intensely but the damage caused might add up to less than the rupture occasioned by straightening out the grammar and wrecking the good mood."

Well, let me put it to you this way:

> Having read that defense, Mailer is utterly unconvincing.

Oh dear.

Having read that defense, I find Mailer to be utterly unconvincing.*

I encounter danglers all the time. They frequently turn up in donated bits of praise generously provided by writers to support other writers—blurbs, that is. "An intoxicating mix of terror and romance, Olga Bracely has penned her best novel yet!"

No.

9.

A sentence whose parts are misarranged to inadvertent comic effect can be a kind of dangler, but mostly I think of it simply as a sentence whose parts are misarranged to inadvertent comic effect.

Or to advertent comic effect, if you're Groucho Marx: "One morning I shot an elephant in my pajamas. How he got into my pajamas, I'll never know."

Or perhaps you've met that famous man with a wooden leg named Smith.

10.

You'd be amazed at how far you can get in life having no idea what the subjunctive mood is—as if it's not bad enough that English has rules, it also has moods—but as long as I've brought the subject up, let's address it.

The subjunctive mood is used to convey various flavors of nonreality. For instance, it dictates the use of "were" rather

---

* When *Harlot's Ghost* was first published, and before Mailer's apologia, the suggestion was ignobly and publicly bruited about by someone who should have been or at least known better that the error had slipped past the manuscript's copy editor. It may well have, but there's no reason to publicly hang an underpaid copy editor out to dry. I know what you're thinking, and: No, it wasn't me. But—now it can be told—I was one of the book's freelance proofreaders. Did I heroically and brilliantly note the error, only to be ignored? I have absolutely no recollection. And I'll bet I didn't.

than "was" in the *Fiddler on the Roof* song "If I Were a Rich Man" and in the frankfurter jingle that begins "I wish I were an Oscar Mayer wiener."

"I wish I were" rather than "I wish I was" seems to come naturally to most people, so let's simply say amen to that and leave it be. The tricky part comes with the juxtaposition of:

"if"

"I," "he," or "she"*

"was" or "were"

Now, if you're lucky enough to be writing a sentence that includes not merely "if" but "as if," you can simply grab on to "were" and run with it:

I felt as if I were a peony in a garden of dandelions.

He comports himself as if he were the king of England.†

But when you've got only an "if" in your hands, when do you use "was" and when do you use "were"?

Well, here's the thing: When I was a baby copy editor, I was told by my betters not to impose the subjunctive on writers who did not naturally use it. That is, if a writer wrote, "If I was president of the United States, I'd spend a bit more time in the Oval Office and a bit less time in Florida," one should leave that writer, and that "was," alone.

That was a marching order I could, for a good long while, march with, and if you're satisfied with it as well, then by all means march away.

---

* To be sure, "you" and "we" and "they" are always matched with "were," so that's one less problem—or three less/fewer problems—to contend with.

† It's indeed "the king of England," not "the King of England." One capitalizes a job title when it's used as an honorific, as in "President Barack Obama," but otherwise it's "the president of the United States," "the pope," and the various other et ceteras. I know that this sort of thing makes royalists and excessively deferential writers go gray in the face, but let's please turn down the hierarchical thinking and styling, OK?

But if you're feeling a little itchy, let's make another run at it. Try this on for size: If you're writing of a situation that is not merely not the case but is unlikely, improbable, or just plain impossible, you can certainly reach for a "were."

> If I were to win the lottery tomorrow, I'd quit my job
> so fast it would make your head spin.

If you're writing of a situation that is simply not the case but could be, you might opt for a *was.*

> If he was to walk into the room right now, I'd give him
> a good piece of my mind.

I tend to think of it thus: If I could insert the words "in fact" after "if I," I might well go with a "was" rather than a "were."

Also, if you're acknowledging some action or state of being that most certainly did occur—that is, if by "if" what you really mean is "in that"—you want a "was":

> If I was hesitant to embrace your suggestion yesterday,
> it was simply that I was too distracted to properly
> absorb it.

CHAPTER 7

The Realities of Fiction

PUTTING ASIDE THE EXTENSIVE MECHANICAL WORK of attending to the rudiments of spelling, punctuation, grammar, etc., the styling of prose is very much about listening. An attentive copy editor should become attuned to and immersed in a writer's voice to the point where the copy editor has so thoroughly absorbed the writer's intentions that the process turns into a sort of conversation-on-the-page.

Nowhere is this conversation more crucial than in the copyediting of fiction, where artistry, however you want to define that slippery concept, can outrank and outweigh notions of what might conventionally be deemed "correct"; where voice—eccentric, particular, peculiar as it may be—is paramount; and where a copy editor, however well-intentioned, who can't hear what a writer is doing, or at least attempting to do, is apt to wreak havoc. Unfortunately, havoc is occasionally wreaked*: I cringingly recall an instance in which one of the finest copy editors I know—so attentive, so sensitive, so

---

*I don't know why some people insist that the past tense of "wreak" is "wrought"—that's a lie, I *do* know why, but I don't want to encourage them— but it is indeed "wreaked."

adept that editors clamor for her services—crashed and burned on a job in which for some mysterious, unhappy reason she didn't understand what the writer was doing generally and, specifically and perhaps worst of all, didn't get his jokes, which she proceeded to flatten as if with a steamroller.* Happily, this sort of calamity is exceptionally rare, and it was easy enough, in this case, to put the writer's nose back in joint by having his manuscript recopyedited, tip to toe, by another copy editor.

Though I can't here demonstrate in any practical fashion the elusive art of empathic listening, I can certainly let you in on some of the methodology—scrutinizing everything, taking nothing for granted, asking lots of questions, taking lots of notes, and performing scores of little tricks—a copy editor employs in the act of copyediting a work of fiction.† I can, as well, point out to you some of the glitches that, since I've repeatedly come face-to-face with them over the years, you may well find in your own work.

THE REAL REALITY OF FICTION

Fiction may be fictional, but a work of fiction won't work if it isn't logical and consistent.

- Characters must age in accordance with the calendar— that is, someone asserted to have been born in May 1960 must then be twenty-five in May 1985, forty in May 2000, etc.—and at the same pace as other characters: Two characters who meet at the ages of

---

* At least she did not, as cataclysmically happened on one job I have firsthand knowledge of, tell the writer repeatedly that her protagonist wouldn't, because it was out of character, do the thing she'd just done. (Note to copy editors: Never do this.)

† Let's please allow that I'm using the term "fiction" here to include as well the various flavors of narrative nonfiction that spring from a writer's memory banks, rather than the kind of formal reportage that coalesces from years of archival research and sheaves of notes.

thirty-five and eighteen cannot, in a later scene, be fifty and merely twenty-six. Grandparents and great-grandparents, I've occasionally noted, are often said to have lived decades out of whack, in either direction, with what is reproductively possible.

- Keep track of the passage of time, particularly in narratives whose plots play themselves out, crucially, in a matter of days or weeks. I've encountered many a Friday arriving two days after a Tuesday, and third graders in math class on what, once one adds up the various "the next day"s, turns out to be a Sunday.

- Height; weight; eye and hair color; nose, ear, and chin size; right- or left-handedness; etc., mandate consistency.

- Stage management and choreography: Watch out for people going up to the attic only to shortly and directly step out onto the driveway; removing their shoes and socks twice over the course of five minutes; drinking from glasses they quite definitively set down, a few paragraphs earlier, in another room;* and reading newspapers that suddenly transform into magazines.

- While we're here: I recall one manuscript in which fully half the characters had names beginning with the letter *M*. You may not be surprised to learn that the author's given name also began with an *M*. This is not a good thing.†

- I don't know why or how writers end up laboriously and lengthily describing restaurant meals as if they—the writers, that is—have never experienced one, but: Pay better attention.

---

*As a rule, the consumption of beverages is not as interesting as many writers seem to think it is.

†It was a point of ongoing perturbation for me that two characters on the *Downton Abbey* series were both—pointlessly, so far as I could discern—named Thomas and that both their surnames began with a *B*.

• I don't know why or how writers end up laboriously and lengthily counterfeiting newspaper articles as if they—the writers, that is—had never read one. At the least, remember to establish the whowhatwhere-whywhen you were taught in high school, and terse it up a bit too.

Fun tip for counterfeiting newspaper articles with verisimilitude and panache: Yank out all the series commas.

ℛ

Real-world details must also be honored. You may think that readers won't notice such things. I assure you they will.

• If you're going to set your story on, say, Sunday, September 24, 1865, make sure that September 24, 1865, was indeed a Sunday. There are any number of perpetual calendars online.* (Also remember that if you're rummaging through old newspaper archives to see what was going on on September 24, 1865, you'd do well to look at newspapers dated September 25, 1865.)

• I recall copyediting a novel in which the protagonist made a journey by, respectively, cab, train, subway, and a second cab in three hours that couldn't, as I proceeded to plot it out with maps, timetables, and a healthy respect for speed limits, possibly have been completed in fewer than ten.

• If you're going to set your story in, say, New York City, you'd better keep track of which avenues guide vehicles south to north and which north to south, and which streets aim east and which west.

• You've likely noticed that the sun rises and sets at dif-

* I've bookmarked timeanddate.com.

ferent times over the course of a year. Make sure you remember to notice that when you're writing.*

- Not all trees and flowers flourish everywhere on Earth.
- If you want to be terribly precise about characters' moviegoing and TV-watching habits, as many writers seem intent on doing, make sure that, say, *The Sound of Music* was in theaters in the summer of 1965† or that *That Girl* aired on Wednesdays.‡ If you're not up for that sort of thing, you always have the option of giving less rather than more detailed information, or you can just make up fictitious but plausible-sounding movies and TV series, which I think is a lot more fun anyway.
- Five-digit zip codes didn't turn up till the 1960s (and the additional four digits didn't arrive till the 1980s); neither did the two-letter periodless state abbreviations we're all now used to. An envelope in the 1950s would not have been addressed to, say:

Boston, MA 02128

It would have been, using the postal zone system devised in the 1940s, addressed to:

Boston 28, Mass.

If your epistolary novel spanning decades requires this sort of stuff, you'd do well to get this sort of stuff right.§

---

* Google "sunrise sunset" and you'll be led not only to a number of useful sites but to Eddie Fisher's plaintive rendition of the hit song from *Fiddler on the Roof*.

† It was. You can find your own way to IMDb.

‡ It didn't. It aired on Thursdays. Wikipedia is great for this sort of thing.

§ Having, I trust, made my point, I leave you to your own research on the history of phone numbers, exchanges, area codes, mandatory area codes, and the digit 1.

• Period authenticity also mandates technical and societal plausibility, and this covers everything from the invention and obsolescence of phone answering machines (especially the sort on which people were always, to their plot-twisting embarrassment, overhearing messages intended for others as they were being left), to the iterations and capabilities of the iPhone, to pre- and post-9/11 levels of security in airports and office buildings, to the existence and popularity of particular pharmaceuticals.*

• Some historical novelist out there may well find this useful, so here's a bit of trivia for you: Recordings at the dawn of that technology were often introduced, right on the wax cylinder, by a sort of emcee, thus: "'All Going Out and Nothing Coming In,' by Mr. Bert Williams, of Williams and Walker, Edison Records!"

• Period vocabulary is its own issue: A writer working on a novel set in eighteenth-century London certainly isn't restricted to the extant words of that era (or its grammar, or its punctuation), but you do want to be careful not to insert glaring anachronisms. I once encountered the word "maverick" showing up a few centuries in advance of the birth of Samuel A. Maverick, on whom the word was founded, and a reference to a woman's outfit as "matchy-matchy" in 1920s Manhattan, which: no.

Dictionaries are particularly helpful in providing the first known use of any given word, so avail yourself of one.

---

* It's been said, and sometimes I believe it, that the worst things to happen to modern fiction are the invention of the cellphone and the availability of antidepressants. But that's a subject for another book.

- If you're dabbling in historical pastiche—that is, going out of your way to imitate the word conventions of the era in which your story is set—only you can decide how heavily you wish to dabble. A novel set in the early twentieth century might well feature not a lightbulb, as we'd now style that word, but a light bulb or a light-bulb, and you may or may not want to refer to a telephone as a 'phone, an omnibus as a 'bus, or influenza as the 'flu.
- Sometimes you just can't win. Long ago, in the pre-Internet era, when it wasn't quite so easy to know everything in a split second, I copyedited a novel set in the early 1960s that referred in passing to a Burger King. "AU," I wrote in the margin, "PLS. CONFIRM THE EXISTENCE OF BURGER KINGS IN THE 1960S." The author ultimately chose to change the Burger King to some sort of Grilled Sandwich Shack of his own devise, acknowledging to me that though he'd carefully researched the history of the food chain and was accurate in his citation, every single person who'd read the manuscript before I did had asked him the same question, and it wasn't, he decided, worth the reader hiccup.*

THE BASICS OF GOOD STORYTELLING

Many writers rely more heavily on pronouns than I'd suggest is useful. For me this sort of thing comes under the heading Remember that Writing Is Not Speaking. When we talk, we can usually make ourselves understood even amid a flood of vague "he"s and "she"s. On the page, too many pronouns are apt to be confounding. I'd strongly suggest to the point of in-

---

* My copy editor has queried my use above of the phrase "his own devise," wondering whether it's (a) too quaint for its own good, and (b) apt to be mistaken for a typo. It's a good thing we have explanatory, clarifying footnotes, isn't it.

sistence that you avoid referring to two people by the same pronoun over the course of a single sentence; to be frank, I'd suggest that you avoid it over the course of a single paragraph. (I know a few authors of same-sex romance novels who are regularly driven to tears by this sort of thing.) The repetition of characters' names is certainly one possible fallback, and though you as a writer may initially think that that third "Constance" over the course of seven sentences is overkill, I as your copy editor strongly believe that your readers will be happier not to have to puzzle over which "she" you're talking about; I think of this as basic skeletal stuff and believe that it's all but invisible to readers. On the other hand, if your paragraph is awash with names and pronouns and you think it's all too much, hunker down and do the sort of revision that eliminates the need for an excess of either. It can be tricky, but it's worth it, and it may well net you a leaner, stronger bit of prose.

- If your attempts to distinguish between unnamed characters of no particular importance lead to describing what "the first woman" then said or did to "the second woman," you might want to step back and give these women, if not names, at least distinct physical characteristics that can be expressed in one or two words. The redhead. The older woman. Something.
- One writer of my beloved acquaintance possesses, it seems, only one way to denote an indeterminate number of things: "a couple." And not even "a couple of." No, it's a couple hours, a couple days, a couple cookies, a couple guys. Over time I attempted to introduce her to concepts like "few," "several," and "some," but she remained largely unpersuaded, and I largely stopped nagging her about it. I urge the rest of you to strive for variation.
- When you've come up with that piquantly on-the-nose, distinctive, wow-that's-perfect adjective, you may—as

I've noticed—be so pleased with it that you unwittingly summon it up again right away. If an idea is, say, benighted on p. 27, some other idea oughtn't to be benighted on p. 31.* Consider jotting down on a pad your favorite five-dollar words as you use them to ensure that none of them appear more than once per manuscript.

• Keep an eye on the repetition of even garden-variety nouns, verbs, adjectives, and adverbs of only moderate distinction, which you might not want to repeat in proximity—unless you're doing this with a purpose, in which case: Do it.

Here, for instance, is a marvelous example. I've always cherished it, and I like to haul it out whenever I can, as it celebrates the skill of a writer who's not often complimented on his writing.

When Dorothy stood in the doorway and looked around, she could see nothing but the great gray prairie on every side. Not a tree nor a house broke the broad sweep of flat country that reached the edge of the sky in all directions. The sun had baked the plowed land into a gray mass, with little cracks running through it. Even the grass was not green, for the sun had burned the tops of the long blades until they were the same gray color to be seen everywhere. Once the house had been painted, but the sun blistered the paint and the rains washed it away, and now the house was as dull and gray as everything else.

When Aunt Em came there to live she was a young, pretty wife. The sun and wind had changed her, too. They had taken the sparkle from her eyes and left them a sober gray; they had taken the red from her cheeks and lips, and they were gray also.

---

* I was recently advised of a novel in which the word "spatulate"—I didn't recognize it either; it's an adjective that means "shaped like a spatula"—showed up twice in two pages, referring to two entirely unrelated nouns. Oh dear.

She was thin and gaunt, and never smiled, now. When Dorothy, who was an orphan, first came to her, Aunt Em had been so startled by the child's laughter that she would scream and press her hand upon her heart whenever Dorothy's merry voice reached her ears; and she still looked at the little girl with wonder that she could find anything to laugh at.

Uncle Henry never laughed. He worked hard from morning till night and did not know what joy was. He was gray also, from his long beard to his rough boots, and he looked stern and solemn, and rarely spoke.

It was Toto that made Dorothy laugh, and saved her from growing as gray as her other surroundings. Toto was not gray; he was a little black dog, with long silky hair and small black eyes that twinkled merrily on either side of his funny, wee nose. Toto played all day long, and Dorothy played with him, and loved him dearly.

Gray, gray, gray. Nine of them over the course of four paragraphs. They don't make a lot of noise— would you have noticed them had I not set you looking for them?—but they get the job done.*

Even a "he walked up the stairs and hung up his coat" might, if you're so inclined, benefit from a tweak—easy in this case: Just change "walked up" to "climbed."† I'll extend this advice even to the suggestion that you avoid echoing similar-sounding words: a "twilight" five words away from a "light," for instance.‡

---

* Hoorah for L. Frank Baum and *The Wonderful Wizard of Oz*, of which these paragraphs are (nearly) the opening.

† Beyond eliminating the "up" repetition, you've also replaced a prepositional phrase with a more precise single-word verb, which almost invariably declutters and improves a sentence.

‡ How bothersome are these wee repetitions to civilian readers? I can't say, not having been a civilian reader in decades, but as a copy editor I'm highly aware of them and will always point them out. Beyond that it's up to the writer.

- Also be wary of inadvertent rhymes, of the "Rob commuted to his job" or "make sure that tonight is all right" sort. By "be wary," I mean: Don't do them.
- Writers' brains, I've noted, have a tendency to play tricks when the writer isn't paying attention, and in copyediting I've occasionally run across weird little puns, echoes, and other bits of unconscious wordplay. Every time I read Shirley Jackson's "The Lottery," I'm stopped in my tracks by this:

> She watched while Mr. Graves came around from the side of the box, greeted Mr. Summers gravely, and selected a slip of paper from the box.

> Somehow I can't imagine Jackson stooping on purpose to such a thudding little joke.

- With all the nodding and head shaking going on, I'm surprised that half the characters in modern fiction haven't dislocated something. By the way, characters who nod needn't nod their heads, as there's really not much else available to nod. And the same goes for the shrugging of unnecessarily-alluded-to shoulders. What else are you going to shrug? Your elbows?
- If everyone in your world is forever pushing their eyeglasses up their collective noses, please send everyone and their eyeglasses to an optician's shop.
- How often do you stare into the middle distance? Me neither.
- A brief, scarcely exhaustive list of other actions that wise writers might do well to put on permanent hiatus:

> the angry flaring of nostrils
> the thoughtful pursing of lips
> the quizzical cocking of the head
> the letting out of the breath you didn't even know you were holding

the extended mirror stare, especially as a warm-up
for a memory whose recollection is apt to go on
for ten pages

Also overrated:

blinking
grimacing
huffing
pausing (especially for "a beat")
smiling weakly
snorting
swallowing
doing anything wistfully

- "After a moment," "in a moment," "she paused a moment," "after a long moment" . . . There are so many
moments. So many.
- This may be a particular peeve of mine and no one
else's, but I note it, because it's my book: Name-
dropping, for no better reason than to show off, underappreciated novels, obscure foreign films, or cherished
indie bands by having one's characters irrelevantly
reading or watching or listening to them is massively
sore-thumbish. A novel is not a blog post about Your
Favorite Things.* If you must do this sort of thing—
and, seriously, must you?—contextualize heavily.
- For fiction written in the past tense, here's a technique
for tackling flashbacks that I stumbled upon years
ago, and writers I've shared it with have tended to get
highly excited: Start off your flashback with, let's say,
two or three standard-issue "had"s ("Earlier that year,
Jerome had visited his brother in Boston"), then clip
one or two more "had"s to a discreet "'d" ("After an
especially unpleasant dinner, he'd decided to return

* Though apparently this book is.

home right away"), then drop the past-perfecting altogether when no one's apt to be paying attention and slip into the simple past ("He unlocked his front door, as he later recalled it, shortly after midnight"). Works like a charm.

- You writers are all far too keen on "And then," which can usually be trimmed to "Then" or done away with entirely.
- You're also overfond of "suddenly."

Yet Another
Shirley Jackson Reference

A few years ago* I had the unforeseen-except-perhaps-in-work-related-dreams honor of copyediting my favorite author, Shirley Jackson, whom I'd not previously had the pleasure of working with because she died when I was in the first grade. Random House had contracted to publish a book of some of Jackson's previously uncollected and/or entirely unseen stories and essays,† and I happily nominated myself to attend to whatever dusting off and polishing up the material needed.

Unsurprisingly, the previously published stuff demanded little of my time: It had been well attended to by the magazines that had been a regular and lucrative source of income for Jackson—*Woman's Day, Good Housekeeping,* and *McCall's,* believe it or not, not to mention *The New Yorker.* Some minor fussings-about aside, those pieces were

---

* Now that I look at my records I can tell you that "a few years ago" was, to be precise, 2014, which I mention only because this is a perfect opportunity for me to remind you that when it comes to information, less is often more. A: It's not particularly interesting that this story occurred in 2014, is it. B: The more specific a writer gets in providing details down to the nuclear level, the more likely it is that at least some of those details are going to be incorrect. "A few" is inapt to be incorrect.

† The collection went through a couple of titles before it was finally named *Let Me Tell You,* and it is now, as they say, available wherever better books are sold.

republished essentially as they had been seen in Jackson's lifetime.

But much of the unpublished material had been presented to us in photocopies of Jackson's characteristic all-lowercase first drafts—I imagine her clattering away at her typewriter in bursts of determined creativity, not bothering to reach for the SHIFT key—and no writer dead or alive deserves to have their material sent to press without at least some review.* To say nothing of capital letters.

I assured the book's editors, who happened to be two of Jackson's grown children and literary executors, that being a lifelong devotee of their mother's work and having read and reread her writing for decades, I knew Jackson's voice as well as any copy editor could hope to know it. I promised them that the material was in safe hands and that I didn't expect to do much more than correct the odd typo.

But: Once I got to work I realized that though the material was, throughout, first-rate—shockingly clean, I'd say, given that it seemed to have moved straight from Jackson's brain to her fingers to the pages and never been touched again—it needed a bit, truly just a bit, of a helping hand.

Having no live author to query—though, to be sure, anything I wanted to do was going to be run past the heirs—I extricated myself from the horns of this dilemma by setting for myself respectful ground rules: I'd allow myself free rein with punctuation, turn the occasional unclear pronoun into a clearer noun (or, if a noun seemed uncalled for, do the reverse), and attempt otherwise never to delete or add more than two words—little words like *the* and *that* and *which* and *and*—at a time.

As it turned out, I was overwhelmingly able to stick to those strictures. Beyond that I found maybe a half dozen knotted-up sentences that were easily untangled—just as, I'm confident, Jackson herself would have untangled them on a second or third run-through. I also quickly discovered that Jackson went to the well of "suddenly" and "and then" rather frequently—there are quite a few fewer of both in the

---

* Just thought I'd test-drive a singular "they" to see how it felt. It felt . . . OK. Not great.

finished book—and occasionally put more pressure on the worthy semicolon than a semicolon can bear.

At one point I stared down a single paragraph for a good twenty minutes, willing its last sentence to be its first. Or was it the other way around? In the event, I eventually realized that the author was right and I was wrong and left the paragraph alone.

Once and only once did I venture to suggest that two substantive words needed to be added to fill out a sentence whose rhythm I couldn't make peace with, and those two words* made it into the book, and I like to flatter myself that I'd ventured so thoroughly into the Shirley Jackson Place by then that the words were not mine but hers. To date, I've experienced no alarmingly blown-open windows or inexplicably smashed crockery, so I like to think that Shirley Jackson is content.

- "He began to cry" = "He cried." Dispose of all "began to"s.
- My nightmare sentence is "And then suddenly he began to cry."

DIALOGUE AND ITS DISCONTENTS

- Fond as I am of semicolons, they're ungainly in dialogue. Avoid them.
- In real-life conversation, how often do you say the name of the person to whom you're speaking?

  Not that much?

  Then why do your characters do it so frequently?
- There's an awful lot of murmuring in fiction nowadays. One writer I repeatedly worked with assured me after a few collaborations that, as he wrote, he let all his characters murmur as much as they wanted to because he knew I would call him out on it, and then

---

* Now it can be told: "garden-variety."

he'd cut back on it. There's also, I note, a great deal of whispering, quite a lot of it hoarse. Perhaps you might offer your hoarse whisperer a cup of tea or a lozenge.

- Italics for emphasis in dialogue can be helpful, but use them sparingly. For one thing, readers don't always relish being told, in such a patently obvious fashion, how to read. For another, if the intended emphasis in any given line of dialogue can't be detected without the use of italics, it's possible that your given line of dialogue could use a bit of revision anyway. Among other solutions, try tossing the bit that needs emphasis to the end of a sentence rather than leaving it muddling in the middle.

Copyediting one masterly novel, I recall gingerly attempting, over the course of a few hundred pages, perhaps a dozen bits of italicization that I thought might be clarifying. The author politely declined, each and every time. (She was right. Authors often are. One of the dangers of copyediting really good writing is that you may find yourself looking to do something to earn your keep and making suggestions that don't need to be suggested.)

- Go light on exclamation points in dialogue. No, even lighter than that. Are you down to none yet? Good.
- Owen Meany may have spoken in all capital letters, but I'll wager your characters can make themselves heard without them. Use italics for shouting, if you must. And, yes, exclamation points—one at a time. No boldface, please, not ever.
- One especially well attended school of thought endorses setting off dialogue with nothing fancier than "he said" and "she said." I've encountered enough characters importuning tearily and barking peevishly that I'm not unsympathetic to that suggestion of re-

straint, but there's no reason to be quite so spartan should your characters occasionally feel the need to bellow, whine, or wheedle. Please, though: moderation. A lot of this:

he asked helplessly
she cried ecstatically
she added irrelevantly
he remarked decisively
objected Tom crossly
broke out Tom violently

is hard to take, and I suppose I should have a chat with F. Scott Fitzgerald, as all of these come from the first chapter of *The Great Gatsby*.

• If your seething, exasperated characters must hiss something—and, really, must they?—make sure they're hissing something hissable.

"Take your hand off me, you brute!" she hissed.
—CHARLES GARVICE, *Better Than Life* (1891)

Um, no, she didn't. You try it.

"Chestnuts, chestnuts," he hissed. "Teeth! teeth! my preciousss; but we has only six!"
—J.R.R. TOLKIEN, *The Hobbit* (1937)

OK, now we're cooking.*

I've seen the argument put forth that any sort of strained constricted whispering qualifies as hissing. To which I can only say that of the approximately 4.3 million ways in which one can characterize speech, "hissed" is not your best bet for s-less utterances. Pick

---

* Alas, shortly thereafter, Gollum—because it's he, who else?—hisses, "Not fair! not fair!" Which is ungreat, but he then goes for the gold with "It isn't fair, my precious, is it, to ask us what it's got in its nassty little pocketses?"

THE REALITIES OF FICTION | 119

another word. Snarled. Grumbled. Susurrated. Well, maybe not susurrated.

As far as I'm concerned:

No sibilants = no hissing.

- Inserting a "she said" into a speech after the character's been rattling on for six sentences is pointless. If you're not setting a speech tag before a speech, then at least set it early on, preferably at the first possible breathing point.

- Something, something, something, she thought to herself.

Unless she's capable of thinking to someone else—and for all I know your character is a telepath—please dispose of that "to herself" instanter.

- In olden times, one often saw articulated thought—that is, dialogue that remains in a character's brain, unspoken—set in quotation marks, like dialogue. Then, for a while, italics (and no quotation marks) were all the rage. Now, mostly such thoughts are simply set in roman, as, say:

I'll never be happy again, Rupert mused.

As it's perfectly comprehensible, and as no one likes to read a lot of italics, I endorse this.*

- Speaking of articulated thought, I'm not entirely persuaded that people, with any frequency, or at all, blurt out the thoughts they're thinking.

And when they do, I doubt very much that they suddenly clap their hands over their mouths.

- "Hello," he smiled.

"I don't care," he shrugged.

No.

---

*Copy editor to me: "You said that before." Me to copy editor: "I say it often."

Dialogue can be said, shouted, sputtered, barked, shrieked, or whispered—it can even be murmured—but it can't be smiled or shrugged.

Occasionally one will even encounter the likes of

"That's all I have to say," he walked out of the room.

The easiest copyeditorial solutions to such things are:

"Hello," he said with a smile.
"Hello," he said, smiling.

or the blunter

"Hello." He smiled.

The better writerly solution is not to employ these constructions in the first place.

"Hello," He Smiled:
The Richard Russo Story

It begins with this:

"Try to preserve an author's style if he is an author and has a style."

That's an editorial maxim from *The New Yorker*'s[*] Wolcott Gibbs dating back to the middish 1930s, and I'd happened upon it in the back pages of *Genius in Disguise*, Thomas Kunkel's irresistible biography of Harold Ross, the magazine's co-founder.[†]

I liked Gibbs's remark so much that I typed it up, printed it out in a great big font, and taped it to my office door. The hallway side, for the record.

---

[*] Be careful not to italicize the apostrophe or the *s* in the possessive of a noun itself set in italics.

[†] The other co-founder? Jane Grant, Ross's wife, who somehow, mysteriously, often goes unmentioned.

It's 1995, I retrocalculate, and I was relatively green as a copy editor and relatively new to Random House as a production editor and possessed of the arrogance of relative if receding youth and of thinking I knew a lot more than I did. And somehow I read Wolcott Gibbs's double-edged sword of an epigram far too often as a mandate not to preserve respectfully but to fix: to take the rules I'd learned and been taught and boned up on and impose them on writers not so blessed with my knowledge and expertise.

I must have been insufferable.

So here I am, with my motto on my door, supervising the production of, let's say, a dozen or so books, including *Straight Man*, a novel by the excellent Richard Russo, who'd go on in the early 2000s to win a Pulitzer Prize for *Empire Falls*. (*Straight Man* is not nearly as well known, I think, as it ought to be, and it's riotously funny. Go find a copy.)

Early on in the process, as the manuscript had just been mailed off to the freelancer I'd contracted to copyedit it, Russo was for some reason or other in the building and, nicely enough, visited me in my office. I can't say I recall what we chatted about, but he was genial and anticipatorily appreciative, and I presume I was deferential and respectful, and off we went.

It's a few weeks later now, and the copyedited manuscript of *Straight Man* has been sent to its author for review and response, and thus it's out of sight and out of mind—out of my mind, at least—as I'm working away on something else, when the phone rings.

"Benjamin, it's Rick Russo."

Pleasantries are exchanged.

"Benjamin, would you say that I'm an author?"

Absolute bafflement. "Well, of course."

"And would you say that I have a style?"

The light begins to break forth, but it's still shadowy inside my head. "Well, of course," I repeat, definitively if warily.

It transpires that my copy editor—who, Rick immediately assures me, has done an exemplary job throughout—has also performed, repeatedly, a standard bit of copyeditorial tweakery, which was to, in encountering the likes of

"Hello," he smiled.

alter it to something like

"Hello," he said with a smile.

or perhaps

"Hello," he said smilingly.

or even, perhaps and simply,

"Hello." He smiled.

The point, as possibly you've inferred, being that one can say hello, and one can smile, but one can't smile hello—or, for that matter, smile any other utterance. One must indeed *say* it. Copyediting 101.

"If I admit," Rick goes on, "that I fully recognize that the copy editor is right and I am wrong, and that this helloing smiling thing is dreadful and insupportable and should never be allowed, might you see fit to allow me to leave it be for no better reason than that I prefer it that way?"

Well, what is one to say in response? He's the author, he's charming, and I'm a pushover in the face of a charm offensive, as any number of writers who've wrapped me around their little fingers have figured out over the years. And, after all and most important, it's his book. At least I know which one of us is the dog and which the tail.

"Of course," I smiled.

And thus Rick Russo had his way, and *Straight Man* was published, and no reviewers, so far as I recall, went out of their way to call out and condemn the helloing smiling construction, and I went right back to doing my best to ensure that the helloing smiling construction never again made its way into print—because, truly, I thought it was awful then and I think it's awful now. But eternal gratitude to Rick Russo for having taught me an invaluable lesson:

The lesson being that notwithstanding all the commonly asserted rules of prose one has been taught in school or read about in stylebooks, authors do, as Wolcott Gibbs recognized and, now, so do I, have their preservable styles, and the role of a copy editor is, above all else, to assist and enhance and advise rather than to correct—indeed, not to try to transform a book into the copy editor's notion of what a good book should be but, simply and with some measure of humility, to help fulfill an author's vision and make each book into the ideal version of itself.

The other lesson being, I suppose, that Rick Russo is terribly observant of the things one posts on one's office door even if he doesn't mention it at the time.

A FEW POINTERS ON UNFINISHED SPEECH

- If one of your characters is speaking and is cut off in midsentence by the speech or action of another character, haul out a dash:

  "I'm about to play Chopin's Prelude in—"
  Grace slammed the piano lid onto Horace's fingers.

- When a line of dialogue is interrupted by an action, note that the dashes are placed not within the dialogue but on either side of the interrupting action.

  "I can't possibly"—she set the jam pot down furiously—"eat such overtoasted toast."

Writers will often do this:

  "I can't possibly—" she set the jam pot down furiously "—eat such overtoasted toast."

and that floating, unmoored narration is, I'm sure you'll agree, spooky-looking.

- If one of your characters is speaking and drifts off dreamily in midsentence, indicate that not with a dash but with an ellipsis.

"It's been such a spring for daffodils," she crooned kittenishly.* "I can't recall the last time . . ." She drifted off dreamily in midsentence.

- When characters self-interrupt and immediately re-sume speaking with a pronounced change in thought, I suggest the em dash–space–capital letter combo pack, thus:

   "Our lesson for today is— No, we can't have class outside today, it's raining."†

- "Furthermore," he noted, "if your characters are in the habit of nattering on for numerous uninterrupted paragraphs of dialogue, do remember that each para-graph of dialogue concludes without a closing quota-tion mark, until you get to the last one.

   "Only then do you properly conclude the dialogue with a closing quotation mark.

   "Like so."

MISCELLANEOUSLY

- If you're writing a novel in English that's set, say, in France, all of whose characters are ostensibly speak-ing French, do not pepper their dialogue with actual French words and phrases—*maman* and *oui* and *n'est-ce pas*—you remember from the fourth grade. It's silly, cheap, obvious, and any other adjectives you might like if they'll stop you from doing this sort of thing. (Whenever I encounter these bits of would-be

---

* I'd originally written "such a *summer* for daffodils." My copy editor cor-rected me.

† The speaker just comma-spliced, and I feel fine about that. The odd comma splice isn't going to kill anyone. You could, if you chose, break up that last bit into two sentences, but it's not as effective, nor does it quite convey the intended sound of the utterance.

local color, I assume that the characters are suddenly speaking in English.)

- Conversely, real-life nonnative speakers of English, I find, rarely lapse into their native tongue simply to say yes, no, or thank you.

- And I implore you: Do not attempt, here in the twenty-first century, to convey the utterance of a character who may be speaking other than what, for the sake of convenience, I'll call standard English with the use of tortured phonetic spellings, the relentless replacement of terminal g's with apostrophes, or any of the other tricks that might have worked for Mark Twain, Zora Neale Hurston, or William Faulkner but are, I assure you, not going to work for you. At best you'll come off as classist and condescending; at worst, in some cases, you'll tip over into racism.

A lot can be accomplished in the conveyance of eccentricity of speech with word choice and word order. Make good use of those.[*]

- You could certainly do worse than to follow the standard of Gore Vidal's immortal Myra Breckinridge: "I am fortunate in having no gift at all for characterizing in prose the actual speech of others and so, for literary purposes, I prefer to make everyone sound like me."

- I've mentioned this before, and it applies to all writing, but I think it applies especially to fiction, whether you're writing it or copyediting it: Reading fiction aloud highlights strengths and exposes weaknesses. I heartily recommend it.

---

[*] Less direly, I'd urge you to avoid as well characterizing speech impediments phonetically. Something like "And if the truth hurtth you it ithn't my fault, ith it, Biff?" (once again: Gypsy Rose Lee, *The G-String Murders*) may—or may not—be funny the first time, but it's tasteless, to say nothing of tiresome.

PART II

The Stuff
in the Back

CHAPTER 8

Notes on, Amid a List of, Frequently and/or Easily Misspelled Words

O NE MORNING IN DECEMBER 2016 the then president-elect of the United States took to Twitter, as was his incessant wont, and accused the Chinese, who'd just, in an act of penny-ante provocation, shanghaied a U.S. drone, of an "unpresidented act." In a flash I was reminded of the importance of knowing how to spell.

The fact is: A lot of people don't type* with autocorrect or spellcheck turned on—or, I gather, heed them even if they do. That said, neither† autocorrect nor spellcheck can save you

---

* Meaning no disrespect to anyone who regularly applies pen or pencil to paper, I haven't in years handwritten anything lengthier than a greeting on a birthday card, and I've come to think of writing as something one does on a computer keyboard. Thus I tend to use the words "write" and "type" interchangeably.

† Please note the first word in this chapter to give the lie to the "*i* before *e,* except after *c*" jingle, which we were all taught in grade school and which is, alongside the spelling mnemonic "The principal is your pal," some major grade school bullshit, if you ask me. ("Or when sounding like *a,* as in 'neighbor' or 'weigh,'" the ditty continues, but you'd stopped listening by then, hadn't you.) There are any number of perfectly common words in the English language featuring the *ei* combination with no *c* (or *a* sound) in sight, from "foreign" to "heist" to "seizure" to "weird." To say nothing of "albeit" and "deify."

from typing a word that is indeed a word but doesn't happen to be the word you mean or should mean to type. For more on that, see Chapter 10: The Confusables.

It goes without saying, though I'm happy to say it, that no one expects you to memorize the spelling of every word in the notoriously irregular, unmemorizable English language. My desk dictionary of choice, and that of most of my copyeditorial colleagues, is the eleventh edition of *Merriam-Webster's Collegiate Dictionary* (affectionately known as *Web 11*); I also keep on a nearby stand a copy of the big *Webster's Third New International Dictionary,* not as *New* now as it was when it was first published in 1961, though mostly it just sits there looking authoritative. You'll also find a number of first-rate dictionaries online, including Merriam-Webster's own, at merriam-webster.com (and if you're a Twitter person, you owe it to yourself to follow the cheekily erudite @Merriam-Webster), and the densely helpful Free Dictionary (thefreedictionary.com). (Google's dictionary, which is where you'll land if you google* any word at all plus the word "definition," is workmanlikely reliable but drab.)

Still and all, I do think that knowing how to spell on one's own is a commendable skill, so for a back-to-elementary-school brushup I offer you a selection of the words I most frequently encounter misspelled—some of which, I don't bother to blush to confess, I've been known to mess up myself—with remarks on some of the general issues of the art of spelling and its pitfalls. If you can, already or afterward, ace all of these, award yourself a shiny foil star.

ACCESSIBLE

The "-ible" words and the "-able" words are easily confusable, and I'm afraid there's no surefire trick for remembering which

---

*It's considered bad copyeditorial form to verbify trademarks, but if you must (and, yes, I know you think you must), I suggest that you lowercase them in so doing. Sorry/not sorry, Xerox Corporation.

are which. Though it is the case that most of the "-able"s are words in their own right even if you delete the "-able" (e.g., "passable," "manageable") and that most of the "-ible"s are not, shorn of their "-ible," freestanding (e.g., "tangible," "audible"), most is not all. As, to be sure, our friend "accessible." And see "confusable," seven lines up. "Confus"?

ACCOMMODATE, ACCOMMODATION

Words with double *c*'s are troublemakers; words with double *c*'s and double *m*'s are invitations to catastrophe.

ACKNOWLEDGMENT

This is the preferred American spelling. The Brits favor (but not by much and only relatively recently) "acknowledgement."*

AD NAUSEAM

Not spelled "ad nauseum."

AFICIONADOS

Copyediting FAQ

Q. How do I know which words ending in *o* are pluralized with an *s* and which are pluralized with an *es*?

A. You don't. Look 'em up.

ANOINT

"Annoint" is a legitimate if obscure and mostly archaic variant spelling, but that doesn't mean you should use it. Same goes for "bannister."

ANTEDILUVIAN

Perhaps not a word you use terribly often, but if you're going to use it, that's how you spell it.

---

* Evidence also indicates that our British cousins are not as fond of the spelling "judgement" as some of them believe or would have you believe. And here is where I send you off (you'll find out why when you get there) to explore the Google Books Ngram Viewer, though I warn you that it's a direly addictive toy.

ASSASSIN, ASSASSINATE, ASSASSINATED, ASSASSINATION
Don't stint on the *s*'s.

BARBITURATE
I'd guess that a popular misapprehension of pronunciation leads to a popular misapprehension of spelling, thus "barbituate," but that's not how you spell it.

BATTALION
Two *t*'s, one *l*, not the other way around. Think "battle," if that helps you.*

BOOKKEEPER
The only legitimate English word I'm aware of that includes three consecutive sets of double letters,† and in writing it you're quite apt to forget the second *k*.‡

BUOY, BUOYANCY, BUOYANT
That oddish *uo*, which somehow never looks right, is easy to flip; thus my periodic encounters with "bouy," "bouyancy," and "bouyant."

BUREAUCRACY
First you have to nail down the spelling of "bureau," which is hard enough. Once you've conquered "bureau," you can likely manage "bureaucrat" and "bureaucratic," but be careful not to crash and burn, as I often do, on "bureaucracy," which always wants to come out "bureaucrasy."

CAPPUCCINO
Two *p*'s and two *c*'s.

Also, there is no *x* in "espresso," but you knew that already.

---

* My problem with mnemonic devices is that I can't remember them.
† Well, yes, "bookkeeping." No, "sweet-toothed" doesn't count.
‡ Or, if you prefer, the first *k*.

CENTENNIAL

And its cousins "sesquicentennial"* and "bicentennial."

CHAISE LONGUE

That's indeed how you spell it, because that's what it is—literally, from the French, a long chair. But the spelling "chaise lounge" took root in English, especially American English, an awfully long time ago, and it's not going anywhere, and one would be hard-pressed anymore to call it an error, particularly when it turns up in novels in the dialogue of characters who would not naturally say "chaise longue."

COMMANDOS

My—and most people's—preferred plural of "commando." (Though "commandoes," which suggests to me a troop of female deer packing Uzis, is, per the dictionary, less incorrect than "aficionadoes.")

CONSENSUS

Not "concensus."

DACHSHUND

Two *h*'s.

DAIQUIRI

Three *i*'s.

DAMMIT

It's not "damnit," goddammit and damn it all to hell, and I wish people would knock it off already.

---

* I'm not sure why English needs a dedicated word for a 150th anniversary, but if it has a word for the thing before the thing before the final thing† and a word for jumping or being shoved out a window,‡ why not.

† "Antepenultimate."

‡ "Defenestration."

DE RIGUEUR

A fancy-schmancy adjective meaning "required or prescribed by fashion"; to misspell it is the ne plus ultra of failed pretension.

DIETICIAN, DIETITIAN

They're both correct. The latter is vastly more popular, though somehow I think the former better evokes the hairnets and lab coats of the elementary school lunch ladies of my distant youth.

DIKE

The things that keep the Netherlands from flooding are dikes. Let's leave it at that.

DILEMMA

Ask a roomful of people whether at any time in their lives they believed this word to be spelled "dilemna," and you will receive in return quite a number of boisterous yeses. But the word is not spelled thus; it's never been spelled thus. Whence, then, "dilemna"? It remains a mystery.

DIPHTHERIA

Not "diptheria." There are two *h*'s here.

DOPPELGÄNGER

The popular error is to transpose the *el* to an *le*.

DUMBBELL

Double *b*. The odds are good that left to your own devices you're going to spell this "dumbell," as you're also likely to attempt "filmaker," "newstand," and "roomate." Well, don't.

ECSTASY

Not "ecstacy." Perhaps you're confusing it with bureaucracy.

ELEGIAC

Not "elegaic," a misspelling that makes it into print with mournful frequency.

ENMITY

I was well into my twenties before I realized that this word was neither pronounced nor spelled "emnity." I have since learned—and I find it retroactively comforting—that I was not, and am not, the only victim of that misapprehension.

FASCIST

Capitalized when referring to an actual member of Mussolini's Fascisti, the British Union of Fascists, or any other organization that thus self-identifies, otherwise lowercased.[*]

FILMMAKER, FILMMAKING

Noted above, under "dumbbell," yet given the frequency with which I encounter "filmaker" and "filmaking," apparently worth repeating.

FLACCID

Pronunciation is not my fiefdom—I don't have to say 'em, I just have to spell 'em—but you may pronounce this either "flaksid" (the original pronunciation) or "flassid" (the more recent, and now more popular, pronunciation).

In any event, two *c*'s.

FLUORESCENCE, FLUORESCENT

There's that peculiar *uo* again.

FLUORIDE

And once again.

FORTY

Rarely to never misspelled on its own, but there's something about a follow-up "four" that leads, occasionally, to "fourty-four."

---

[*] A, on the other hand, and perhaps capriciously, I always refer to capital-*N* Nazis, whether they're of Hitler's party or simply homegrown aspirants. B, if we're to be friends, you and I, please don't ever call me or anyone else a "grammar Nazi," a term that manages to be both direly insulting and offensively trivializing.

FUCHSIA

Commonly misspelled "fuschia," a dishonor to the botanist Leonhard Fuchs, after whom the flower (and color) are named.

GARROTE

Even knowing I've just spelled it correctly, I still think it should be "garotte."

GENEALOGY

I once let this go to print as "geneology" (perhaps I was thinking of geology?), and decades later the memory still stings.

GLAMOUR, GLAMOROUS

When Noah Webster was standardizing American English in the nineteenth century and streamlining "neighbour" into "neighbor," "honour" into "honor," etc., he neglected to transform "glamour" into "glamor"—because, oddly enough, he didn't include the word at all, in any form, in his initial 1828 dictionary or in any of his follow-up volumes. "Glamor" does show up from time to time, but certainly it lacks glamour. Do note, though, that "glamorous" is spelled only thus; it's never "glamourous." And it's "glamorize," never "glamourize."

GONORRHEA

Two *r*'s. See also "syphilis."

GRAFFITI

Two *f*'s rather than, as I occasionally run across it, two *t*'s. It's a plural, by the way. There is a singular, "graffito," but no one ever seems to use it. Perhaps because one rarely encounters a single graffito?

GUTTURAL

Not "gutteral," even though that's how you pronounce it. If you know your Latin, you may recognize this word that refers to throaty or generally disagreeable utterances as deriving from *guttur,* the Latin for "throat." If you don't know your Latin, you'll simply have to remember how to spell it.

HEROES

When one is writing about valiant champions, the plural of "hero" is, invariably, "heroes." The plural of the hero that's the heavily laden sandwich can be given, per the dictionary, as "heros," but I can't say I've run across it much if at all in the wild, and I can't say I care for it.

HIGHFALUTIN

This word, used to describe the putting on of airs, seems (even the dictionary isn't positive) to derive from a merger of "high" and "fluting"; nonetheless, it's not to be taken as some sort of Li'l Abner clipping like "comin'" or "goin'," and there's no apostrophe at its tail end (or, for that matter, a hyphen in its middle).

HORS D'OEUVRE, HORS D'OEUVRES

This one is a nightmare for everyone because of the *oeu.* Drill *oeu* into your head and the rest falls into place. The *s* for the plural is an English-language innovation; French makes do with *hors d'oeuvre* as both singular and plural.

While we're here: Though hors d'oeuvres include all more or less bite-size thingamabobs passable on trays, canapés are a subset of hors d'oeuvres requiring a base of bread, toast, cracker, puff pastry, etc., topped or spread with a topping or a spread. Amuse-bouches, which can be made out of just about anything so long as it's little, are chef-bestowed pre-meal* gifts,

---

*Modern copyeditorial style favors closing up—that is, merging hyphenlessly—prefixes and the words to which they attach (e.g., "antiwar," "postgraduate," "preoccupation," "reelect"), but if the result is difficult to read and/or uncommon, you should feel free to hold on to that hyphen. (The same goes for suffixes, as in the above-used "hyphenlessly.") Thus I opt for "pre-meal" rather than "premeal." (I find the universally accepted "premed" hard enough to make out on the first go, much less "premeal.") You'll note as well, when you cast your eye back up to the text proper, that I'm about to opt for "ladle-like," as (though the

often served in those charming miniature ladle-like spoons. Now you know.

HYPOCRISY
See also "bureaucracy."

IDIOSYNCRASY
Same.

INDISPENSABLE
Microsoft Word's spellcheck believes "indispensible" to be correct; no one else I know does, and it rarely makes it to print.

INDUBITABLY
There's a *b* in the middle, not a *p*.

INFINITESIMAL
Just the one *s*.

INOCULATE
One *n* and one *c* only.

LEPRECHAUN
It doesn't look much more sensible properly spelled than misspelled, but there you have it.

LIAISON
A word with three consecutive vowels is just begging for trouble.

The relatively recent back-formation* "liaise" irritates a lot of people. I think it's dandy and useful.

---

likes of, say, "catlike" or "cakelike" is dandy) "ladlelike" would, I think, try one's eyes' patience. (P.S. You can't ever do "dolllike," because look at it.)

* A back-formation is a neologism—that is, a newly coined word—derived from an already existing word, generally by yanking off a bit at the beginning or the end. Among the many common back-formations in the English language:

LIQUEUR

Another word with three consecutive vowels! If you're looking to blame someone for this sort of thing, blame the French.

Also, there's no *c* before the *q*, as is occasionally attempted.

MARSHMALLOW

Two *a*'s, no *e*'s.

MEDIEVAL

Even the Brits don't use "mediaeval" much anymore, much less mediæval.*

MEMENTO

Not "momento." Think of memory, because you buy and/or hold on to a memento so as to remember something.

MILLENNIUM, MILLENNIA, MILLENNIAL

Two *l*'s, two *n*'s. In each. It's always fun online to catch someone attempting to insult millennials yet unable to spell "millennials."

MINUSCULE

Not "miniscule," however much that seems to make sense.

MISCHIEVOUS

The spelling—and pronunciation—"mischievious" go back centuries, but they're persistently considered nonstandard. They're also unbearably twee. Woodland elves might opt for "mischievious"; mortals should not.

"aviate" (from "aviator"), "burgle" (from "burglar"), "laze" (from "lazy"), "tweeze" (from "tweezers") . . . Well, there are a lot of them. For all the back-formations that slip effortlessly into popular use, though, many never cease to raise dander and/or hackles: "conversate" and "mentee," for instance, both of which I find grotesque, and "enthuse," which I find harmless but which some people have loved to hate since it was coined nearly two hundred years ago.

* That fused-letter thing is called a ligature.

MISSPELL, MISSPELLED, MISSPELLING
To misspell "misspell" is, to borrow a phrase from the playwright Tennessee Williams,* slapstick tragedy.

MULTIFARIOUS
With an *f*, that is, not a *v*.

NAÏVE, NAÏVETÉ
Though the dictionary might (begrudgingly) let you get away
with dropping the accent marks, there's no fun in spelling
"naïve" or "naïveté" without them, and "naivety," though
ratified by the dictionary, is just plain sad-looking.

NEWSSTAND
Two *s*'s, please. Two *s*'s.

NON SEQUITUR
Not "non sequiter." And no hyphen.

OCCURRED, OCCURRENCE, OCCURRING
Pretty much everyone can spell "occur." Pretty much no one
can spell "occurred," "occurrence," or "occurring."

ODORIFEROUS, ODOROUS
They're both words. So is "odiferous," for that matter, but one
rarely runs across it. They all mean the same thing: stinking.†

OPHTHALMIC, OPHTHALMOLOGIST, OPHTHALMOLOGY
Eye-crossingly easy to misspell.

---

* There's nothing to be gained by referring to the playwright Tennessee Williams as "the famous playwright Tennessee Williams." If a person is famous
enough to be referred to as famous, there's no need to refer to that person as
famous, is there. Neither is there much to be gained by referring to "the late Tennessee Williams," much less "the late, great Tennessee Williams," which is some
major cheese. I'm occasionally asked how long a dead person is appropriately
late rather than just plain dead. I don't know, and apparently neither does anyone else.

† Though "moist" often tops lists of the most viscerally unpleasant words in
the English language, I turn my nose up at "stinky" and "smelly."

OVERRATE

Also overreach, override, overrule, etc.

PARALLEL, PARALLELED, PARALLELISM

As a young person, I desperately wanted "parallel" to be spelled "paralell" or at least "parallell"; somehow it never was.

PARAPHERNALIA

That *r* just past the midpoint has a tendency to fall out.

PASTIME

Just the one *t*. (If it helps, consider that the two words being portmanteaued are "pass" and "time," not "past" and "time.")

PEJORATIVE

Perhaps confusing the contemptuous "pejorative" with the lying "perjury," some people attempt "perjorative."

PENDANT

It's not that "pendent," as occasionally turns up when "pendant" is meant, isn't a word; it's that it's usually not the word you want. "Pendant" is a noun; "pendent" is an adjective meaning hanging or dangling—that is, what a pendant does. Pendulously.

PERSEVERE, PERSEVERANCE, PERSEVERANT

I note a tendency to slip an extra *r* in, just before the *v*.

PHARAOH

Reading, a few years back, a facsimile first edition of Agatha Christie's 1937 novel *Death on the Nile,* I was amused to note an instance of the misspelling "pharoah," which till then I'd figured was a recent problem.* Apparently not.

The 2015 Triple Crown triumph of the horse whose name

---

* I occasionally receive aggrieved correspondence, with much "Whither publishing?" teeth gnashing, from readers who've stumbled upon a typo in one of our books. I don't like typos any more than you do—likely I like them quite a

is officially (mis)spelled American Pharoah (and whose sire's name, even more grislily, is, for reasons I won't go into, Pioneerof the Nile) called much popular attention to the error, so perhaps ongoingly the word will show up properly spelled more often.

PIMIENTO
The popular spelling "pimento" cannot be called incorrect, though copy editors will persist in changing it. Interestingly, Web 11 has a separate entry for "pimento cheese." It contains pimientos.

POINSETTIA
Neither "poinsetta" nor "poinsietta."

PREROGATIVE
It is not spelled "perogative," though it's often misspelled— and mispronounced—thus.

PROTUBERANCE, PROTUBERANT
Not "protruberance" or "protruberant." Yes, you're thinking of "protrude." We all are. That's why the misspelling keeps showing up.

PUBLICLY
The vastly less popular "publically" is generally if not universally held to be nonstandard, which is a nice way of saying that by any decent standards it's incorrect.

RACCOON
The variant "racoon"—rarely seen now but once quite popular—cannot be taken as incorrect, but it can surely be taken as weird-looking.

---

bit less—but as long as there have been books, there have been typos. Nobody's perfect.

RASPBERRY
With a *p*.

REMUNERATIVE
Not "renumerative." I tend to avoid "remunerative" altogether, not only because I can't remember how to spell it but because I can't pronounce it without choking on it, and so I'd rather go with "lucrative."

RENOWN, RENOWNED
Not "reknown" or "reknowned."

REPERTOIRE, REPERTORY
Three *r*'s each.

RESTAURATEUR
It's not "restauranteur," and the floor is not open to debate.

ROCOCO
Neither "roccoco" nor "rococco." Nor, not that you would, "roccocco."

ROOMMATE
See "dumbbell" and "filmmaker," above. And just keep seeing them till you get these right.

SACRILEGIOUS
One wants to spell it "sacreligious." One can't.

SEIZE, SEIZED
Easily and not infrequently misspelled, by people who get hung up on that damned "*i* before *e*" thing, as "sieze" and "siezed."

SEPARATE, SEPARATION
Not "seperate" and "seperation."

SHEPHERD

Some people may be named Shepard, but sheep watchers are shepherds and certain dogs are German shepherds and potato-crusted meat dishes are shepherd's pies.

SIEGE

Even if you dodge the bullet of a misspelled "seize," you may still (counterintuitively) trip and misspell "siege" as "seige." Don't.

SKULDUGGERY

The variant "skullduggery" has, at least in the United States, lately become the more popular. That the word derives from a Scots term for fornication and not from grave robbery leads me to favor the nonmisleading single-*l* spelling.

STOMACHACHE

It's peculiar-looking as one word, I suppose, but it sits cheek by jowl with "earache" and "headache," and no one seems to find them peculiar-looking at all.

STRAITJACKET

"Strait" as in constricted, not "straight" as in not curvy.* Also: straitlaced.

STRATAGEM

It starts off like "strategy"; it just doesn't finish like "strategy."

SUPERSEDE

Not "supercede." I have never in my life spelled "supersede" correctly on the first go.

---

*The title of the 1964 Joan Crawford axe-murderess thriller—which you really ought to see, it's the damnedest thing—is *Strait-Jacket*. (The generally preferred American spelling is "ax," but I'd much rather be an axe-murderess than an ax-murderess. You?)

SURPRISE, SURPRISED, SURPRISING
In any of them, don't forget the first *r*, which is omitted with surprising frequency.

SYPHILIS
One *l*.

TAILLIGHT
Two *l*'s.

TENDINITIS
Not "tendonitis," though that's likely an unstoppable respelling of the word (and I note that the local spellcheck has refused to call it out with the Red Dots of Shame).

THRESHOLD
It's not "threshhold." I bet you're thinking of "withhold."

TOUT DE SUITE
It's not "toute suite," and correctly or incorrectly spelled, it's as irksome as *n'est-ce pas,* as noted in Chapter 5: Foreign Affairs. You know what's a good word? "Now."

UNDERRATE, UNDERRATED, UNDERRATING
(And any other "under" + *r*–commencing compounds you can think of.)

UNPRECEDENTED
For pete's sake, how hard was that?

UNWIELDY
Not "unwieldly," as I occasionally run across it.

VILLAIN, VILLAINOUS, VILLAINY
That's *ai,* not *ia.*

VINAIGRETTE
Not "viniagrette." Also not, for that matter, "vinegarette."

WEIRD
I run across "wierd" more often than I ever expect to.

WHOA
It's been rendered online as "woah" so often that one might be persuaded that that's an acceptable alternate spelling. It is not.

WITHHOLD
See "threshold."

Y'ALL
Never "ya'll."

Somewhat to my Yankee surprise, there's scant consensus (and much feuding) among my southern confederates as to whether "y'all" may properly be applied to just one person (and I leave discussion of the death-defying "all y'all" for another day) but near unanimity that non-southerners ought not to use it at all, y'all.

CHAPTER 9

Peeves and Crotchets

An Englishman's way of speaking absolutely classifies him.
The moment he talks he makes some other Englishman despise him.
—ALAN JAY LERNER, "Why Can't the English?"

I'VE NEVER MET A WRITER OR OTHER WORD PERSON who didn't possess a pocketful of language peeves and crotchets—words or uses of words that drive a normally reasonable person into unreasonable fits of pique, if not paroxysms of rage—and I doubt I'd trust anyone anyway who denied having a few of these bugaboos stashed away somewhere.

As they adore or abhor olives, opera, and the acting of Leonardo DiCaprio, people like what they like wordwise and abominate what they abominate. They're not, I've discovered, apt to be dissuaded from their prejudices by the evidence of centuries of literate literary usage or recitations from the bracingly peeve-dismantling *Merriam-Webster's Dictionary of English Usage*. And they're certainly not likely to be moved by the suggestion that English is in a constant state of evolution and that if our great-grandmothers ever caught us using the noun "store" when what we should have said was "shop" or using "host" as a verb, they'd wash our mouths out with soap. Well, I concede with a shrug, if the English language itself is notoriously irregular and irrational, why shouldn't its practitioners be too?

The thing is, everyone's peeves and crotchets* are different. People who couldn't care less about "could care less" will, faced with the use of "impact" as a verb, geschrei the house down, and that mob that sees fifty shades of red, scarlet, and carmine over the relatively newfangled use of "begs the question" to mean "raises the question" may well pass by a "comprised of" without so much as batting an eye.

As a copy editor, I tend to steer writers toward geschrei-proof language because, I feel, if you're going to irritate readers, you might as well irritate them (a) on purpose and (b) over something more important than the ostensible difference between "eager" and "anxious." Also I believe, because many of them have told me so, that writers are as a rule averse to being carped at by readers, justifiably or un-, over inconsequential matters and appreciate the safety net/security blanket offered them by somewhat conservative copyediting. (Though not so conservative, to be sure, as to impose daft nonrules like the aforementioned ones about not splitting infinitives or using "And" to begin sentences.)

Cracking my knuckles in preparation for writing this chapter, I made my way one Saturday morning to that agora of the twenty-first century, Twitter, where an awful lot of writers who should be writing and editors who should be editing hang out. There I put in a request for what I gingerly, tactfully referred to as "personal usage flashpoints," tossing out as examples "literally" (when used to mean "metaphorically") and "irregardless" (when used at all), which make for highly effective chum when you're trying to attract language piranhas.

Half a day and a few hundred colorful responses later, I'd amassed a list, which, whittled down somewhat, I offer you

---

*A tip of the hat to my copyeditorial colleague John E. McIntyre, of *The Baltimore Sun*, who coined the splendid term "peeververein," defined as "the collective group of self-appointed language experts whose complaints about errors in grammar and usage are generally unfounded or trivial." As insults go, it's quite sporty, don't you think? And certainly a step up from "stickler," "pedant," or "grammar Nazi."

here, with the inevitable commentary. Some of these entries, I admit, are peeves and crotchets I share, because I'm no more or less irrational than anyone else, while some, vigorously adhered to by people whose judgment I otherwise respect, make me furrow my brow, hike my eyebrows, and look askance—or, to put it in the current parlance, give side-eye to.

Oh, and this is crucial: The important thing to remember about peeves and crotchets is that your own peeves and crotchets reflect sensible preferences based on a refined appreciation of the music and meaning of the English language, and that everyone else's are the products of diseased minds.

OK, let's roll.

AGGRAVATE

If you use "aggravate" to mean not "make a bad thing worse" but "piss the living daylights out of," though it has for centuries been used thus, you will irritate a goodly number of people, so you might well stick, in such cases, with "irritate." If "irritate" bores or otherwise aggravates you, can you avail yourself of one of its synonyms—among them "annoy," "exasperate," and, my favorite, "vex"—and save yourself, as Jewish mothers have expressed it from time immemorial, the aggravation?

AGREEANCE

This is not, as its deriders may think, a Johnny-come-lately distortion of the English language but an ancient term, long since tossed onto the junk heap, that resurfaces every now and then where most people would say "agreement." One sees it so rarely that it scarcely qualifies as a worthy target of ire, but it bothers those whom it bothers.

ANXIOUS

The utterly common and exceptionally long-established use of "anxious" to describe anticipation of a happy sort makes some people anxious, and not in a good way. As an anxious type myself, I don't think it's worth the kerfuffle and reserve "anxious" for things I'm nervously battening down the hatches over and use "eager" to express, well, eagerness. That said, "anxious" comes in handy for things you're excited about that are nonetheless spawning stomach butterflies. A first date, say.

ARTISANAL

As can happen with any word that is suddenly, explosively ubiquitous, "artisanal," when used to refer to things made by hand for which you pay an arm and a leg, has quickly devolved from a selling point to an object of eye-rolling derision. Not being in the pickle, beer, or soap business, I rarely encounter it professionally, but if you're on the verge of using it, you might want to think twice. Then thrice.*

ASK

The nouning of the verb "ask"—"That's a big ask," "What's the ask on this?"—makes me chortle appreciatively, though I can't help but note that "request" is a perfectly charming word as either noun or verb. Verb-to-noun transformations—"nominalization" is the formal term for the process—can grate as well as amuse, as can many of the other attempts, often hailing from the worlds of business and academia, to gussy up shopworn ideas by replacing conventional language with overreaching—and arguably unnecessary—coinages.†

BASED OFF OF

No. Just no. "An intentional tremor, with prepositions," as a friend described it. The inarguably—so don't argue with me—correct phrase is "based on."

---

* This would have been the perfect place for a snickering reference to Brooklyn hipsters, but snickering references to Brooklyn hipsters are trite and tired, so I refrain. By the way, the rhetorical trick of referring to something by denying that you're referring to it is called "apophasis."

† Speaking out of the other side of my face, I might also argue that if you're not making up words every now and then, you're not doing your job. "Nouning," by the bye, is not one of mine. It's out there already.

BEGS THE QUESTION

When used to mean "raises the question," this one's no mere peeve; it's a nuclear threat. So duck and cover and listen up.

Begging the question, as the term is traditionally understood, is a kind of logical fallacy—the original Latin is *petitio principii*, and no, I don't know these things off the top of my head; I look them up like any normal human being—in which one argues for the legitimacy of a conclusion by citing as evidence the very thing one is trying to prove in the first place. Circular reasoning, that is. To assert, say, that vegetables are good for you because eating them makes you healthy or that I am a first-rate copy editor because clearly my copyediting improves other people's prose is to beg the question.

Except hardly anyone anymore recognizes, much less uses, "begs the question" for that sort of thing, and the phrase has been overwhelmingly repurposed to mean "leads to an inevitable query," as in, say, "The abject failure of five successive big-budget special-effects-laden films begs the question, Is the era of the blockbuster over and done with?"[*]

People who are in the business of hating the relatively new-fashioned use of "begs the question" hate it vehemently, and they hate it loudly. Unfortunately, subbing in "raises the question" or "inspires the query" or any number of other phrasings, fools no one; one can always detect the deleted "begs the question," a kind of prose pentimento, for those of you who were paying attention in art history class or have read Lillian Hellman's thrilling if dubiously accurate memoir.

BEMUSED

The increasing use of "bemused" to mean "wryly, winkingly amused, as if while wearing a grosgrain bow tie and sipping a Manhattan" rather than "bothered and bewildered" is going to—sooner rather than later, I fear—render the word mean-

---

[*] "Begs the question" has also taken on a part-time job to mean "evades the question," but I confront that vastly less frequently.

ingless and useless, and that's too bad; it's a good word. My own never-say-die attitude toward preserving "bemusement" to mean perplexity, and only that, is beginning to give me that General Custer vibe.

CENTERED AROUND
Even as a spatially challenged person who doodled and dozed his way through geography class, I recognize that "centered around" doesn't make any sense, so I will always opt for "centered on" or "revolved around." You should too.

CHOMPING AT THE BIT
Yes, it's traditionally "champing at the bit." Yes, many people now write "chomping," likely because the word "champing" is unfamiliar to them. In that "champing" and "chomping" are as virtually indistinguishable in meaning as they are in spelling, the condemnation of "chomping" strikes me as trifling.

CLICHÉ
It's a perfectly lovely noun. As an adjective, it rankles. You can afford the extra letter in "clichéd." Use it.

COMPRISE
I confess: I can barely remember which is the right way to use this word and which the wrong way, so every time I cross paths with it—or am tempted to use it—I stop to look it up.

"The English alphabet comprises twenty-six letters." This is correct.

"Twenty-six letters compose the English alphabet." This is also correct, though "make up" would sound a bit less stilted than "composed," don't you think?

"The English alphabet is comprised of twenty-six letters." Cue the sirens, because here come the grammar cops.

Use plain "comprise" to mean "made up of" and you're on safe ground. But as soon as you're about to attach the word "of" to the word "comprise," raise your hands to the sky and edit yourself. Once you've lowered your hands.

COULD CARE LESS

Use this phrase at your own peril to express utter indifference, because it inspires, from many, furious condemnation. I appreciate its indirect sarcasm, and the more people hate on it, the more apt I am to use it.

CURATE

This is what "curate" is good for: to serve as a noun identifying a junior clergyperson or (pronounced differently) as a verb describing the work of a museum's staff organizing and presenting works of art.

This is what "curate" is not so good for: to portray what you're doing when you're organizing a playlist of motivating songs for gym use, selecting smoked fishes for a brunch, or arranging displays of blouses, espadrilles, and picturesque thrift-shop books at Anthropologie.

DATA

It's a plural, it's a singular, it's a breath mint, it's a dessert topping.

The data supports the consensus that "data" is popularly used as a singular noun, and it's worth neither fussing over this nor raising the existence of the word "datum."

Move on already.

DECIMATE

There are those who would use "decimate" only to describe the punishment by death of one in ten—not one in nine, not one in eleven—mutinous soldiers.

There are those who would use it to describe, generally, destruction.

The latter group certainly gets more use out of the word.

DIFFERENT THAN

There's nothing wrong with "different than," and don't let anyone tell you otherwise.

If you say "different to," you're likely a Brit, and that's OK too.

DISINTERESTED

I'd be happier if you'd restrict your use of "disinterested" to suggest impartiality and, when speaking of lack of interest, make use of the handy "uninterested." I don't think that's asking a lot.

ENORMITY

There are those who insist on using "enormity" only in cases of monstrous evil ("the enormity of her crimes"), which is more or less how the word arrived in the English language, and would have you use "enormousness" (or "largeness" or "immensity" or "abundance" or some such) in descriptions of size.

I'll meet you in the middle. Feel free to use "enormity" to describe something that is not only big but monstrously, freakishly so or to describe something arduous ("the enormity of my workload"). Avoid it in positive uses ("the enormity of her talent") because it's a needless eyebrow raiser.

ENTHUSE

If you don't like "enthuse," wait till we get to "liaise."

EPICENTER

Strictly speaking, an epicenter is the place on the Earth's surface directly above the place an earthquake is occurring.

Less strictly speaking, an epicenter is a hub of activity, often but not always malignant activity.

You're on relatively safe metaphorical ground referring to, say, the epicenter of a plague; a reference to Paris as the epicenter of classic cooking may not sit well on some stomachs.

I myself don't care much for fanciful uses of "epicenter," mostly because I think that "center" does the job just fine.

FACTOID

If you use the word "factoid" to refer to a bite-size nugget of authentic information of the sort you'll find in a listicle,[*] you'll sadden those of us who hold to the word's original meaning: According to Norman Mailer, who should certainly know as he was the one who invented the word in the first place, factoids are "facts which have no existence before appearing in a magazine or newspaper, creations which are not so much lies as a product to manipulate emotion in the Silent Majority." That the Great Wall of China is visible from the Moon (or even from your plain-vanilla astronaut orbit) is a factoid, as are the existence of George Washington's wooden teeth, the nationwide panic caused by Orson Welles's "War of the Worlds" broadcast, and the execution by burning at the stake of Salem's condemned witches.[†]

FEWER THAN/LESS THAN

Perhaps you've turned this distinction into a fetish. The strict—and, really, not all that hard to remember—differentiation is that "fewer than" is applied to countable objects (fewer bottles of beer on the wall) and "less than" to what we call exclusively singular nouns (less happiness, less quality) and mass nouns (fewer chips, less guacamole).

Except—and there's always an "except," isn't there—one does use "less than" in discussions of distance (less than five hundred miles) and time (completing a test in less than sixty minutes—if you're not already saying "in under sixty min-

---

[*] I love "listicle." If a coinage truly captures a concept for which no extant word will do, if it truly brings something fresh to the table, I say let it pull up a chair and make itself comfortable.

[†] Washington's dentures were made of ivory, metal, and teeth appropriated from animals and other humans; nah, it didn't; and (a) they weren't witches, and (b) they were hanged.

utes," which you probably are and go ahead). And one likely uses "less than" in discussions of money and weight; *The New York Times Manual of Style and Usage* refers, efficiently, to this use of "less than" as appropriate for "a quantity considered as a single bulk amount." Thus "I have less than two hundred dollars" or "I weigh less than two hundred pounds" or "a country that's gone to hell in less than five months," because it's not really the individual months one's interested in, merely the relative brevity of the decline.

That said—and there's always a "that said," isn't there—one does not say "one fewer," both because it's achingly unidiomatic and because it wrecks the title of the Bacharach-David classic "One Less Bell to Answer."

As to people who object to supermarket express-lane signs reading "10 ITEMS OR LESS"? On the one hand, I hear you. On the other hand, get a hobby. Maybe flower arranging, or decoupage.

FIRSTLY, SECONDLY, THIRDLY
Like nails on a blackboard.

If you decline to write "firstly," "secondly," and "thirdly" in favor of "first," "second," and "third," not only are you saving letters but you can tell all your friends about this amazing thing called a flat adverb—an adverb that matches in form its sibling adjective, notably doesn't end in *-ly*, and is 100 percent correct, which is why we're allowed to say "Sleep tight," "Drive safe," and "Take it easy." Though not in that order.

FOR ALL INTENSIVE PURPOSES
I didn't intend to include "for all intensive purposes" on this list because I've never, so far as I can recall, encountered anyone saying or writing it except as a joke about people saying or writing "for all intensive purposes." But it's out there (and

has been since the 1950s, another reason to dislike that decade), and it turns up intermittently in print.

It's "for all intents and purposes."

FORTUITOUS

As to the use of "fortuitous" to mean fortunate or favorable, it's universally acceptable so long as the good fortune or favor is accidental, because that's what "fortuitous" means: by chance (though, in its original sense, with no guarantee of a happy ending). If you achieve something good by the sweat of your brow, find a word that better honors your achievement.

FULSOME

A word that over the centuries has picked up more meanings than are good for it, or for you: among them abundant, generous, overgenerous, excessive, offensive, and stench-ridden. (It can also be applied to the sort of interior decorating taste that leans toward gilt and gold-plated everything, though the best word for that sort of thing remains *ungapatchka*.) Though you may be tempted to apply "fulsome" unambiguously positively, if you allude to a "fulsome expression of praise," a hefty chunk of your audience will have visions of oleaginous brown-nosing dancing in their heads. So just skip it.

GIFT (AS A VERB)

If you're bored with "bestow," "proffer," "award," "hand out," "hand over," or any of the other excellent verbs the English language has come up with over the years to describe the act of giving a person a thing, by all means make use of "gift," which I wouldn't even consider describing as odious because I'm not that sort of person and because, I assure you, many other people are already lined up eagerly to do so.[*]

---

[*] "Regift," on the other hand, is a gorgeous coinage because it does something no other word can properly do.

GROW (TO MEAN "BUILD")

You can't argue, as some people attempt to do, that you can't properly use the phrase "grow a business" (rather, that is, than "build a business") because "grow" is only an intransitive verb (the sort that doesn't take an object). Why not? Because it is also, or at least can be, a transitive verb, as you'll surely note as you grow dahlias or a mustache.

You are free, though, to dislike such bureaucratese phrases as "grow the economy" because they're, to use the technical term, icky.

HOI POLLOI, THE

"Hoi polloi" is ancient Greek for "the many," and it's a term some people haul out when they're looking to insult those they think they're better than and want something jazzier than "the great unwashed" or "proles." Since the term, by derivation and definition, already includes the article "hoi" it's often asserted, and not only by ancient Greeks, that to refer to "the hoi polloi" is barbarously repetitive and offensive. I can't say that "the hoi polloi" bothers me much (which is to say, it doesn't bother me at all), though I might well be bothered to hear that something or other is favored by hoi polloi.

What does bother or at least bemuse me is the use of "hoi polloi," with or without the "the," to refer to rich people, as one runs across every now and then. A favored explanation for this confusion is that "hoi polloi" in such cases is being confused with "hoity-toity," which you may recognize as a synonym for "fancy-shmancy,"* but its being explicable doesn't make it right.†

---

* "Hoity-toity" and "fancy-shmancy" are examples of what's called reduplication, if that's a thing you'd like to know. See also, among many others, "easy-peasy," "knickknack," and "boogie-woogie."

† In the 2013 film *Philomena,* Judi Dench, as the heroine I will attempt to neutrally describe as being of the working classes, does at one point refer to the aristocratic people she's reading about in a romance novel as "the hoi polloi."

HOPEFULLY

If you can live with "There was a terrible car accident; thankfully, no one was hurt," you can certainly live with "Tomorrow's weather forecast is favorable; hopefully, we'll leave on time."

"Thankfully" and "hopefully" are, in these uses, disjunct adverbs, meaning that they modify not any particular action in the sentence (as they would in, say, "she thankfully received the gift" or "he hopefully approached his boss for a raise") but the overall mood of the speaker of the sentence (or simply the sentence itself).

I'm not sure how "hopefully," among all such disjunct usages, got singled out for abuse, but it's unfair and ought not to be borne.

By the way: "Frankly, my dear, I don't give a damn."

Ahem.

ICONIC

A word whose overuse has rendered it as dull and meaningless as "famous." Moreover, while "famous" is at least applied to people who are at least reasonably celebrated and widely recognized, "iconic" seems lately to be desperately applied to people who are barely even well known.

IMPACT (AS A VERB)

The use of the verb "impact," in the sense of "affect," when "affect" might be deemed perfectly appropriate and sufficient, is a true scream inducer. Perhaps you're already screaming.

I'm not sure that my job is necessarily impacted by a change in, say, working hours, but perhaps you're more time sensitive.

I don't necessarily hold with the notion that the verb "impact" should never be used for anything less, um, impactful

---

Possibly, I suppose, that's an error on the part of the screenwriter; I prefer to think that it's a deft and expressive bit of characterization.

than an asteroid wiping out the dinosaur population of the Earth, but do try to reserve it for big-ticket items.

IMPACTFUL

Yet another of those words that carry that unmistakable whiff of business-speak, and it's not, to my nose, a pleasant scent. If everyone stopped using it, I bet that no one would miss it.

INCENTIVIZE

The only thing worse than the ungodly "incentivize" is its satanic little sibling, "incent."

INVITE (AS A NOUN)

If your life expectancy is so limited that you don't have the time to issue an invitation, you might not be up to throwing that party.

IRONY

Funniness is not irony. Coincidence is not irony. Weirdness is not irony. Rain on your wedding day is not irony. Irony is irony. I once copyedited a work in which the author, if he used the phrase "deliciously ironic" once, used it a dozen times. The problem was, nothing he ever said was either delicious or ironic. Which, as a colleague pointed out, was deliciously ironic.

IRREGARDLESS

This grim Brundlefly, a genetic mash-up of "irrespective" and "regardless," is wholly unnecessary. Plus—and don't pretend otherwise, you're not that opaque—you know you use it only to irritate people.

LEARNINGS

Have you no sense of decency? At long last, have you no sense of decency?

They're lessons.

LIAISE

This back-formation, extracted from "liaison," bugs some people. I think it's dandy. I don't think that its cousins "cooperate" and "collaborate" quite do the trick of describing go-betweening (really, do you want me to say "go-betweening"?), and it's a damn sight better than the personal-boundary-crossing "reach out."

LITERALLY

A respectable word that has been distorted into the Intensifier from Hell. No, you did not literally die laughing. No, I don't care that all your cool friends use "literally" thus. If all your cool friends literally jumped off the Empire State Building, would you?*

LOAN (AS A VERB)

The use of "loan" as a verb has always carried, to my ears, a certain Bowery Boys noise—"Hey, Sach, can you loan me a fin?"—and when I see it in text, I tend to automatically change it to "lend." I will not be put out if you stet me, because there's absolutely nothing wrong with the use of "loan" as a verb.

MORE (OR MOST) IMPORTANTLY

If you have a stick up your fundament about "firstly," "secondly," and "thirdly," you likely have a similar stick there re "more importantly," and I hope you have the room for it.

MORE THAN/OVER

This distinction, specifically insofar as counting is concerned, is less controversial than that between "less than" and "fewer than," mostly because so few people observe it, and also because one is hard-pressed to find anyone in the word biz to defend it. So whether a book is over six hundred pages long or more than six hundred pages long, or whether little Jimmy is

---

* I have now officially turned into my mother.

suddenly more than six feet tall or suddenly over six feet tall . . . Do as you like. It's nothing to get worked up more than.

MYRIAD

"Myriad" was a noun well before it was an adjective, so though I appreciate that referring to "myriad travails" is more efficient than referring to "a myriad of travails," either is just fine, and the noun objectors don't have much of a leg to stand on here. Feel free, if you're that kind of person, to point out that John Milton used "myriad" as a noun. Also Thoreau.

NAUSEATED (VS. NAUSEOUS)

I don't think I knew till I was well beyond my college years that there was even such a word as "nauseated." On those occasions when I was about to heave, I was content to be nauseous. Eventually I learned the traditional differentiation between "nauseous"—causing nausea—and "nauseated"—preparing to heave—but it was too late for me to mend my ways, so I'm still happy, as it were, to be nauseous.

NOISOME

"Noisome" means "stinking." And "harmful." And, I suppose, "nauseating." One doesn't, just this moment, have to peeve about its being mistaken for a synonym for "noisy," because no decent person asserts or accepts that it is one. But in a world in which "nonplussed"—look down!—has increasingly come to mean "cool as a cucumber," I say: Better safe than sorry.

NONPLUSSED

So then, "nonplussed." To be nonplussed is to be confused, startled, at a loss for words. Lately the word's devolved into a synonym for relaxed, cool as a cucumber, chill, and that's a problem. How has this come to be? Presumably the "plussed" part strikes some eyes/ears as meaning "excited," so the "non" part seems to turn that on its head, and there you have "non-plussed" serving as its own antonym.*

ON ACCIDENT

Yes, it's "on purpose." No, it's not "on accident." It's "by accident."

ONBOARD

The use of "onboard" as a verb in place of "familiarize" or "integrate" is grotesque. It's bad enough when it's applied to policies; applied to new employees in place of the perfectly lovely word "orient," it's worse. And it feels like a terribly short walk from onboarding a new employee to waterboarding one.

PASS AWAY

In conversation with a bereaved relative, one might, I suppose, refer to someone having passed away or passed. In writing, people die.

PENULTIMATE

"Penultimate" is not a fancyism for "ultimate." It does not mean "like totally ultimate, bro." It means "the thing before the last thing."

PERUSE

I've given up on "peruse," because a word that's used to mean both "read thoroughly and carefully" and "glance at cursorily" is as close to useless as a word can be.

PLETHORA

People who use "plethora" to describe something of which there's too much—it started out in English as the name of a

---

* A word that means its own opposite is a contronym, though the term "Janus word"—you remember two-faced Janus, looking ahead and behind at the same time, yes?—is also applied, and it packs a thrill. "Sanction" (to allow

condition involving an overabundance of blood—sneer grimly at those who use it simply (and positively) to mean "a lot of something." I have no dog in this fight.

REFERENCE (AS A VERB)
You can just say "refer to."

RESIDE
You mean "live"?

'ROUND
If she's approachin' by way of circumnavigatin' a mountain, she's comin' round it, and one can do nicely without a preceding apostrophe. I'm talking to you, people who like to write "'til" or, worse, "'till."

STEP FOOT IN
For your own safety, I'm telling you, just say "set foot in." You'll live longer.

TASK (AS A VERB)
I'd rather be assigned to do something than tasked to do it.

'TIL
Once again, for the people in the cheap seats: "Till" is a word. "Until" is a word. "Till" is an older word than "until." They both mean the same thing. There's no justification whatsoever for the prissyism "'til."

TRY AND
If you try and do something, someone will immediately tell you to try *to* do it, so you might as well just try to do it so no one will yell at you.

---

and to penalize) and "cleave" (to hold fast *and* to cut up) are classic Janus words. And though context will easily indicate for these two which meaning is being used, I wouldn't say the same re "nonplussed," so let's hold on to just the one meaning, OK?

UTILIZE

You can haul out "utilize" when you're speaking of making particularly good use of something, as in utilizing facts and figures to project a company's future earnings. Otherwise all you really need is "use."

VERY UNIQUE

In the 1906 edition of *The King's English,* H. W. Fowler declared—and he was neither the first nor the last person to so declare—"A thing is unique, or not unique; there are no degrees of uniqueness; nothing is ever somewhat or rather unique, though many things are almost or in some respects unique."

I will allow that something can be virtually unique but can't be more than—not very, not especially, not really—unique.

You might as well hang a KICK ME sign on your writing.*

---

* My editor wants me to tell you here never to use the words "yummy," "panties," or "guac." Mission accomplished.

CHAPTER 10

The Confusables

"When I use a word," Humpty Dumpty said, in rather a scornful tone,
"it means just what I choose it to mean—neither more nor less."
"The question is," said Alice, "whether you can make words
mean so many different things."
"The question is," said Humpty Dumpty, "which is
to be master—that's all."
—Lewis Carroll, *Through the Looking-Glass, and*
What Alice Found There

SPELLCHECK IS A MARVELOUS INVENTION, but it can't stop you from using the wrong word when the wrong word you've used is a word (but the wrong word). A great deal of copyediting entails catching these sorts of errors, which I assure you even the best writers commit.

A LOT/ALLOT, ALLOTTED, ALLOTTING
A lot of something is a great deal of it.
     To allot is to assign.

ADVANCE/ADVANCED
To advance is to move forward. The past tense of "advance" is "advanced."
     An advance is a forward movement, as of an army, or a preliminary payment, as to writers who have not yet finished writing their books or children seeking to get ahead on their allowances.
     As well, "advance" means beforehand (as in "supplied in advance").
     On the other hand, "advanced" refers to being ahead of

the norm in progress or complexity, as an exceptionally clever student is advanced.

The mistaken use of "advanced" for "advance" (not least in publishing, where bound galleys* are too commonly misreferred to as "advanced editions") is constant and unfortunate.

ADVERSE/AVERSE

"Adverse" means unfavorable or harmful, as in "We are enduring adverse weather."

"Averse" means opposed to, repulsed by, or antipathetic toward, as in "I am averse to olives and capers."

AFFECT/EFFECT

The traditional snap differentiation between "affect" and "effect" is that "affect" is a verb ("This martini is so watery, it doesn't affect me at all") and "effect" is a noun ("This martini is so watery, it has no effect on me at all"). Which is true as far as it goes. But only that far.

Because "affect" is also a noun: "a set of observable manifestations of a subjectively experienced emotion." One may speak, for instance, of a psychiatrist's commenting on a traumatized patient's affect.

And "effect" is also a verb, as in "to effect change"—that is, to cause change to happen.

Other uses of these words and their variants—as an affected person affects a posh accent; one's personal effects (the things you're carrying around on your person); "in effect" in the sense of "virtually"—seem to cause less confusion.

AID/AIDE

To aid is to help.

An aide is an assistant.

---

* Bound galleys are early bind-ups of typeset text—prettily designed but not yet proofread—sent out to reviewers, bookstore buyers, and people who, hopefully, will provide the publisher with burbling blurbs of praise with which to festoon the finished books. Alliteration, amirite?

AISLE/ISLE

This is a relatively new mix-up, at least so far as I've witnessed it, so let's put a brisk stop to it.

Aisles are the passages between seating areas in theaters and houses of worship and airplanes, and between display shelves of groceries in supermarkets.

Isles are islands (usually small ones).

ALL RIGHT/ALRIGHT

Gertrude Stein made bemusing (or amusing, if you find Stein amusing) use of "alright" in her 1931 book *How to Write:*

> A sentence is alright but a number of sentences make a paragraph and that is not alright.

As well, Pete Townshend wrote a song for the Who called "The Kids Are Alright."*

These and other uses notwithstanding—and quite possibly you don't want to write like Gertrude Stein†—"alright" is objected to, by some, as slovenly, and its appearance in print remains rare relative to that of "all right." That said, that I'm regularly asked my opinion of the acceptableness or un- of "alright" suggests to me that it's making inroads, like it or not. I continue to wrinkle my nose at the sight of it, perhaps because I can't see that it has a worthwhile enough distinction from "all right" to justify its existence, as, say, "altogether" and "already" are distinctly distinct from "all together" and "all ready." You may feel otherwise.‡

---

* The 2010 film starring Annette Bening and Julianne Moore is *The Kids Are All Right.*

† Or perhaps you do. "Why is a paragraph not alright. A paragraph is not alright because it is not alight it is not aroused by their defences it is not left to them every little while it is not by way of their having it thought that they will include never having them forfeiting whichever they took. Think of a paragraph a paragraph arranges a paraphanelia [*sic*]. A paragraph is a liberty and a liberty is in between. If in between is there aloud moreover with a placed with a placing of their order. They gave an offer that they would go. A paragraph is meant as that."

‡ OK, I'm hiding this down here in a footnote because I almost feel, copyeditorially speaking, as if I'm giving comfort to the enemy: When it comes to exas-

ALLUDE/ALLUSION/ALLUSIVE/ELUDE/ELUSIVE

To allude is to refer obliquely, to hint at, as one alludes to a painful subject rather than discussing it explicitly.

An allusion is such an indirect, or allusive, reference.

To elude is to escape, as a bank robber eludes a dragnet.

A dream one half-recalls on waking that then slips entirely from one's consciousness might be called elusive. That is, it's difficult to hold on to.

ALTAR/ALTER

An altar is a raised structure on which, in religious ceremonies, sacrifices are made or gifts are left.

To alter is to change.

ALTERNATE/ALTERNATIVE

The Strictly Speaking Club, of which I'm an on-again, off-again member, will tell you that, strictly speaking, an alternate is a thing that replaces a thing, and alternatives—which travel in packs, or at least pairs—are options, any one of which might be viable. That is, if, owing to an accident, I'm forced off the road in Connecticut and must find my way to Boston via Pawtucket, I'm mandated to travel an alternate route, but on another day, should I opt to make my way to Boston on local streets rather than highways, I am simply choosing an alternative route.

As well, to do something every other Wednesday is to do that thing on alternate Wednesdays, to blow hot and cold in one's feelings is to alternately like and dislike something, and constructing a lasagna with tiers of noodles, sauce, and cheese is to build it with alternate layers. "Succeeding by turns," as the dictionary helpfully phrases it.

Also as well, an option beyond normalcy[*] is an alternative:

_____

peration, "Alright already" looks all right to me. But that's as far as I can go. Today.

[*] Or normality, if you prefer that alternative.

alternative music, alternative medicine, alternative lifestyle, etc. (This use can carry a whiff of disapproval, so be careful how you apply it.)

One's alternate identity (Percy Blakeney's Scarlet Pimpernel, Bruce Wayne's Batman, Paul Reubens's Pee-wee Herman) is one's alter ego.[*]

AMBIGUOUS/AMBIVALENT

To be ambiguous is to lack clarity, to be murkily open to misinterpretation.

To be ambivalent is to have mixed feelings.

One's meaning may be ambiguous, but one's attitude is ambivalent.

AMOK/AMUCK

To run amok is, in its original sense, to launch, after a bout of brooding, into a murderous frenzy—a phenomenon, I find in my encyclopedia, particularly observed in Malaysia, whence the word "amok" derives. In its current, less homicidal context, the word evokes, for instance, what occurs when a mob of six-year-olds sugar themselves into howling agitation.

"Amuck" is simply a variant spelling of "amok," and for quite some time it was the more popular English-language spelling. "Amok" overtook it in the 1940s, and I'd like to think that the 1953 Merrie Melodies classic *Duck Amuck,* featuring the eponymous Daffy, finished off "amuck" in any other but comical contexts.

AMUSE/BEMUSE/BEMUSED

To amuse is to entertain, delight, divert.

To bemuse is to perplex, befuddle, preoccupy, nonplus.

The rising use of "bemused" to describe, as I noted earlier,

[*] Pseudonyms are not alternate *identities* but simply alternate *names* used for professional, literary, political, or, occasionally, terroristic purposes: Currer Bell for Charlotte Brontë, Lewis Carroll for Charles Dodgson, Leon Trotsky for Lev Davidovich Bronstein, Carlos the Jackal for Ilich Ramírez Sánchez, etc.

a sort of wry, unflappable, tuxedo-wearing, cocktail-sipping amusement may be unstoppable, but unstopped it will certainly kill off the usefulness of the word entirely—just as the redefinition of "nonplus," which properly means to confuse-startle-unnerve, to mean its precise opposite ("I wasn't frightened at all; I was completely nonplussed"), will, unchecked, render that word unusable in any fashion. Don't say I didn't warn you.

ANYMORE/ANY MORE

"Anymore" = any longer or at this time, as in "I've a feeling we're not in Kansas anymore."

"Any more" = an additional amount, as in "I don't want any more pie, thank you."

You don't have to search back too many decades to find frequent use of "any more" where we'd now, at least in America, write "anymore." (The Brits remain less keen on the fused version.)

APPRAISE/APPRISE

To appraise is to assess or evaluate, as one has a gem appraised to determine its worth.

To apprise is to inform, as one apprises one's boss of one's vacation plans.

ASSURE/ENSURE/INSURE

One assures another person so as to relieve doubt: "I assure you we'll leave on time."

To ensure is to make something certain—some*thing,* not some*one:* "The proctor is here to ensure that there is no talking during the test."

"Insure" is best reserved for discussions of compensation in the event of death or dismemberment, monthly premiums, and everything else involved in our betting that something terrible is going to happen to us.

BAITED/BATED

A trap is baited—that is, outfitted with bait.

"Bated," which you are unlikely to chance upon disattached from the word "breath," means reduced or moderated or suspended. To await something with bated breath is to await it with thrilled tension, to be on (to use a grand old word) tenterhooks.

BAKLAVA/BALACLAVA

Baklava is a Middle Eastern pastry made of filo dough, chopped or ground nuts, and an awful lot of honey.

A balaclava is a hood that covers the entire head (except, for the sakes of practicality and respiration, the eyes and the mouth). A ski mask, more or less.

Neither "baklava" nor "balaclava" should be confused with baccalà, which is dried, salted cod; a balalaika, which is a stringed instrument; or Olga Baclanova, the actress best known for being turned into a human duck in the 1932 horror film *Freaks*.

BAWL/BALL

To bawl one's eyes out is to weep profusely.

To ball one's eyes out would be some sort of sporting or teabagging mishap.

BERG/BURG

A berg is an iceberg.

"Burg" is a slangish, old-fashioned, often uncomplimentary term for a town or a city. If a town or a city is particularly dreary and puny and backward, it's not merely a burg but a podunk burg.

BESIDE/BESIDES

"Beside" means "next to" (as in "Come sit beside me").

"Besides" means "other than" (as in "There's no one left besides Granny who remembers those old days").

I've found that "beside" is frequently used when "besides" is meant, and I wonder whether people who have had it drilled into their heads to use "toward" rather than "towards," "backward" rather than "backwards," etc., view "besides" as a Briticism-to-be-avoided. Or, thinking it a relative of "anyways," view it as an outright error.

BLACK OUT / BLACKOUT

The verb is "black out," as one may black out after binge drinking.

The noun is "blackout," meaning a loss of consciousness, an electrical power failure, or a suppression of information (as in a news blackout).

BLOND / BLONDE

"Blond" is an adjective: He has blond hair; she has blond hair.

"Blond" and "blonde" are also nouns: A man with blond hair is a blond; a woman with blond hair is a blonde. "Blonde" carries some heavy cultural baggage by way of the moldy pejorative "dumb blonde," so use it thoughtfully and carefully, if at all.

I won't pretend that "blonde" is unknown as an adjective. Here, plucked, via a random Internet search, from Emma Embury's "The Interesting Stranger," c. 1841: "the blonde hair, rosy cheeks and somewhat dumpy person of her merry sister."*
If you insist on using "blonde" as an adjective, I must insist that you apply it only to women, as the concluding *e,* via the French, marks the word as feminine.

BOARDER / BORDER

A boarder is a person who rents a room in a boardinghouse.

A border divides one geographical entity from another.

(My editor, looking over my shoulder, which is his job,

---

* That's not a nice thing to say about someone's merry sister.

suggested that this differentiation was obvious and thus delet-able from this admittedly lengthy list. I wish.)

BORN/BORNE

The word you want for discussions of birth, actual or meta-phorical, is "born," whether one was born yesterday, born in a trunk or out of wedlock, or New York–born.

Otherwise, things that are carried or produced are borne. Diseases are insect-borne. A tree that bears fruit has, then, borne fruit. The right to bear arms is the right to have borne them.

And though triumph may be born out of tragedy, one's grand schemes may not be borne out in reality.

BREACH/BREECH/BROACH/BROOCH

To breach is to break open or pierce.

A breach is a rupture or violation, as in a breach in a dam or a breach of etiquette. When Shakespeare's Henry V cries, "Once more unto the breach, dear friends, once more," he's literally referring to the gap his English troops have opened in the walls of a French city under siege. Note, please, that it's "unto the breach," not, as it's often misquoted, "into" it.

A breach is also the leaping of a whale out of the ocean; the whale is thus said to be breaching.

"Breech" is an outmoded term for buttocks; thus trousers were once breeches. A breech birth is one in which the baby emerges buttocks (or feet) first.

To broach a subject is to raise it.

A brooch is a piece of decorative jewelry.

BREATH/BREATHE/BREADTH

"Breath" is a noun; "breathe" is a verb. One loses one's breath. One breathes one's last breath. Et cetera.

"Breath" is often written when "breathe" is called for. This is an especially easy error to commit and, once committed, difficult to catch, so I urge you to be on your guard about it.

No one ever seems to get "breadth" wrong—though it comes up every now and then in "Hey, how come it's 'length' and 'breadth' and 'width' but not 'heighth'?" conversations*—so I simply note its existence.

BULLION/BOUILLON
The former is metal, the latter broth (which you may sometimes encounter dehydrated into little cubes).

CACHE/CACHET
A cache is a place for hiding one's valuables or a collection of things so hidden. As a verb, then, to cache means to hide. One might, I suppose, cache one's cache of cash in an underground cache.

Cachet is the quality of prestige and distinction, as Edith Wharton's avaricious, ambitious Undine Spragg, in *The Custom of the Country,* marries for social cachet. And for cash.

Though the pronunciation of words, as opposed to their spelling and use, is, as I've mentioned, outside my bailiwick, I'm happy to point out that "cache" is pronounced exactly like "cash," whereas "cachet" has two syllables: "ka-shay."

CALLOUS/CALLUS
To be callous is to be hard-hearted.

A callus is a thickening of the skin.

Many, many, many people get this wrong, so if you can get it right you'll earn a slew of brownie points.[†]

CANVAS/CANVASS
Canvas is cloth, of the sort used to make sails or to paint on.

To canvass is to secure votes or opinions.

---

* It used to be "heighth" and now it's not, and these days "heighth" is generally characterized as "nonstandard" or "dialectical." How's that for an unsatisfactory answer?

† Whence the term "brownie points"? No one's 100 percent certain; it's one of those wonderful word mysteries. I like the idea that not everything can be or needs to be known.

CAPITAL/CAPITOL

A capital is an important city, or a large letter as one would find at the beginning of a sentence or a proper noun, or one's accumulated funds, or, architecturally, the crown of the shaft of a column. It is also an adjective describing a serious crime (often, though not invariably, punishable by death) and something that approving British people used to exclaim—"Capital!"—before they all started exclaiming "Brilliant!"

A capitol is a building housing a legislature, like the great domed Capitol (capitalized in this case, as that is its name) in our nation's capital.

CARAT/KARAT/CARET/CARROT

A carat is a unit of weight applied to gemstones.

The proportion of gold in an alloy is measured in karats, the purest gold being 24-karat.

A caret is a copyediting and proofreading symbol (it looks like this: ∧) showing where new text is to be inserted into an already set line.

Carrots are what Bugs Bunny eats.

CASUAL/CAUSAL

Be careful with these, as one doesn't want to write of a causal relationship (in which one thing causes another thing or is caused by it) when one means to write of a casual—easygoing, informal—relationship, and vice versa. The words are visually almost indistinguishable, their meanings anything but.

CHORD/CORD

In music, a chord is a number of notes played simultaneously; "chord" is also used to refer to an emotional response, as a plaintive melody may be said to strike a chord.

A cord is a woven string of threads.

To strike a blow against an exceptionally popular error: One has vocal cords, not (no matter how musical one is) "vocal chords."

CITE/SIGHT/SITE

The confusion between "cite" and "site" seems to be on the rise. To cite something is to quote or attribute it, as one cites a reference book or a website. And, aha, there's the potential for confusion: In citing a fact one's found on a (web)site, the desire to "site" it is increasingly compelling (but still incorrect).

Further confusion arises between "site"—as a noun, the property on which a structure is constructed; as a verb, the action of placing that structure—and "sight," a thing one goes to see, e.g., the sights of Paris one views while sightseeing.

A sight is also the dojigger on a firearm that helps you aim, thus "I've got you in my sights."

CLASSIC/CLASSICAL

A classic is an excellent or defining version of something, as "Wouldn't It Be Nice" is a classic pop song by the Beach Boys and the classic (if inadvisable) cure for a hangover is to recommence to drink.

"Classical" is best reserved for descriptions of things like the civilizations of ancient Greece and Rome or the orchestral music of the eighteenth and nineteenth centuries.

CLIMACTIC/CLIMATIC

The former relates to narrative thrills, spills, and chills on the way to a denouement; the latter concerns, perhaps (and hopefully) less thrillingly, meteorological phenomena.

COME/CUM

Sexually speaking, there are no hard-and-fast[*] rules about this, but I think that "come" works nicely as a verb in the sense of "to climax." If one is then going to use the common term for the product of male orgasm, "cum" is your man.[†]

As a staid conjunction, "cum" suggests dual use, as one

---

[*] As it were.
[†] As it were.

might speak of a desk-cum-bureau. It's best set between the things it's conjoining with hyphens.* After centuries of use, the Latin-derived "cum" is surely a proper English word, so set it in roman rather than italicizing it. It also tends to inspire, in the chronically immature,† the giggles, so give it a good thought before you choose to use it at all.

COMPLEMENT/COMPLEMENTARY/COMPLIMENT/ COMPLIMENTARY

To complement something is to go nicely with it, the way a diagonally striped tie may complement a vertically striped shirt.

If I am telling you how natty you look in your spiffily complementing shirt and tie, I am paying you a compliment.

An ability to spell and an ability to type rapidly and accurately might be thought of as complementary skills in secretarial work—that is, each serves the other.

If I am offering you my spelling and typing skills free of charge, I am giving you access to a complimentary service.

CONFIDANT/CONFIDANTE

If you're not a fan of gendered nouns, you can certainly apply "confidant" to anyone with whom you share confidences. Don't, though, refer to a man as a confidante; confidantes are, solely, women.

(Most people discern correctly between "fiancé" and "fiancée," but most is not all.)

CONSCIENCE/CONSCIOUS

Your conscience is the little voice within that helps you differentiate between right and wrong. If you are Pinocchio in the Disney version, you possess an externalized conscience in the

---

* Or, if any of the things being conjoined are multiword things, en dashes, e.g., "a memoir–cum–murder mystery."

† Pretty much everyone I know.

person—well, in the insect—of Jiminy Cricket, whose name derives from the euphemistic oath that is a polite alternative to bellowing "Jesus Christ!"

To be conscious is to be awake and alert, also to be particularly aware and mindful.

CONTINUAL/CONTINUOUS

"Continual" means ongoing but with pause or interruption, starting and stopping, as, say, continual thunderstorms (with patches of sunlight) or continual bickering (with patches of amity).

"Continuous" means ceaseless, as in a Noah-and-the-Flood-like forty days and forty nights of unrelenting rain.

CORONET/CORNET

A coronet is a small crown; a cornet is a trumpetlike musical instrument.

CRITERION/CRITERIA

"Criterion" is singular: a standard upon which one can make a decision. A number of criterions (it's a word, really, though I can't think of the last time I saw it used) are criteria.

I frequently encounter the plural "criteria" where the singular "criterion" is meant. Perhaps people think it's fancier.

CROCHET/CROTCHETY/CROTCHET

To do needlework with a crochet hook is to crochet. Crocheting is not knitting (neither is it tatting, which is the making of lace), and people who do either get peeved, or even crotchety, if you mix them up.

To be crotchety, then, is to be grouchy, cantankerous, prickly, tetchy.*

---

* Is there any particular difference between "tetchy" and the perhaps more familiar "touchy"? Not particularly. They both mean irritable. That said, "tetched" means something quite different: slightly deranged.

One's crotchets are one's unreasonable notions or one's eccentric habits. (As well: What we Americans call a quarter note, the Brits call a crotchet; the Brits have all kinds of interesting names for perfectly normal musical things.)

I note no widespread confusion between a salmon croquette and a game of croquet, so we'll pass those by.

CUE/QUEUE

These two are not so alike in appearance, but confusion between them is, in my experience, on the rise.

A cue is a signal, as to an actor, to make an entrance, commence a speech, or perform some action. "You sockdologizing old man-trap," a line in Tom Taylor's 1858 comedy *Our American Cousin,* may be the most notorious cue in history, as the audience laughter it inspired was expected by John Wilkes Booth—an actor, but not in this particular play—to smother the sound of his gunshot as he assassinated Abraham Lincoln.

To cue is to give a cue. To take a cue is to model one's behavior or actions on someone else's.

A queue is a ponytail, often braided, of the sort traditionally worn by, among others, Chinese men. More commonly, a queue is a line of people waiting for something. (Did you know that a line of people walking in pairs is called a crocodile?) A queue is also the lineup of DVDs you have waiting for you at Netflix, if you happen to still watch DVDs.

To queue, then, is to get in line. This is often phrased "queue up," which should not be confused with "cue up," which is to get a thing ready to commence (as, say, a PowerPoint presentation or what older people would call a slide show).

"Queue" was, not long ago, a terribly British verb, and for Americans to say that they were "queuing up" for this or that was the height of pretension. I'm not certain when the term arrived in the United States, but it certainly seems to have its green card by now.

DAIRY/DIARY

You are unlikely to confuse their meanings; you may well confuse them while typing. Nuff, as they say, said.

DEFUSE/DIFFUSE

To defuse is, literally, to remove a fuse, as from a bomb, to keep it from blowing up. Figuratively, if you're trying to calm down a roomful of ornery people, you're defusing a thorny situation.

The adjective "diffuse" means unconcentrated (as, say, "diffuse settlements in a vast territory"). As a verb it means "to spread" (as air freshener may diffuse, or be diffused, through a room).

DEMUR/DEMURE/DEMURRAL

To demur is to voice opposition or objection; perhaps because the word, spoken, makes a gentle burring noise (or perhaps because it looks like "demure"), it's often used to suggest polite opposition.

"Demur" is also a noun, as one may accept someone else's decision without demur (or, if you prefer, demurral). "Demur" and "demurral" also carry a less frequently used meaning: delay.

To be demure is to be modest or reserved.

DESCENDANT/DESCENDENT

Use the former as a noun, for progeny and progeny's progeny; use the latter as an adjective to describe said progenies, or to describe something moving downward.

Each is occasionally, and unhelpfully, defined as meaning the other.

(Vastly more often than not, you want the former. The latter rarely shows up.)

DESERT/DESSERT

Most of us can correctly discern between a desert (that hot and dry place) and a dessert (that sweet and soul-satisfying complement to one's meal).

Many go wrong in their attempt to haul out the venerable*
phrase referring to people receiving their comeuppance. Such
people are getting not their "just desserts" but their just
deserts—they are getting precisely what they *deserve*.

Though if a few of us drop by a restaurant with the sole
intention of enjoying a couple of slices of pie and a goblet of
chocolate mousse, we may surely be said to be receiving just
desserts.

DISASSOCIATE/DISSOCIATE

They mean the same thing—sever—and they showed up in
English around the same time. For reasons I can't discern,
"disassociate" gets a lot of rocks thrown at it; I can't say that
it bothers me. If you're aware of the psychological meaning of
dissociation—a separation from reality that occurs in crisis—
you may come to think of "disassociation" as better suited to
more everyday severances, as, say, disassociating oneself from
an offensive statement made by one's racist uncle at Thanks-
giving dinner.

DISCREET/DISCRETE

Discreet people possess discretion; they kiss but don't tell.
They are circumspect, chary, and wary.

This thing over here and that thing over there are discrete—
separate and distinct—things.

"Discreet" and "discrete" are often mixed up, not only but
particularly by the authors of frisky personal ads.

EEK/EKE

"Eek!" is what you exclaim when you see a mouse.

To eke (as in "to eke out a living") is to secure something
with difficulty and, as a rule, barely. I suppose one could,
feigning fright, eke out an eek.

---

* I've occasionally seen "venerable" used to mean, solely, eminent or to
mean, solely, old. I'd say that it's best used to mean both, together.

EMIGRATE/IMMIGRATE

One emigrates from a place; one immigrates to a place. My paternal grandfather emigrated from Latvia; he immigrated to the United States. The terms are used to describe movement from one nation or continent to another; one does not, say, emigrate from Chicago to New York, or even from Chicago to Paris.

EMINENT/IMMINENT/IMMANENT

To be eminent is to be renowned, famous.

To be imminent is to be on the way and arriving any moment now.

To be immanent is to be inherent—built in, so to speak. One most frequently, when at all, sees the term applied to constitutional rights and the existence and influence of God.

ENVELOP/ENVELOPE

"Envelop" is the verb, as in to surround or encompass, "envelope" the noun, as in the paper doohickey into which one puts a letter.

EPIGRAM/EPIGRAPH

An epigram is a succinct, smart, and, as a rule, humorous statement, of the sort Oscar Wilde used to toss about like Ritz crackers to stray ducks. For instance, from the irresistibly quotable *The Importance of Being Earnest:* "All women become like their mothers. That is their tragedy. No man does. That's his."

An epigraph is an evocative quotation—rarely humorous but generally succinct—set at the beginning of a book, often immediately after the dedication, or at the beginning of a chapter.

EVERYDAY/EVERY DAY

"Everyday" is an adjective ("an everyday occurrence"), "every day" an adverb ("I go to work every day").

"Everyday" is increasingly often being used as an adverb; this is highly bothersome, and please don't you dare speed up the trend.

EVOKE/INVOKE

To evoke is to call to mind, as the smell of coconut or rum (or coconut *and* rum) may evoke a fondly remembered tropical vacation or the ghost stories of a present-day horror writer may be said to evoke those of Edith Wharton or M. R. James.*

To invoke is to summon in actual practice, as a warlock invokes demons to destroy his enemy, or to call upon for protection or assistance, as one invokes one's Fifth Amendment right to remain silent and avoid self-incrimination.

To put it as simply as I can, if you confine evoking to the figurative and invoking to the actual, you'll do fine.

EXERCISE/EXORCISE

Not, truth to tell, a lot of confusion abounding between that which one does at the gym and that which one does to demons, but:

If you are agitated and worked up about something, you are not exorcised but exercised.

FARTHER/FURTHER

As a rule, or at least what passes for a rule, "farther" is reserved for literal physical distance ("I'm so exhausted, I can't take a step farther") and "further" is used figuratively, as a measure of degree or time ("Later this afternoon we can discuss this weighty matter further").

In the face of ambiguity, go with "further." Our friends the Brits alleviate the ambiguity by mostly using "further" for everything.

---

* I recommend both enthusiastically. They're superb, and elegant, and unnerving.

FAUN/FAWN

A faun is a mythical creature, part man and part goat, a less intimidating version of a satyr.

A fawn is a young deer; fawn is also a pale yellow-brown color.

To fawn is to be obsequious in a quest for favor, to apple-polish, to bootlick, to suck up.

FAZE/PHASE

To faze is to bother, or to disturb, or to discompose, as someone is fazed by the prospect of speaking in public.

A phase is a stage of development, as a child may go through a phase of refusing to eat vegetables; to phase is to perform an action over time, as in phasing out outmoded textbooks.

FERMENT/FOMENT

One ferments (alcoholizes) beer or wine; one foments (stirs up) discord. That said, one's anger can ferment, and an agitated group of people can be described as being in a state of ferment.

The use of the verb "ferment" as a synonym for the verb "foment" agitates many people; it cannot, however, be said to be incorrect. Sorry, agitated people.

FICTIONAL/FICTITIOUS

"Fictional" describes the nature of works of imaginative art and their constituent parts. The characters in a novel are fictional.

"Fictitious" describes something not in imaginative art that is made up. The dead grandmother you concocted in fifth grade to get out of school on a test day was, may she rest in peace, fictitious.

FLACK/FLAK

A flack is a press agent. Flak is antiaircraft weaponry and, especially, the gunfire propelled therefrom.

If you're being roundly criticized, you're catching not flack but flak.

FLAIL/FLAY/FLOG

To flail is to wave about wildly, as a drowning man might flail his arms; to flail is also to wallop. The verb relates to a noun: A flail is a threshing tool, a longer staff with a shorter stick loosely attached to it that gets swung about. It's the other thing you see pharaohs holding in paintings and sculpture—the one that doesn't look like a shepherd's crook—and it's also the shiversome stick-with-spiky-metal-balls-attached medieval weapon.

As verbs of punishment, "flail" and "flog" are given as synonyms, though to me the former evokes the stick and the latter the whip. Whatever the terms evoke for you is your own business.

To flay, on the other hand, is to peel or tear the skin off something or someone, or to do that sort of thing figuratively, as, say, with words.

FLAIR/FLARE

The former is a knack (as, say, a flair for the dramatic) or stylishness (as someone dresses with flair); the latter is a burst of light or flame, an emergency signal, or a widening, as of one's bell-bottom trousers.

FLAUNT/FLOUT

To flaunt is to show off: yourself or some thing. Wealth and power are popularly flaunted.

To flout is to show contempt for or to defy; the word seems to be more or less permanently attached to either "the law" or "the rules."

FLESH OUT/FLUSH OUT

To flesh out is to add substance, as one fleshes out a business proposal by offering substantive details of intended action.

To flush out is to clean something by forcing water through it, as one flushes out a wound, or to expose something or someone by forcing it out of hiding, as one might use a smoke bomb to flush out a gang of criminals holed up in their lair.

FLIER/FLYER

A flier is a person or thing that flies. When it comes to pieces of paper you don't want handed to you by people whose causes you're not interested in, some opt for "flier" and some for "flyer." I suggest reserving "flier" for the soaring-in-the-air thing and "flyer" for the sheet of paper heading imminently into the recycle bin.

If you're risking something, you may be said to be taking either a flyer or a flier. I, with no particular reason in mind, would go with the former (which is slightly more popular in print).

FLOUNDER/FOUNDER

To flounder is to struggle clumsily; to founder is to sink or to fail. Floundering may precede foundering; thus the terms are sometimes confused.

FORBEAR/FOREBEAR

To forbear is to refrain from doing something, as one may forbear from eating chocolate during Lent, or to exhibit self-control in the face of difficulty (thus to demonstrate forbearance).

One's forebears are one's ancestors.[*]

FOREGO/FORGO

To forego is to precede.

To forgo is to do without.

---

[*] One of the unlikelier confusions I've run across as a copy editor is that between "ancestors" (the family members who preceded you) and "descendants" (one's direct progeny, and theirs). Nonetheless I encounter it once or twice a year, so: Fair warning.

FOREWORD/FORWARD

A foreword is an introductory section of a book; the term is generally used to refer to a brief essay written by someone other than the book's principal author.*

Forward is a direction: not backward. It's also an adjective often applied to children, suggesting bratty presumptuousness, or to people getting above their station or being aggressive (often sexually).

GANTLET/GAUNTLET

A gauntlet is a kind of glove, particularly useful for hurling to the ground in challenge when mortally insulted, or for picking up to accept such a challenge.

If you're forced to make your way between two parallel lines of people armed with clubs who are intent on thrashing the living daylights out of you and you don't have the option to sprint like hell in the opposite direction, you are running either the gantlet or the gauntlet, depending upon whom you ask. I'm a "gauntlet" fellow. I find the very sight of "gantlet" fussy and prissy, as if those two lines of assailants are raring to smack you around with doilies.

GEL/JELL

A gel is a jelly; it is also a transparent colored sheet, usually made of plastic, used in stage lighting.

When Jell-O sets, or when one's master plan takes shape, it either gels or jells. I like "jells."

GIBE/JIBE/JIVE

There's a lot of etymological muddiness here, but you'll be on solid ground if you use "gibe" to mean (as a noun) a sneering taunt or (as a verb) to deride, and "jibe" to mean agree with or align.

---

* Confidential to publishing professionals: You've *got* to stop referring to forewords as "forwards" or, worse, "forwords." I thank you.

The periodically encountered use of "jive" to mean "jibe" ("I'm so pleased that our plans for the weekend jive") is unsupportable, etymologically or any other -ly.

GRAVELY/GRAVELLY

"Gravely" is an adverb denoting seriousness, as one may become gravely ill.

"Gravelly" is an adjective characterizing a collection of pebbles and other bits of rock, as in a gravelly road, or roughness, as in a raspy, gravelly voice.

GRISLY/GRISTLY/GRIZZLY/GRIZZLED

Gory crimes are grisly.

Tough meat is gristly.

Some bears are grizzly.

Mistaken references to "grizzly crimes" (unless committed by actual bears, in which case OK) are extremely popular, always good for a chuckle, and to be avoided strenuously.

"Grizzled" refers to hair streaked with gray—and, by extension, it makes a decent synonym for "old." It does not mean, as many people seem to think it does, either unkempt or rugged.

HANGAR/HANGER

One puts a plane in a hangar.

One hangs a coat on a hanger.

The underappreciated cut of beef found suspended[*] from a cow's diaphragm is hanger steak.

HANGED/HUNG

Criminals are hanged.

Paintings are hung. Some. Also men. Some.

---

[*] Hanging, get it?

HARDY/HEARTY

Hardy people are able to cope with hardship; they are plucky, doughty, intrepid, indomitable.

Hearty people have a lot of heart; they are spirited and ebullient and cheerful, often in a loud, demonstrative, and irritating fashion.

A rich, nourishing soup or stew is hearty.

HAWK/HOCK

Verbwise, to hawk (outside discussion of birds, that is) is to sell and to hock is to pawn.

As to loogies, you may either (traditionally) hawk them or (popularly) hock them.

To hork, should you need to know this, is to vomit or to . . . well, there are a few other definitions, most of them disgusting.

HISTORIC/HISTORICAL

"Historic" denotes significance, as the passing of the Civil Rights Act was a historic event.

"Historical" simply denotes presence in the past.

Note, please: "a historic event," not "an historic event." Unless you're in the habit of saying or writing "an helicopter" you've got no cause to say or write "an historic."

HOARD/HORDE

To hoard is to amass, often with an eye toward secrecy; that which one hoards is one's hoard. J.R.R. Tolkien's Smaug is a hoarder of gold. New York's legendary Collyer brothers, Homer and Langley, were hoarders of just about anything they could cram into their Fifth Avenue townhouse. Their hoarding ultimately led to their grisly deaths, Langley crushed by a would-be defensive booby trap and poor blind, helpless Homer subsequently starving to death. The More You Know.

"Horde" is most often used as an uncomplimentary term for a teeming crowd of something or other: Mongol invaders, say, or sidewalk-blocking tourists in Times Square, or zombies.

HOME/HONE

Birds of prey and missiles home in on their targets.

To hone is to sharpen.

The phrase "hone in on" is one of those so-many-people-use-it-that-it-has-its-own-dictionary-entry-and-can-scarcely-anymore-be-called-an-error things, but that doesn't mean I have to like it.

HUMMUS/HUMUS

Hummus is a Middle Eastern dip made from mashed chick-peas.

Humus is decaying organic matter in soil.

You will find fifty-seven varieties of the former at your local Whole Foods. Be careful never to eat the latter.

IMPLY/INFER

To imply is to suggest, to say something without saying it.

To infer is to draw a conclusion from information perhaps obliquely offered, to figure out, to deduce.

Think of "imply" as an outward action and "infer" as an inward one. Or: Speakers imply; listeners infer.

INTERNMENT/INTERMENT

Internment is imprisoning or confining, particularly during wartime—as Japanese Americans were interned during World War II.

Interment is ritual burial, as a child might laboriously and with great ceremony inter a deceased pet. (To put something into an urn—particularly ashes after a cremation, which I hope you don't call cremains—is to inurn it.)

IT'S/ITS

"It's" is "it is," as in "It's a lovely day today."

"Its" is the possessive of "it," as in "It rubs the lotion on its skin."

No matter the perspicacity of any statement you may ever present publicly in print or, especially, online, an inability to discern between "its" and "it's" (and, see below, "your" and "you're") will make you a target for thunderous belittling. It's not fair, I suppose, but neither is life generally, I find.

KIBITZ/KIBBUTZ

To kibitz is to chitchat. Used with a bit more shade, it's to offer meddlesome advice from the sidelines, particularly at a card game.* Note that it's spelled with a single *b*.

A kibbutz, with two *b*'s, is an Israeli socialistic farming collective.

LAMA/LLAMA

The South American domesticated ungulate, cousin to the alpaca and the vicuña, is a llama.

A Buddhist priest or monk of Tibet or Mongolia is a lama. Lamas live in lamaseries.

LAY, LIE, LAID, LAIN, AND THE REST OF THE CLAN

Loath as I am to haul out the grammatical jargon, we're not going to get through the lay/lie thing without it.

So, then: One notes that "lay" is a transitive verb, which means that it demands an object. A transitive verb doesn't merely do; it must do *to* something. One does not merely lay; one lays a thing.† I lay my hands on a long-sought volume of poetry. I lay blame on a convenient stooge. I lay (if I am a hen) an egg.‡

---

*From Tennessee Williams's *A Streetcar Named Desire:*
BLANCHE: Poker is so fascinating. Could I kibitz?
STANLEY: You could not.
† Or, yes, a person. Get it out of your system.
‡ That said, one does occasionally speak, simply, of hens laying, as a vocation; this is one of those instances in which "lay" is an intransitive verb: No object is called for.

What does this mean to you? Well, for a start: If you're hesitating between "lie" and "lay" and (a) your sentence has a thing to act upon and (b) you can replace the verb you're in a quandary about with a less confusingly transitive verb like "place," you need a "lay."

"Lie," on the other hand, is an intransitive verb. I lie, period. Works for both recumbence and fibbing. No object needed. "Lie" can handle an adverb (I lie down, I lie badly) or a place on which to do it (I lie on the couch); it just doesn't need a thing, a what, attached to it.

Unfortunately, both verbs can and must be conjugated, and this is where the trouble kicks in.

Let's run through them, tensely.

to lay

present	lay	I lay the bowl on the table.
present participle	laying	I am laying the bowl on the table.
past	laid	Earlier, I laid the bowl on the table.
past participle	laid	I have laid the bowl on the table.

to lie (in the sense of to recline)*

present	lie	I lie down.
present participle	lying	Look at me: I am lying down.
past	lay	Yesterday, I lay down.
past participle	lain	Look at me: I have lain down.

That the past participle of "lie" is "lain," which never looks right to anyone, is bad enough. That the past tense of "lie" is "lay," the very word we are trying so hard not to misuse in the first place, is maddening. I know. I'm sorry.

With practice, you may be able to commit all of these to memory. Or you may dog-ear this page and keep it handy. I know I would.

---

* Conjugating "to lie" in the sense of to tell a whopper is pretty easy, so I'm parking it down here at the bottom of the page: I lie, I am lying, I lied, I have lied.

Bonus Lay/Lie Facts

The action of lying down does not require that one be a person, as some people mistakenly (and, I think, oddly) believe. I lie down. Fiona the hippopotamus lies down. Pat the bunny lies down.

One doesn't, in present-tense hiding, lay low or, in ambush, lay in wait. It's "lie" all the way: I lie low; I lie in wait.

That said, one does lay a trap for one's enemy, and given the chance, one will lay that enemy low.

To lay a ghost is to exorcise it.

You're not going to like this: Up until the late eighteenth century or so, no one particularly cared whether you chose to lie down or lay down, so long as you got horizontal. Then some word busybodies got wrought up on the subject, a rule was born, and schoolchildren (and writers) have been tortured on the subject ever since.

LEACH/LEECH

To leach is to drain one substance out of another by means of a percolating* liquid, as rainwater may leach nutrients out of soil.

To leech, literally, is to apply leeches, those nasty-looking bloodsucking worms, to a patient in order to advance healing.

To leech, figuratively, is to make a habit of exploiting another person—to suck that person dry in a leechlike manner or, to mix invertebrates, to sponge.

LEAD/LED

The past tense of the verb "lead" is not "lead" but "led." Today I will lead my troops into battle; yesterday I led them.

---

* The word "percolate" is so strongly linked in the modern mind to the pop-pop-popping of a coffee percolator that many people, I find, are surprised to learn that percolating is not bubbling but the filtering of a liquid (e.g., water) through a solid (e.g., ground coffee). Percolation is not what occurs in the dome at the top of a percolator; it's what's going on underneath.

I wouldn't point out something that seems so elementary but for the vast number of times I've seen, published, "lead" where "led" was called for. The error is not mysterious—for one thing, they sound the same; for another, compare "read," which is the past tense of "read"—but error it is.

LIGHTENING/LIGHTNING

If you're carrying your mother's suitcase to the train station, you are nobly lightening her load.

If on your way to the train station a thunderstorm descends, you should seek shelter, not only to stay dry but to avoid being struck by lightning.

LOATH/LOATHE

I am loath—that is, reluctant—to make comments, snide or otherwise, about people I loathe—that is, detest.

Use "loath" as an adjective; use "loathe" as a verb.

LOSE/LOOSE

To mislay something is to lose it.

Something that is not tight or severe—a dress, one's morals—is loose.

To loose something is to set it free. Oddly, to unloose something is also to set it free.

LUXURIANT/LUXURIOUS

Something lush or plentiful is luxuriant: Rapunzel's hair, say, or kudzu.

Something luxurious is lavish and elegant and expensive, like a Lamborghini or a stateroom on the *Titanic*.

MANTEL/MANTLE

A mantel is a shelf above a fireplace.

A mantle is a sleeveless, capelike garment. Metaphorically, it's the thing you don when you're assuming some responsibility.

MARITAL/MARTIAL

The former refers to marriage, the latter to the military. Unless your marriage is militaristic, in which case word choice probably isn't your biggest problem.

MASTERFUL/MASTERLY

Somewhere along the path you may have been taught, as I was, that "masterful" is an adjective meaning bossy or domineering and that "masterly" is an adjective that means adept or virtuosic. Experience has shown me, though, that writers tend to use "masterful" to mean accomplished—gushing book blurbs are forever calling out "masterful prose"—and do not take kindly to having it changed to "masterly," which they tend not to use at all. (I suppose that part of the discomfort with "masterly" is that, with that -ly finale, it looks like an adverb.)

Reading up on the subject to write up this pair, I learned this: Both words have carried both meanings for centuries, and only in the early twentieth century did one particularly influential wordsmith take it upon himself to neaten things up by segregating them into the separate roles I've mentioned above. Which is to say: The distinction is sort of kind of utterly insupportable.

So feel free to maintain the division if you're so inclined— you won't be wrong if you do—but feel free not to.

MILITATE/MITIGATE

To militate is to prevent or to counteraffect, as the presence of heavily armed soldiers will militate against public unrest.

To mitigate is to alleviate, as the presence of the Red Cross will mitigate the suffering of hurricane victims.

No matter how many times you see "mitigate against," which is all the time, it is never correct.

MILLENNIUM/MILLENNIA

One millennium, two or more millennia. Be careful with the spelling as well: two *l*'s, two *n*'s.

In downtown Manhattan, there's a Millenium Hilton. I would never stay there.[*]

MINER/MINOR
Miners labor underground.

Minors are children.

An inconsequential detail is minor. So, musically, is a chord, scale, or key that the ear tends to associate with melancholy.

MUCOUS/MUCUS
Re "mucous," I couldn't possibly improve upon this elegant dictionary definition: "relating to, covered with, or of the nature of mucus."

That is, "mucous" is an adjective, "mucus" a noun. Mucous membranes produce mucus.

NAVAL/NAVEL
People rarely err when they mean to type "naval" in the seafaring sense, but when the talk turns to belly buttons, many forget to switch from *a* to *e*. Your innie or your outie is a navel.

ONBOARD/ON BOARD
Remember "everyday" and "every day"? Well, here we are again.

"Onboard" is an adjective (onboard refueling, for instance, or an onboard navigation system); "on board" is an adverb, literally denoting presence on a vessel ("The crew was on board the ship") or figuratively denoting agreement ("This department is on board with the new regulations").

The use of "onboard" as a verb was, you may recall, covered on p. 163, and let's not encourage it via repetition.

---

[*] According to a 2000 *Wired* article, whose author spoke to the hotel's PR flack, "The building's current name dates back to the early 1990s . . . when its former owner deliberately chose to spell 'Millennium' with a single *n*. . . . He was well aware that the spelling was wrong [but] figured the small aberration in nomenclature would make the hotel stand out from the crowd." In the immortal words of Maureen McCormick, "Sure, Jan."

ORDINANCE/ORDNANCE

An ordinance is a decree or a piece of legislation.

"Ordnance" refers to military supplies—not only artillery but ammunition, armor, vehicles, all the practical stuff of warfare.

PALATE/PALETTE/PALLET

Your palate is the roof of your mouth or your sense of taste.

A palette is an array of color or the board onto which artists lay their paint.

A pallet is a platform onto which items are loaded, as in a warehouse; "pallet" is also a somewhat outmoded term for a small bed.

PASS/PASSED/PAST

As a verb, "passed" is the past tense of "pass."

"Past" is both noun and adjective, as in William Faulkner's "The past is never dead. It's not even past." It's also a preposition, and an adverb, and just about anything else you can think of *except a verb*.

"Passed" is *never* an adjective, and "past" is *never* a verb.

PEAK/PEEK/PIQUE

Mixing these up is direly easy. A peak is a summit; a peek is a glance. The *ea* in "sneak" inspires many an erroneous "sneak peak." No, please: It's "sneak peek." (Unless you find yourself jetting through a cloud and suddenly about to collide with a mountain, in which case, sure, that's a sneak peak.)

A fit of pique is a peeved little tantrum; to pique one's interest is to stimulate and excite it.

PEAL/PEEL

You probably don't need to be reminded that bells peal and potatoes are peeled. You might need to be reminded that what you're doing when you're being watchful is keeping your eyes peeled—wide open and lids up.

The thing itself—of a potato, a banana, a lemon, an orange—is a peel. Plus—and this is why we have the verb "peel"—one removes it before eating. As opposed to a skin—an apple's, say—which outside of cooking one is apt to eat.

PEDAL, PEDDLE, PEDDLER, ET AL.

A pedal is something you operate with your foot. If you are operating something with your foot, you are a pedaling pedaler. Those cropped calf-length trousers you're wearing, whether you're riding a bicycle or not, are pedal pushers.*

To peddle is to go from place to place selling things—often, small things: gewgaws, doodads, trinkets, the odd tchotchke. Peddlers peddle. (In Great Britain, sometimes it's pedlars who peddle.) Perhaps because itinerant merchants might be seen as untrustworthy—otherwise, why don't they own a proper store?—to peddle is also to promote a shaky or shady notion. ("Go peddle your nonsense elsewhere.")

When you attempt to distance yourself from an action or (mis)statement, you are backpedaling. When you're trying to fudge a fact or minimize the unpleasantness of a situation, you're soft-pedaling. The former derives from bicycling, the latter from playing the piano. Why is "backpedaling" closed up and "soft-pedaling" hyphenated? Because dictionaries are whimsical.

The segment of a flower—likely you've got this down already, but better safe than sorry—is a petal.

PHENOMENON/PHENOMENA

As with "criterion" and "criteria" or "millennium" and "millennia" above, this is simply a matter of singular and plural: one phenomenon, two or more phenomena.

PIXILATED/PIXELATED

To be pixilated is to be confusedly crazy; it's a silly-sounding word (derived from "pixie") so perhaps best reserved for silly

---

* Also known as clam diggers or Capri pants.

sorts of craziness. "Pixilated" was famously used in Frank Capra's 1936 screwball comedy *Mr. Deeds Goes to Town,* in which it was applied to Gary Cooper's tuba-playing character, Longfellow Deeds.

A pixelated image, on a computer or television screen, is one whose tiniest individual elements (often dots or squares; the term "pixel" is a portmanteau of "picture" and "element") are expanded to the point where one can no longer make sense of the bigger picture.

I like to think that "pixelated" derived specifically and intentionally from "pixilated"; otherwise we'd just call it "pixeled." I have no evidence to support that perhaps pixilated notion.

PLUM/PLUMB/PLUMMY

The adjective "plum," deriving from the name of the summer-enhancing fruit, means choice and desirable. One speaks of, say, securing a plum role in a play or a plum political appointment.

To plumb is to determine depth, as of a body of water, and, by extension, to deeply explore or examine, as in, say, plumbing the horrors of modern warfare.

As an adverb, "plumb" means utterly or squarely, as in plumb loco or landing plumb in the middle of a ghastly situation.

A plumb is the weight on the end of a line that one uses to plumb, and, "plumb," as an adjective, means precisely vertical.

Also, what a plumber does for a living is plumb.

A plummy speaking voice is too rich, too proper, too self-conscious—that is to say, too-too.

POKEY/POKY

The pokey is the hoosegow, the clink, the slammer, the big house—a prison.

Something poky is irritatingly slow, or provincial, or frumpy.

In America we do the hokey pokey (and we turn ourselves around). In England they do the hokey cokey (and they turn themselves around).

POPULACE/POPULOUS

"Populace" is a noun; it means population or, particularly, the so-called common people.

"Populous" is an adjective; it means well and densely populated.

PORE/POUR

To pore over something is to examine it closely. Pores are those things on your face that get clogged.

To pour something is to tip it—water, wine, salt, sugar, what have you—out of a container.

PRECEDE/PROCEED

To precede is to come before.

To proceed is to move forward.

PREMIER/PREMIERE

As an adjective, "premier" means first or top-ranked; as a noun, it's a head of state.

A premiere is a debut, as of a play. To premiere a movie is to open it.

PRESCRIBE/PROSCRIBE

To prescribe is to authorize medical treatment or the taking of medication, or otherwise to direct authoritatively.

To proscribe is to forbid.

PRINCIPAL/PRINCIPLE

How many times was it explained to you in elementary school spelling lessons that "the principal is your pal"? And what was your level of horror when you realized that the principal was not your pal but a terrifying martinet?

Consider that realization a principal (that is to say, primary) life lesson. In fact, you might deem it a principle—a fundamental truth from which more advanced truths derive—on the road to mature cynicism.

One's principles are one's amassed moralities; villains are unprincipled.

One's principal is, as well, one's amassed bank holdings that one aspires not to touch so that one can live entirely on one's interest. Good luck with that.

PRONE/SUPINE

Obviously there's no confusion of vowel order or consonant doubling here, but I include these terms because they are frequently mixed up and I can't figure out where else to park them.

For the record:

To be supine is to be lying on one's back.

To be prone is to be lying on one's stomach.

Beyond "lead" when "led" is meant, I'd say that "prone" for "supine" (or vice versa) is the commonest error to get past writers, copy editors, and proofreaders and find its way to print.

You can devise all the mnemonics you like (if you're supine you're lying on your spine, if you're prone you're . . . oh, the heck with it), but I never—never—fail to consult the dictionary whenever I'm faced with either word.

PROPHECY/PROPHESY

"Prophecy" is the noun, "prophesy" the verb. An oracle prophesies a prophecy. The plural of "prophecy" is "prophecies"; the third-person singular of the verb "prophesy" is "prophesies." (I prophesy, you prophesy, he prophesies, she prophesies, they shall have prophesied, we all scream for ice cream.)

RACK/WRACK/WREAK

Setting aside the meanings pertaining to cuts of meat, the storage of clothing and spice tins, the corralling of billiard balls, the accumulation of points, and rude references to a woman's bosom, let's focus on "rack" in the sense of pain: A rack is a nasty device (we may think of it as medieval, but it has a long and distinguished history going back at least to the first century A.D.) to which one is fastened by the wrists and the ankles and, well, you know all the shrieking, limb-dislocating rest. To be put to the rack, then, is to be tortured, and thus one's body is racked with pain. One contemplates effortfully by racking one's brains. A painful cough is a racking one. And an anxiety-inducing experience is nerve-racking.

Or is it?

To wrack is to wreck, to destroy. Was that awful hour you spent locked in a room full of rambunctious kindergartners simply nerve-racking, or was it utterly nerve-wracking? Is your moldering ancestral manse going to wrack and ruin, or merely rack and ruin?

You'll be either elated or pained to the point of destruction to learn that the differences between "rack" and "wrack" have become so confused over time that many dictionaries simply list them as synonyms, and many stylebooks, after halfhearted attempts to nudge a few meanings in the direction of either, shrug resignedly and move on.

The suggestion of *The New York Times Manual of Style and Usage* to avoid "wrack" entirely and use "wreck" when you mean wreck is, all things considered, not a bad one.

And what of "wreak"? To wreak is to cause (in an unnice way) or to inflict. An army wreaks havoc. A storm wreaks damage. The preferred past tense of "wreak," I should note, is not "wrought" (which is an ancient past tense of "work"; it still turns up in the phrase "wrought iron") but, simply, "wreaked."

REIGN/REIN

Monarchs reign.

Horses are reined.

If one is granted the freedom to make one's own decisions and run one's own life, one is given free rein. Free rein, please, not free reign: The phrase is taken not from the devil-may-care actions of kings or queens but from permitting one's mount to do what it likes—the opposite of maintaining a tight rein. Unfortunately, "free reign" makes a kind of sense, so it's frequently—though, still, incorrectly—used.

RELUCTANT/RETICENT

To be reluctant is to be resistant, unwilling.

To be reticent is to be silent, uncommunicative.

One is reluctant to do X; one is reticent about subject Y.

"Reticent" is increasingly often used to mean "reluctant." I see no good reason to allow the distinction between these two to collapse, though many have given up on it.

RETCH/WRETCH

To retch is to heave, to gag, to nearly vomit. I think it's wonderful that the English language has a word for "to nearly vomit." (The word can also be used flat out to mean "to vomit," but there are so many other colorful synonyms for that action that surely we can leave "retch" for the preface rather than the conclusion.)

A wretch is a person on the darker side of the happiness/niceness spectrum, from the muddy gray of the deeply miserable poor unfortunate to the full-tilt blackness of the scoundrel and the miscreant. And the blackguard.

RIFFLE/RIFLE

This duo plays well to the onomatopoeia/mnemonics crowd, because to riffle something is to thumb lightly through it, as, say, through the pages of a book or a deck of playing cards, and the word "riffle," at least to my ears, has that lovely susurrating sound built right into it. To rifle through something—a room, a desk drawer—is to rummage with criminal intent to steal. That the verb "rifle" is the same as a noun for a firearm should also make it easier for you to remember which one of these is which.

ROGUE / ROUGE

Careful there, you typing fingers.

A rogue is a scoundrel, a ne'er-do-well.[*] (See also "wretch," above.)

Rouge is that which one applies to the lips or the cheeks to redden them.

SEGUE / SEGWAY

The music-derived "segue" means, as a verb, to transition seamlessly and, as a noun, such a seamless transition. Before the invention of the motorized two-wheeled *Arrested Development* punchline—the Segway—"segue" was, lacking a homophone, likely never misspelled. Now it is. A lot. A smooth change is not a "segway." Ever.

SENSUAL / SENSUOUS

"Sensual" pertains to the physical senses; "sensuous" involves aesthetic matters. The *Oxford English Dictionary* tells us that John Milton is thought to have coined "sensuous" in the mid-seventeenth century so as to have a word for the pleasure of the finer senses that would have, unlike "sensual," no sexual connotation. Unfortunately, hardly anyone then or since has been able to remember which is supposed to be which, and the publication in 1969 of the racy how-to bestseller *The Sensuous Woman*—which should, according to Miltonian rules, have been called *The Sensual Woman*—likely muddied the distinction forever. If you're leaning toward the use of either word and fear that your reader will be confused, you might do well to simply choose another term altogether.

---

[*] I love a word with an assortment of punctuation, don't you?: no-man's-land, will-o'-the-wisp.

SHONE/SHOWN

"Shone" is the past and past participle of shine (so is "shined," if you like "shined"). "Shown" is the past participle of "show."

STANCH/STAUNCH

These two derive from a single root, and each is occasionally offered as a synonym for the other, but if you're, as I perennially am, in a compartmentalizing mood:

Use "stanch" when you mean to stop the flow of something, as blood from a wound, or to hold something in check, as to stanch the rising violence in a war-torn country.

And use "staunch" to describe someone who is indomitable, steadfast, loyal, and strong.*

STATIONARY/STATIONERY

To be stationary is to be unmoving.

Stationery is writing paper (and, often included in the idea, the full array of envelopes, pens, pencils, and ink).

SUBTLY/SUBTLETY

Be careful to discern between the adverb ("She insinuated herself subtly into the conversation") and the noun ("He wheedled money out of his parents with great subtlety").

This one involves less definition confusion than typing confusion, but it's a massively popular example of the latter.

TENANT/TENET

A tenant is a rent payer.

A tenet is a belief, a principle.

THAN/THEN

Beyond mixing these up with a slip of the fingers, many people mix them up syntactically when they mistype "No sooner

---

* Best use of "staunch" ever? Out of the mouth of Edith "Little Edie" Bouvier Beale, in the 1975 documentary *Grey Gardens,* by Albert and David Maysles. "A staunch woman . . . S-T-A-U-N-C-H. There's nothing worse, I'm telling you. They don't weaken. No matter what." You should watch it. Go. I'll wait here.

had we placed our order with the waiter *then* the restaurant caught on fire" when they should be adhering to the correct construction "no sooner had x *than* y."

THEIR/THERE/THEY'RE

"Their" is a possessive meaning belongs to them: I can see their house from here.

"There" is a direction indicating a place that is not here: I can see their house, which is over there.

"They're" is a contraction for "they are": They're walking to their house.

As with "it's/its" (above), "to/too" (below), and "your/you're" (yet further below), you simply need to get this right. It's not enough to know the differences, one must also apply them.

TO/TOO

I know I shouldn't have to clear this up, but you'd be saddened to learn how frequently adults get it wrong.

"To" is, among many things, a preposition, as in "He walked to the store"; what is called an infinitive marker, as in the verb "to be"; and an occasional adverb, as in "She yanked the door to"—which is to say, she pulled it shut—or "He came to"—meaning he became conscious.

"Too" means also (as in "eating one's cake and having it too") and excessively (as in "Slow down, you move too fast").

TOOTHY/TOOTHSOME

To be toothy is to have prominent teeth, or simply a lot of them.

To be toothsome is to be tasty; often the term is used to describe things that seem, in anticipation and as yet untasted, to be tasty, as a toothsome morsel. And that sense of anticipatory salivation is why "toothsome" is also applied to people who are sexually appealing, I imagine.

TORTUOUS/TORTUROUS

The former means twisty, winding, serpentine; the latter means like torture. A tortuous journey can be torturous, but there is no judgment inherent in "tortuous"; it's merely descriptive. "Torturous," no matter how you slice it, or are sliced (see "flay," above), is unpleasant.

UNDERWAY/UNDER WAY

As above, with "everyday" and "every day" and "onboard" and "on board," "underway" is an adjective, "under way" an adverb. You won't have much (or any) use of the former, so odds are you want the latter. The voyage is under way, the project is under way, your life is under way. More and more lately, "underway" is used as an adverb. Bummer, I say.

VALE/VEIL

A vale is a valley; a veil is a face covering.

As picturesquely funereally evocative as the notion of a "veil of tears" might be, the phrase—going all the way back to Psalm 84—is properly "vale of tears."

VENAL/VENIAL

"Venal" means mercenary, bribable, corrupt.

"Venial" means pardonable; a venial sin is one that will not send you to hell.

WAIVE/WAVE/WAVER

To waive is to renounce or cede, as one waives one's right to a trial by jury.

To wave is to flap one's hand about (or to curl one's hair).

A customs inspector who lets you pass without examining your luggage is waving—not waiving—you through.

To waver (not to be confused with a waiver, which is a document of relinquishment) is to tremble or to vacillate.

WHOSE/WHO'S

"I don't know whose books those are." "Whose" is a pronoun denoting belonging.

"Who's on first?" "Who's" means "Who is."

WORKOUT/WORK OUT

The former is a noun; the latter is a verb. You're not on the way to the gym to "workout." You're on the way to the gym to work out. And to give yourself a workout.

YOUR/YOU'RE

Just like "whose" and "who's." "This is not your book but one stolen from the library. You're in a world of trouble."

CHAPTER 11

Notes on
Proper Nouns

I THINK I CAN SAFELY SAY that no rational person is hubristic enough to type "Zbigniew Brzezinski" or "Aleksandr Solzhenitsyn" or "Shohreh Aghdashloo" without first checking the spelling of the name, but the number of less formidable-looking proper nouns that wind up misspelled in manuscripts and, if copy editors and proofreaders are not vigilant, in finished books is vast. In response to a few near misses and at least one published oops, which I cop to below, I began keeping this list years ago; in fact, it's the germ of the book you're now reading, and I have a great sentimental attachment to it. And I never seem to be able to stop adding things to it.*

I suppose I might just say "If it starts with a capital letter, look it up" and end this chapter right here, but where would be the fun in that?

---

* The list, you'll note, leans heavily toward the performing arts. As Popeye once said: I yam what I yam. Also, I've found over time that many writers about the performing arts are irksomely cavalier about spelling. And dates.

PEOPLE*

BUD ABBOTT
Of the comedy team Abbott and (Lou) Costello, whose "Who's on first?" routine is an acknowledged delight but whose perhaps lesser-known Bagel Street sketch (also known as the Susquehanna Hat Company sketch) is one of the funniest things in the history of Western civilization.

Two *t*'s in Abbott.

A single-*t* abbot, for the record, is the fellow in charge of a monastery.

PEDRO ALMODÓVAR
Film director.

The acute accent† sits over the second, not the first, *o* in his surname.

HANS CHRISTIAN ANDERSEN
Fairytalist.

Not "Anderson."

ANN-MARGRET
Actress.‡ Singer. Erstwhile kitten with a whip.

Not "Margaret," and: Mind the hyphen.

ATTILA
Hun.

Not "Atilla."

DAN AYKROYD
Comedian. Half of the Blues Brothers.

---

* Also a fairy, a bear, and a few other beings that can't quite be called people.

† The accent mark that slants the other way is a grave accent.

‡ Though unnecessarily female-gendered nouns—"comedienne," "murderess," "poetess," "sculptress," the delectable "aviatrix"—are increasingly a thing of the past, "actress" persists and likely will so long as award-giving guilds persist in categorically segregating male actors and female actors. That said, many female actors refer to themselves, and are referred to, as just plain actors.

Not "Ackroyd" (though that's the correct spelling for Agatha Christie's Roger-who-was-killed).

"Ghostbuster" is one word, by the way.

ELIZABETH BENNET
Headstrong heroine of Jane Austen's *Pride and Prejudice*.

Just the one *t* in Bennet.

It's not "Jane Austin." Does that bear mentioning? I fear that it does.

PIETER BRUEGEL THE ELDER
Sixteenth-century Flemish painter, the Matthew McConaughey of his era, as no one can ever quite remember how to spell his name, likely because it is also spelled Brueghel or Breughel. His eldest son, also named Pieter, generally referred to as Pieter Brueghel the Younger, also vacillated on the spelling of the family name. Which happily suggests that no matter how you spell it, you can defend your choice.

GAUTAMA BUDDHA
A.k.a. Siddhartha Gautama, a.k.a. the Buddha.

Sage.

Not "the Bhudda."

Also, then, not "Bhuddist" but "Buddhist."

WARREN BUFFETT
Billionaire.

Not "Buffet," which would make him a serve-yourself meal.

Here's a head-scratcher, though: Why does no one seem ever to misspell singer Jimmy Buffett's name?

JULIUS CAESAR
Roman emperor after whom caesarean delivery was likely not named.

Not "Ceasar."

The salad—born, untraumatically, not in Rome but in Mexico—is also Caesar.

The Messrs. Chavez (activist) and Romero (Joker), among many others, were Cesars.

NICOLAS CAGE
Film actor.

> Not "Nicholas."

> Nephew of film director Francis Ford Coppola and cousin of FFC's daughter, film director Sofia Coppola, whose surname is occasionally misspelled "Copolla." (Italian words with double consonants seem to confound people; be on your guard.)

ROSANNE CASH
Singer/songwriter/writing writer.

> Most definitely not "Roseanne."

HILLARY RODHAM CLINTON
Tragically lost opportunity.

> A two-*l* Hillary.

> Novelist Mantel and actress Swank are one-*l* Hilarys.

PATRICIA CORNWELL
Novelist and Jack the Ripper obsessive.

> Not "Cornwall."

NOËL COWARD
Actor, playwright, composer, lyricist, director, generally busy fellow.

> The diaeresis—the *New Yorker*–beloved mark often affectionately but, in this and all other non-German-language cases, inaccurately referred to as an umlaut—is not optional.

ALEISTER CROWLEY
Pansexual occultist.

You'll more often run into Alistairs and Alastairs (Alastair Sim, for instance, the preeminent cinematic Scrooge).

E. E. CUMMINGS
Edward Estlin Cummings, in full. Poet.
His name is not "e. e. cummings."*

A Note on Initials

Random House style favors even spacing overall for names featuring two initials, that is:

E. E. Cummings (rather than E.E. Cummings)
T. S. Eliot (rather than T.S. Eliot)
H. L. Mencken (you get the point)

to say nothing of

George R. R. Martin

For names featuring three initials, go with the more compact

J.R.R. Tolkien

for instance, because on the page, J. R. R. Tolkien, not unlike the Peter Jackson films taken from his books, goes on for bloody ever.

More and more often I'm seeing, for people who truly use their initials as a first name, such stylings as

PJ Harvey

and

KT Tunstall

which I think look spiffy and make good sense, an enviably fine combination.

Mostly one wants to strike a balance between one's editorial preferences and the preferences of the people who own the names.

---

* Though in styling his name publishers and text designers occasionally mimicked Cummings's penchant for writing all in lowercase by styling his name "e. e. cummings," the writer himself far more often than not favored standard capitalization insofar as his name was concerned.

CECIL B. DEMILLE

Spectacular director.

The family name was de Mille, and that's how Cecil B. signed his name. But for business purposes and onscreen credits, he used the more imposing DeMille, so thus we refer to him.

Cecil's brother, also a director (and a screenwriter), was William de Mille.

William's daughter was the choreographer Agnes de Mille.

CRUELLA DE VIL

Puppy-coat-craving archvillainess.

Not "de Ville," as I often encounter it.

While we're here: Dodie Smith's 1956 novel is *The Hundred and One Dalmatians*. The 1961 Disney animated film thereof was first released as *One Hundred and One Dalmatians*; it's now generally marketed as *101 Dalmatians*, which is the official title of the 1996 live-action remake.

The spotted dogs are not "Dalmations," though that error attempts to happen every so often.

W.E.B. DU BOIS

Writer and civil rights activist.

His surname is correctly rendered "Du Bois" and not (as for Tennessee Williams's Blanche) "DuBois."

And it's pronounced not "doo-BWAH" (which would be correct for Blanche) but "doo-BOYZ."

T. S. ELIOT

Person ultimately responsible for *Cats*.

This is your reminder always to look up Eliots, Elyots, Elliots, and Elliotts.

PHILEAS FOGG

Hero of Jules Verne's *La tour du monde en quatre-vingts jours*, a.k.a. *Around the World in Eighty Days*.

Not "Phineas."

MAHATMA GANDHI

Nonviolent revolutionary.

Born Mohandas Karamchand Gandhi.

"Mahatma," by the way, isn't a name per se. It's a Sanskrit honorific, meaning "great soul."

All that taken into account, the surname is not "Ghandi," as it's misspelled with dismaying frequency.

THEODOR GEISEL

A.k.a. Dr. Seuss.

Cat in the Hat creator.

Not a Theodore with a second *e*.*

There are more Theodors out there than one might at first imagine, including the philosopher surnamed Adorno and the Zionist surnamed Herzl.†

ALLEN GINSBERG

Beat poet.

Always verify the name of anyone who is named Allen, Allan, Alan, Ginsberg, Ginsburg (Ruth Bader, for instance), or even Ginzburg.

JAKE GYLLENHAAL

Actor.

Also, for that matter, Maggie Gyllenhaal, his sister. Actress.

GEORGE FRIDERIC HANDEL

Composer.

This, above, is his own anglicized version of his name; in the original German he's Georg Friedrich Händel.

---

* Whenever you're about to write something like "Not a Theodore with an *e*," as I was just about to, make your way back to the beginning of the word, count up your letters, and adjust your math accordingly.

† I might simply have written "the philosopher Adorno and the Zionist Herzl," but the crash of discrete proper nouns is always to be avoided. See also "June Truman's secretary of state," p. 27.

LILLIAN HELLMAN

Playwright, screenwriter, memoirist, of whom writer Mary McCarthy once commented, "Every word she writes is a lie, including 'and' and 'the,'" which is one of the most jaw-droppingly deft insults ever hurled (and for which Hellman sued; wouldn't you?).

Only one *n* in Hellman.

Hellmann's, with two *n*'s, is a brand of mayonnaise.

O. HENRY

Pen name of twisty-ending-short-story writer William Sydney Porter.

Not "O'Henry."

The candy bar is Oh Henry!; it was not, as many people think, named after baseball player Henry Louis "Hank" Aaron.

KATHARINE HEPBURN

Radiant personality and occasionally brilliant actress.

Not "Katherine."

PEE-WEE HERMAN

Alter ego of comedian Paul Reubens. Note the hyphen, note the lowercase *w*.

The nickname of the major-league shortstop Harold Peter Henry Reese is Pee Wee.

ADOLF HITLER

Genocidal maniac democratically elected to run an ostensibly enlightened nation.

It's not "Adolph."

I can't, apparently, say that enough.

BILLIE HOLIDAY

Goddess.

One *l* in Holiday.

JUDY HOLLIDAY
Actress.
> Two *l*'s in Holliday.

ANJELICA HUSTON
Actress.
> Not "Angelica."
> Lot of actresses in this list, are there not.

ALEJANDRO G. IÑÁRRITU
Mexican filmmaker.
> The back-to-back diacriticals are distinctive.
> The full title of his Academy Award–winning film *Birdman* is, please note, *Birdman or (The Unexpected Virtue of Ignorance),* which manages to be both distinctive and bothersome.

COUSIN ITT
Short, hirsute Addams relation.

SCARLETT JOHANSSON
Actress.
> Two *t*'s in Scarlett, like in Scarlett O'Hara.

MADELINE KAHN
Actress, often outrageously funny.
> Not "Madeleine."
> While we're here:
> Ludwig Bemelmans's storybook schoolgirl ("In an old house in Paris, that was covered with vines," etc.) is also Madeline.
> The Proustian pastry is a madeleine.
> The first female secretary of state in U.S. history was Madeleine Albright.

NIKITA KHRUSHCHEV
Soviet shoe banger.
> You'd think that people would always look up a tricky name like Khrushchev. You'd be wrong.

FREDDY KRUEGER

Frequenter of Elm Street.

Not "Kreuger." And not "Kruger." And not "Kroger."

SHIA LABEOUF

I appreciate people who take the time to spell this odd actor's odd name correctly. In a more sensible French-cognizant world, it would be spelled LeBoeuf.

K. D. LANG

Musician.

All-lowercase names are a matter of copyeditorial delicacy. I lean toward honoring the preference of the name's owner. One might, on first mention, to avoid any possible confusion, drop in a parenthetical along the lines of "(who styles her name thus)," but you probably won't be happy with how fuss-budgety it looks. This sort of thing is, I suppose, a matter of taste, of context, of fame, of reader familiarity.

(Same indeed goes for people who make their way through life mononymically, e.g., Cher and Beyoncé, neither of whom, to be sure, requires a "who styles her name thus.")

VIVIEN LEIGH

Actress.

Not "Vivian."

LEONARDO DA VINCI

Quite literally, Renaissance man.

He's set here between Leigh and Lévi-Strauss rather than up among the *D*'s because his name is, indeed, Leonardo and he oughtn't to be referred to as "Da Vinci." Vinci is where he was from; it's not his name. That novel by Dan Brown has done much to blunt this particular point, but getting this right remains a laudable thing to do.

CLAUDE LÉVI-STRAUSS

Anthropologist.

(The unrelated company that makes the jeans is Levi Strauss.)

ROY LICHTENSTEIN

Pop artist.

I occasionally see the spelling of his name confused with that of the little landlocked European country hemmed in by Switzerland and Austria, which are themselves landlocked, and which is the Principality of Liechtenstein.

PATTI LUPONE

Singing actress.

Not "Lupone."

This is not a woman you want to mess with, so get it right.

MACBETH

Thane.

Not "MacBeth."

It's the wise writer who looks up any name starting with Mac- or Mc-, whether it belongs to an apple (McIntosh) or to a computer (Macintosh), or to James Abbott McNeill Whistler (painter), Fred MacMurray (actor), or John D. MacDonald (author).

While we're here: The theatrical superstition against uttering the name Macbeth is often misrepresented. One may safely utter it, say, walking down Forty-fourth Street or at a table at Sardi's. Or while reading this book aloud. One may not utter it, except during rehearsals or performances, in a theater. Thus the euphemisms "the Scottish play," "the Scottish lord," etc.

MATTHEW MCCONAUGHEY

Actor.

His surname is impossible to spell correctly.

IAN MCKELLEN
Actor.

His name is—inexplicably, I'd say; one might just as easily get it right as get it wrong—often misrendered "McKellan."

STEPHENIE MEYER
Writer.

Not "Stephanie."

LIZA MINNELLI
Star.

Two *n*'s, two *l*'s.

Same, happily enough, goes for her father, Hollywood director Vincente.

ALANIS MORISSETTE
Singer-songwriter.

In her surname: one *r*, two *s*'s, two *t*'s. Very easy to get wrong.

See also "irony," p. 160.

ELISABETH MOSS
Actress.

Not "Elizabeth."

FRIEDRICH WILHELM NIETZSCHE
Trouble-causing philosopher.

There are, I've learned over the years, so many, many ways to misspell Nietzsche.

GEORGIA O'KEEFFE
Artist.

Two *f*'s.

LAURENCE OLIVIER
Actor.

Laurence with a *u*. Knighthood made him Sir Laurence Olivier, or Sir Laurence for short. Not Sir Olivier, an error Americans are prone to. (He was also eventually Lord Olivier, but that's a different honour [*sic*].)

EDGAR ALLAN POE
Writer.

I'd venture to say that Poe's is the most consistently misspelled author's name in the Western canon. His central name is not "Allen."

CHRISTOPHER REEVE
Actor.

Played Superman.

GEORGE REEVES
Actor.

Also played Superman.

Thus, I imagine, the frequent misrendering of Christopher Reeve's surname.*

While we're here, let's also take note of:

KEANU REEVES
Star of Bill & Ted comedies, Matrix uncomedies, and John Wick unintentional comedies.

CONDOLEEZZA RICE
Politician.

Mind the double *z*.

RICHARD RODGERS
Composer of numerous landmark musicals, most famously partnered with lyricists Lorenz Hart (*The Boys from Syracuse,*

---

* I've generally noticed the odd tendency to slap an *s* onto the surname of people whose surnames don't end with one. Thus actor Alan Cumming becomes Alan Cummings, etc.

Pal Joey, etc.) and Oscar Hammerstein II (*Oklahoma!*, *Carousel*, *The King and I*, etc.).[*]
Not to be confused with Richard Rogers, the architect of London's Millennium Dome.

ROXANE

The love object of Edmond Rostand's 1897 play *Cyrano de Bergerac*. One *n*.
The writer Roxane Gay is also a one-*n* Roxane.
The eponymous heroine of both the 1978 Police song and Steve Martin's 1987 film (inspired by Rostand's play) is Roxanne. Two *n*'s.

PETER SARSGAARD

Actor.
Wasn't the vampire in *True Blood*.

FRANZ SCHUBERT

Austrian composer.
The American theatrical impresario brothers Sam, Leo, and J.J. were the Shuberts. Same goes, then, for the Shubert Theatre (and Shubert Alley) in New York, and the Shubert Organization.

MARTIN SCORSESE

Director.
Not "Scorcese."

ALEXANDER SKARSGÅRD

Actor.
Was the vampire in *True Blood*.
The ring diacritic in his surname is often omitted, perhaps

---

[*] The habit of identifying people by dropping a specifying parenthetical into their name—e.g., Lorenz (*Pal Joey*) Hart—is unsightly, so don't do it, whatever you're writing. You're not a 1930s columnist.

because no one can bother to figure out where it's hiding in their keyboard.

SPIDER-MAN
Superhero.

Note the hyphen, note the capital *M*.

DANIELLE STEEL
Prolific novelist.

Before I came to work for the company that publishes her, I managed, in a book referring to her, to let her name go to print not once but a half dozen times as "Danielle Steele." Yeesh.

BARBRA STREISAND
It's a bit late in the history of Western civilization for people to misspell her first name as "Barbara," but it still happens.

MOTHER TERESA
Nun, missionary, now a Catholic saint.

No *h*.

TERESA OF ÁVILA
Nun, mystic, now a Catholic saint.

Nope. Still no *h*.

If you're utterly jonesing for a saintly *h*, I commend to you Thérèse of Lisieux.

TINKER BELL
Fairy.

Two words, the latter conveying the sound of her communication, the former conveying that her job was to mend pots and pans. Really.

HARRY S. TRUMAN
President on whose desk the buck stopped.

The middle initial doesn't stand for anything, so for decades copy editors have amused themselves, if no one else, by styling his name as Harry S Truman. Truman seems to have (mostly) signed his name with a perioded *S*, so let's do it that way.

TRACEY ULLMAN
Funny actress. Note the *e* in Tracey.

LIV ULLMANN
Less funny, but no less remarkable, actress.

FELIX UNGAR
In Neil Simon's 1965 Broadway comedy *The Odd Couple* and the 1968 film thereof, the quintessential fussbudget is Felix Ungar, with an *a*.

In the later TV series, he is Felix Unger, with an *e*.

NATHANAEL WEST
Author of *The Day of the Locust.*
Not "Nathaniel."

WINNIE-THE-POOH
Bear.

A. A. Milne styled the bear's full name with hyphens (though the character is also called, hyphenlessly, Pooh Bear). The Disney folk do not.

ALFRE WOODARD
Actress.
Not "Woodward."
Joanne Woodward, though.

VIRGINIA WOOLF
Writer, though it hardly does her justice to refer to her so plainly.

Neither "Wolfe" nor "Wolf." Perhaps you're thinking of, respectively, Thomas and the Man.*

---

* The 1941 Universal horror film starring Lon Chaney, Jr., is *The Wolf Man.* The 2010 remake starring who can even remember? is *The Wolfman.*

ALEXANDER WOOLLCOTT

New Yorker contributor, Algonquin Round Table denizen, and compulsive quipster, the inspiration for the character Sheridan Whiteside in the George S. Kaufman–Moss Hart comedy *The Man Who Came to Dinner*, a role originated by the actor Monty Woolley (and eventually played by Woollcott himself). Called, for short, Alec.

Neither Woollcott nor Woolley is to be confused with the writer Wolcott Gibbs, a longtime editor at *The New Yorker*, who described Woollcott as "one of the most dreadful writers who ever existed"—and who, you may recall, is the author of every copy editor's favorite maxim, "Try to preserve an author's style if he is an author and has a style."

FLORENZ ZIEGFELD

Impresario.

Frequently misspelled (and mispronounced) "Ziegfield."

PLACES

ANTARCTICA

Two *c*'s.

ARCTIC

Also two *c*'s.

BEL AIR

The name of the Westside Los Angeles neighborhood is generally given unhyphenated. The Hotel Bel-Air is, though, hyphenated.

While we're here: Los Angeles has, unofficially, an Eastside and a Westside. New York City has, more or less officially, an East Side (including an Upper East Side and a Lower East Side) and a West Side (including an Upper West Side, but only people who refer to Manhattan's Sixth Avenue as Avenue of the Americas would ever refer to a "Lower West Side"). Discerning fans of *Law & Order: Special Victims Unit* will note, in the show's opening credits, the eternally incorrect newspaper headline "EASTSIDE RAPIST CAPTURED."

BLEECKER STREET
In New York's Greenwich Village.

Not "Bleeker," though one occasionally, even on local signage, encounters it misspelled.

BRITTANY
The French province Bretagne, that is.

Or the late actress Brittany Murphy.

Not Britney Spears, though.

An increasing number of women whose parents were clearly not paying attention are named Britanny.

CAESARS PALACE
Hotel and casino.

There's no apostrophe in Caesars because, we are told, Caesars founder Jay Sarno decreed, "We're all Caesars."

CINCINNATI
Not "Cincinatti."

COLOMBIA
South American country. Two *o*'s.

Columbia, with a *u*, is, among other things, a New York university, a recording company, a Hollywood movie studio, the District also known as Washington, the Gem of the Ocean, and the female representation of the United States.

FONTAINEBLEAU
Both a French château and a Miami Beach resort hotel.

GRAND CENTRAL TERMINAL
Magnificent Beaux Arts structure located at the junction of Forty-second Street and Park Avenue in New York City—

a junction and not an intersection because the streets meet but do not cross.

That the building is often referred to as Grand Central Station does not make that its name. That said, if you're going to characterize a busy and/or crowded place by saying "It's like Grand Central Station in here!," you should go ahead and do that because that's what everyone does, and there are occasions when idiom outweighs* accuracy.

LaGuardia Airport
Hellhole.

The person after whom the thing was named is fabled New York City mayor Fiorello H. La Guardia, but there is no space in the airport's official name.

While we're here: The official name for that *G* in LaGuardia (or for any midword capital letter, whether it's the *D* in MacDonald or the *P* in iPhone or the *S* in PlayStation) is "medial capital," though it may also be called a camel case (or, more self-reflexively, CamelCase) capital.

Middle-earth
Nerd heaven.

Hyphenated, and the "earth" is lowercased.

Mississippi
Some people, present company included, cannot ever spell it correctly without singing the song.

Piccadilly Circus
All told, four *c*'s.

Romania
The spellings Roumania and Rumania are obsolete.

That said, if you're quoting the last line of Dorothy Park-

---

* I'd originally written here "idiom trumps accuracy," but I've developed an aversion to that verb.

er's poem "Comment," it remains, inarguably, "And I am Marie of Roumania."

SAVILE ROW
Not "Saville."

SHANGRI-LA
The hidden Tibetan paradise in James Hilton's 1933 novel *Lost Horizon*. Note the hyphen, note the capital *L*. That some dictionaries offer it as "Shangri-la," with a lowercase *l*, strikes me as effrontery. Surely Hilton, who made up the name, knew best how to spell it.

TUCSON, ARIZONA
Not "Tuscon."

OTHER BITS AND PIECES OF SOCIAL, CULTURAL, AND HISTORICAL ARCANA THAT TURN UP, WITH REASONABLE FREQUENCY, IN MANUSCRIPTS, OFTEN MISRENDERED

ALICE'S ADVENTURES IN WONDERLAND
The full title of Lewis Carroll's 1865 deceptively lighthearted fantasy,* though it cannot be denied that people have been calling it *Alice in Wonderland* pretty much since it was published. The 1871 sequel is *Through the Looking-Glass, and What Alice Found There*. You may drop the second half of that title; don't drop the hyphen in "Looking-Glass."

THE BEAUTIFUL AND DAMNED
There's only one "the" in the title of this F. Scott Fitzgerald novel.

---

*I'd suggest avoiding the "deceptively [adjective] [thing]" construction entirely, because it's often impossible to tell whether a deceptively [adjective] [thing] is extremely that [adjective] or entirely not that [adjective]. What's a deceptively large room, for instance?

THE BRIDGE OVER THE RIVER KWAI

The English-language title of Pierre Boulle's novel *Le pont de la rivière Kwai*. (Boulle was also the author of *La planète des singes*, first published in English as *Monkey Planet*. You may know it best as *Planet of the Apes*.)[*]

David Lean's film thereof is *The Bridge on the River Kwai*.

BULFINCH'S MYTHOLOGY

Written by single-*l* Thomas Bulfinch, not by a double-*l* passerine bird.

THE DIARY OF A YOUNG GIRL

The title under which Anne Frank's journal was first published in English.

The Diary of Anne Frank is the title of a play by Frances Goodrich and Albert Hackett, as well as of its film adaptations.

FINNEGANS WAKE

A novel by James Joyce that you've either not read, not comprehended, or both, despite what you tell people.

No apostrophe.

I repeat: No apostrophe.

FLORODORA

A onetime cultural touchstone, now a nugget of obscure and frequently misspelled trivia,[†] *Florodora* was a musical that played in London's West End in 1899, ran even more successfully in New York beginning in 1900, then enjoyed numerous tours and revivals for decades. (Little Rascals aficionados may recall its shout-out in *Our Gang Follies of 1936*.) Its hit number, "Tell Me, Pretty Maiden (Are There Any More at Home Like You?)," was performed by a sextet of identically gowned,

---

[*] Monkeys are not apes; neither are apes monkeys. Monkeys have tails.

[†] Perhaps my single favorite nugget of obscure trivia, thus the surely-uncalled-for two hefty paragraphs I'm devoting to it, plus this footnote and the three that follow.

parasol-wielding young ladies accompanied by six identically suited, top-hatted gentlemen.

According to theatrical legend (this one, rara avis,[*] seems to check out as accurate), all the original Florodora Girls married millionaires. One of the replacement Florodoras, Evelyn Nesbit,[†] not only bagged a millionaire, the unstable, to say the least, Harry Kendall Thaw, but achieved lasting notoriety when Thaw shot to death Nesbit's lover, the architect Stanford White, in a rooftop theater at Madison Square Garden in 1906. Thus ensued the Trial of the Century, not to be confused with the 1921 Trial of the Century of Sacco and Vanzetti, the 1924 Trial of the Century of Leopold and Loeb, the 1935 Trial of the Century of Bruno Hauptmann, or the 1995 Trial of the Century of O. J. Simpson, shortly after which, thankfully, the century decided to call it quits.[‡]

FRANKENSTEIN

The title of the novel by Mary Shelley (in full: *Frankenstein; or, The Modern Prometheus*). Also the title of (among other adaptations) the 1931 Universal film directed by James Whale and starring Boris Karloff.

Though confusion between the two commenced almost immediately upon the novel's publication, Frankenstein is not the name of the manmade man concocted and brought to life by scientist Victor Frankenstein (Henry Frankenstein in the Karloff film and its immediate sequels) from dead tissue secured in "charnel-houses . . . the dissecting room and the slaughter-house." Shelley calls him, among other things, "creature," "monster," "vile insect" (that's a good one), and "daemon." The 1931 film bills him, simply, as "The Monster."

---

[*] Latin for "rare bird," and a remarkably pretentious way of saying that something is unusual.

[†] Not to be confused with Edith Nesbit, who as E. Nesbit wrote many books for young people, including *The Railway Children*.

[‡] When did the twentieth century end? Not on December 31, 1999, but on December 31, 2000. And don't you forget it.

It's not OK to call Frankenstein's monster "Frankenstein," and people who willfully advocate for this make me cross.

GUNS N' ROSES
That the name of this band is not Guns 'n' Roses is vexing, but so, I suppose, is being named Axl, much less Slash.

IMMACULATE CONCEPTION
The issue here is not of spelling but of definition. The Immaculate Conception is the doctrine that Mary, the future mother of Jesus, was conceived in her mother's womb (by the standard biological means) without the taint of original sin.

The belief in the virgin birth[*] of Jesus is the belief that Jesus was conceived through the Holy Spirit, without a human father, and while his mother was, indeed, still a virgin.

The former is not the latter. In the words of Christopher Durang's homicidal nun Sister Mary Ignatius: "Everyone makes this error; it makes me lose my patience."

JEOPARDY!
With an exclamation point!

JESUS CHRIST SUPERSTAR
No exclamation point. Or comma, for that matter.

THE JUILLIARD SCHOOL
You learn to spell it correctly the same way you get to nearby Carnegie Hall: Practice.

LADY CHATTERLEY'S LOVER
Smutty D. H. Lawrence novel.

Note the second *e* in "Chatterley."

---

[*] "Immaculate Conception" is always initial-capped. For some reason, "virgin birth" tends not to be.

LICENCE TO KILL

The 1989 James Bond film. Universally spelled, Brit-style, with two *c*'s.

LOVE'S LABOUR'S LOST

Americanizing out the *u* in *Labour's* is impudent; omitting either apostrophe is just plain wrong.

MOBY-DICK; OR, THE WHALE

Much confusion swirls around that hyphen, which in the original 1851 publication of Herman Melville's novel appeared on the title page but nowhere else. If you hyphenate the novel's title and otherwise leave the whale's name open as Moby Dick, you'll be safe. That said, just about every film adaptation I can track drops the hyphen entirely.

OKLAHOMA!

The exclamation mark in the title of this Rodgers and Hammerstein musical should not be neglected, nor should the exclamation marks in *Hello, Dolly!*; *Oh! Calcutta!*; *Oh Lady! Lady!!*; *Piff! Paff!! Pouf!!!*; and similarly excitable Broadway shows.

"OVER THE RAINBOW"

The song MGM head honcho Louis B. Mayer wanted cut from *The Wizard of Oz* because he thought it was slowing the picture down.

The "somewhere" is in the lyric; it's not in the title.

THE PICTURE OF DORIAN GRAY

Eminently quotable[*] novel by the eminently quotable Oscar Wilde.

---

[*] "There is no such thing as a moral or an immoral book. Books are well written, or badly written. That is all." Even for the epigrammatically adept Wilde, that's spectacular.

234 | THE STUFF IN THE BACK

Not "Portrait."

Not "Grey."

PUBLISHERS WEEKLY

Misrendered with alarming frequency by people in the publishing industry as *Publisher's Weekly.*

REVELATION

The New Testament's Book of Revelation, also known as the Apocalypse.

Not "Revelations."

SEX AND THE CITY

It's *and,* not *in.*

The TV series and the films having run their course, I'd gone quite some time not encountering this, either correctly or incorrectly rendered, but actress Cynthia Nixon's announcement, in early 2018, that she was running for governor of New York State brought this one back into the fore.

Unless you're such a devotee that you'd never get this wrong, you'd do well to check and recheck this one. I always do.

SHOW BOAT

The Edna Ferber novel, and the Jerome Kern–Oscar Hammerstein II musical adapted from it.

Two words.

SUPER BOWL

Two words.

"THE WASTE LAND"

T. S. Eliot's 1922 poem.

Your standard-issue barren swath of territory is, per modern spelling style, simply a wasteland.

While we're here: Though April may indeed be, per standard modern American spelling, the cruelest month, Eliot wrote "cruellest," and in quoting him you must honor his spelling.

THE WONDERFUL WIZARD OF OZ

The full title of L. Frank Baum's 1900 cyclonic fantasy novel.

Gale, the surname of the story's heroine, Dorothy, is not given in Baum's first Oz novel or in *The Marvelous Land of Oz,* its superb first sequel, though it turns up in later volumes. It debuted in a 1902 Broadway musical in which, perhaps because little dogs are intractable and hard to see in a large theater, a cow named Imogene was subbed in for the beloved Toto.

No, not a real cow. Don't be silly.

WOOKIEE

Everyone gets it wrong. It's not "Wookie."

Also on the subject of the world of *Star Wars,* "lightsaber" is one word, "dark side" is lowercased (oddly enough), and "A long time ago in a galaxy far, far away. . . ." ends with a period and three ellipsis points, even though it is a fragment and not a complete sentence, because that is how the *Star Wars* people like it. And if you challenge them on any of these points, they'll cut your hand off. True story.

ASSORTED BRAND NAMES AND TRADEMARKS YOU'LL WANT TO SPELL CORRECTLY

Trademarks tend over the long haul to lose their capital letters, thus transforming from proper nouns to—no, not improper, though that would be fun—common nouns, sometimes because the company that established them vanishes, often because the trademark becomes so utterly synonymous with the thing itself that the transformation is irresistible. Thus we have the genericized aspirin, cellophane, heroin, kerosene, teleprompter (formerly and jauntily TelePrompTer), thermos, zipper, and—the copy editor's delight—dumpster (which, once upon a long time ago, was the Dempster-Dumpster manufactured by Dempster Brothers).

One should do one's best to honor extant trademarks (and the companies that own them), but I know firsthand that attempting to persuade a writer that a wee plastic bag is a Baggie rather than a baggie is an exercise in futility.[*]

More even than dropping capital letters from trademarked things, it's considered bad form to allow the verbification of trademarks. Thus, copy editors have long attempted (and long failed) to stop writers from using the common verb extracted from the photocopying machines devised by the Xerox Corporation. But it's scarcely possible anymore to argue that that which one does at the Google site is not googling. If you absolutely must make a verb out of a trademark—not that I am endorsing this, because it's the wrong thing to do—I do suggest that you lowercase it.[†]

Mostly I just want you to spell/style these correctly:

BREYERS
There's no apostrophe in the name of this ice cream brand. Not to be confused with Dreyer's,[‡] which does have an apostrophe.

BUBBLE WRAP
A brand of what one might otherwise choose to call bubble pack.

CAP'N CRUNCH
Not "Captain."

Nostalgia alert: This one always particularly reminds me of how in the pre-Internet era I used to jot down all the house-

---

[*] In full they're Hefty Baggies Sandwich & Storage Bags, so strictly speaking there's no such thing as a Baggie, much less a baggie.

[†] Department of There's an Exception to Everything: I'd still say that I FedExed rather than fedexed a package, even if I sent it via UPS.

[‡] I always find parenthetical "(no relation)"s bothersomely adorable, but: (no relation).

holdy brand names mentioned in whatever manuscript I was working on, then take a trip to the supermarket, notepad in hand, to walk the aisles, peer at packaging, and verify spellings. So as not to seem completely mad, I would also, in between peering and verifying, do my shopping.

CRACKER JACK

Many (most?) people call this classic combination of candied popcorn and peanuts "Cracker Jacks," but to do so wrecks the rhyme "Buy me some peanuts and Cracker Jack / I don't care if I never get back." It's also not the name of the product.

CROCK-POT

You probably don't even know that it's a brand, and you probably spell it "crockpot." You might avail yourself of the generic "slow cooker." Or you might not.

DR PEPPER

The absence of a period in the name of this soda pop is much discussed at copyediting bacchanals.

FRIGIDAIRE

That many people call any old refrigerator a "frigidaire" is a testament to the onetime supremacy of the Frigidaire brand, but if you're indeed talking about any old refrigerator, call it a refrigerator. Or an icebox, if you're a hundred years old. Or a fridge, which term is up for grabs.

FROOT LOOPS

An intentionally comic misspelling (as "Froot") is called a cacography.

HÄAGEN-DAZS

The name of the ice cream manufacturer is not Danish but gibberish intended to sound Danish.

JCPENNEY
They're still officially J. C. Penney Company, Inc., so if you can't bear the sight of that smushed JCPenney, feel free to use the more formal version.

JEEP
The vehicle whose name was eventually trademarked by Willys-Overland and is now manufactured by Chrysler may be a Jeep, but lowercase jeeps have been around since the early part of the twentieth century. There's no reason to retroapply the trademark to vehicles that predate it.

JOCKEY SHORTS
They own the "Jockey" but not the "shorts." You can always call them tighty-whiteys.

KLEENEX
You can always just say "tissue."

KOOL-AID
The phrase "drinking the Kool-Aid," meaning to willfully if heedlessly follow some dogma, must surely rankle Kraft Foods, particularly in that the cyanide beverage Jim Jones's devotees drank in the 1978 mass suicide at Jonestown seems to have been concocted largely if not entirely from the also-ran brand Flavor Aid.

MEN'S WEARHOUSE
Not "Warehouse." It's a joke. Get it?

ONESIES
Onesies is a Gerber Childrenswear brand of what can be, but never is, generically referred to as diaper shirts or infant bodysuits. The Gerber people are adamant that the term is theirs alone and should not be genericized into "onesie"; in this case I fear not only that the barn door is open but that the horse is halfway across the Atlantic on the *Queen Mary 2*.

PING-PONG

Once I learned that the term "ping-pong," for table tennis, predates the trademark, I gave up trying to enforce the caps on authors whom it invariably irritated.

PLEXIGLAS

Plexiglas is a brand name; "plexiglass" is a wannabe generic name derived from it.

POPSICLE

The Popsicle people also make the Creamsicle, the Fudgsicle (note the absence of an *e* after the *g*), and something called a Yosicle.

PORTA-POTTY

There seem to be as many trademarked names for portable toilets as there are portable-toilet puns. Perhaps you should just make up one of your own and then check that it doesn't already exist—as I once, for reasons I can no longer recall, concocted an Indian brand called "Vend-A-Loo."

POST-IT

Note the lowercase *i*.

Q-TIPS

The generic term is "cotton swabs," and Unilever personnel are mighty proprietary about their trademark.

Did you know that the *Q* stands for "Quality"?

REALTOR

A registered trademark of the National Association of Realtors. Not every real estate agent is a Realtor, and I see no reason to write "realtor" when you can just as easily write "real estate agent."

REDDI-WIP

I'm trying to imagine the meeting in which someone inquired, "How much can we misspell two perfectly simple words?"

ROLLS-ROYCE
Hyphenated. Also expensive.

7-ELEVEN
A numeral, a hyphen, and a word. Home of the Slurpee.

SHEETROCK
Or opt for the generic "plasterboard," "drywall," or "wallboard."

STARBUCKS
No apostrophe.

STYROFOAM
Styrofoam is the trademarked name for a type of polystyrene foam used as a thermal insulation material. Those items we layfolk often refer to as styrofoam cups and styrofoam coolers are in fact not made of Styrofoam at all.

TARMAC
A trademark, but good luck trying to get anyone to keep the cap.

TASER
Though University of Florida student Andrew Meyer, in the process of resisting arrest, might have generically and respectfully pleaded, "Don't stun me with that electroshock weapon, Officer," what he did in fact cry was "Don't tase me, bro." (The unofficial verb is more logically spelled "tase" than "taze," I'd say.)

VOLKSWAGEN
Keep an eye on that *e;* it's not a second *o.*

XBOX
Not X-Box or XBox.

MISCELLANEOUS FACTY THINGS

- The people* convicted of and executed for witchcraft in late-seventeenth-century colonial Massachusetts were not burned at the stake, as one persistently sees asserted, but hanged. The accused Giles Corey, who refused to plead to charges one way or the other, was, grotesquely, tortured to death as stones were piled on him. His defiant last words were, we're told, "More weight."
- DEFCON 5 is "I have a hangnail, but otherwise everything is fine." DEFCON 1 is "We're all about to die." There is no such thing as DEFCON 8, DEFCON 12, etc.
- *Krakatoa, East of Java* is a 1969 film about the eruption of the eponymous volcano. Krakatoa, unfortunately, is west of Java.
- The rain in Spain doesn't fall mainly on the plain; it stays mainly in the plain.

---

* Mostly but not exclusively women, though one tends to forget that.

CHAPTER 12

The
Trimmables

THERE'S A LOT OF DELETING IN COPYEDITING, not just of the "very"s and "rather"s and "quite"s and excrescent "that"s with which we all encase our prose like so much Bubble Wrap and packing peanuts, but of restatements of information—"AS ESTAB'D," one politely jots in the margin.

Much repetition, though, comes under the more elementary heading of Two Words Where One Will Do, and here's a collection of easily disposed of redundancies. Some of these may strike you as obvious—though their obviousness doesn't stop them from showing up constantly. Others are a little more arcane—the sorts of things you could likely get away with without anyone's noticing—but they're snippable nonetheless.

In either case, for those moments when you're contemplating that either you or your prose could stand to go on a diet and your prose seems the easier target, here's a good place to start.

(The bits in italics are the bits you can dispose of.)

ABM *missile*
ABM = anti-ballistic missile.

absolutely certain, *absolute* certainty, *absolutely* essential

added bonus

advance planning, *advance* warning

all-time record
As well, one doesn't set a "new record." One merely sets a record.

assless chaps
The garment, that is. Not fellows lacking in dorsal embonpoint. I'm not sure how often this will come up in your writing—or in your life—but chaps are, by definition, assless. Look at a cowboy. From behind.

ATM *machine*
ATM = automated teller machine, which, one might argue and win the argument, is redundant enough as it is.

blend *together*

cameo *appearance,* cameo *role*

capitol *building*

closed fist
A closed hand is, I suppose, a thing. But as there are no open fists, neither are there closed ones.

close proximity
Like "from whence" (see below), "close proximity" can be defended simply by its lengthy history of turning up in competent prose, but to be proximate is, inarguably, to be close, so if you need to emphasize intimacy, perhaps find a less galumphing way to do it.

CNN *network*
CNN = Cable News Network.

consensus *of opinion, general* consensus
The word "consensus" has the "general" and the "of opinion"
baked right in. It doesn't need any help.

continue *on*
The airlines like it. I don't.

crisis *situation*

depreciated *in value*

direct confrontation

disappear *from sight*

earlier *in time*

end product

end result
I can appreciate the difference between a midprogress result
and an ultimate result, but "end result" is cloddish.

equally as, equally *as*
Use one or the other, not both. Alan Jay Lerner's "I'd be
equally as willing for a dentist to be drilling / than to ever let
a woman in my life," from *My Fair Lady*, is often pointed out
by aficionados as one of the prime grammatical calamities in
musical theater lyric writing—not only the "equally as" but
that "than" that should certainly be an "as." That the singer
of the lyric is the persnickety grammarian Henry Higgins only
adds to the ironic fun.

erupt (or explode) *violently*

exact same
To be sure, "exact same" is redundant. To be sure, I still say it
and write it.

fall *down*

What are you going to do, fall up?

fellow countryman

fetch *back*

To fetch something is not merely to go get it but to go get it and return with it to the starting place. Ask a dog.

few *in number*

fiction novel

Appalling. A novel is a work of fiction. That's why it's called a novel.

That said, "nonfiction novel" is not the oxymoron it might at first seem. The term refers to the genre pioneered—though not, as is occasionally averred, invented—by Truman Capote with *In Cold Blood,* that of the work of nonfiction written novelistically.

I once—and, happily, to date, only once—encountered the term "prose novel," which is as brain-clonking a redundancy as "fiction novel" but which I eventually realized was meant as a retronym:* In a world full of graphic novels, the user of the term had apparently decided, one must identify a work of fiction containing a hundred thousand words, give or take, but lacking pictures as a "prose novel."

Decency forbids. One need no more refer to a novel as a "prose novel" than one need refer to a concoction of a lot of

---

* "Retronym" is a term coined by the journalist Frank Mankiewicz in 1980 to identify a new term coined to replace a term whose meaning, once clear, has become clouded or outmoded, often by some technological advance. For instance: What was once simply a watch became, with the invention of digital watches, an analog watch. Ordinary guitars were dubbed, after the electric ones showed up, acoustic guitars. No one ever referred to a landline till mobile phones became the thing. Closer to home, one had no cause to refer to a hardcover book till paperbacks were invented, nor to refer to a mass-market paperback (those are the little ones you find in spinning drugstore racks) till those larger, svelter, more expensive editions we call trade paperbacks appeared.

gin and as little vermouth as is humanly possible as a "gin martini." Martinis, by definition, are made with gin. The burden is on misguided people who make them with vodka to append those two extra syllables.

Lately one encounters people referring to any full-length book, even a work of nonfiction, as a novel. That has to stop.

final outcome

follow *after*

free gift
A classic of the redundancy genre, much beloved of retailers and advertisers.

from whence
Whence means "from where," which makes "from whence" pretty damn redundant. Still, the phrase has a lot of history, including, from the King James Version of the Bible, "I will lift up mine eyes unto the hills, from whence cometh my help." So I suppose you can write "from whence" if you're also talking about thine eyes and the place your help is comething from.

For a dazzling (and purposeful) use of "from whence," consider Frank Loesser's *Guys and Dolls* lyric "Take back your mink / to from whence it came"—gorgeously appropriate for the tawdry nightclub number in which it's sung.

frontispiece *illustration*
A frontispiece is an illustration immediately preceding, and generally facing, a book's title page.

full gamut
A gamut is the full range or scope of something, so the word needs no modifier. Ditto "complete range," "broad spectrum," "full extent," and their cousins.

fuse *together*

future plans

gather *together*
Yes, I know: "We Gather Together (to Ask the Lord's Bless-ing)" and "For where two or three are gathered together in my name, there am I in the midst of them" (Matthew 18:20). Two wrongs, even sacred ones, do not make a divine right.

glance *briefly*
Indeed, that's what your garden-variety glance is: brief.

HIV *virus*
HIV = human immunodeficiency virus.

hollow tube
Bet you hadn't thought of that one, had you.

hourly (or daily or weekly or monthly or yearly) *basis*

integrate *with each other*

interdependent *upon each other*

join *together*

kneel *down*

knots *per hour*
One knot = one nautical mile per hour.

last *of all*

lesbian *woman*
Come on, folks. Think.

lift *up*

low ebb

One may properly (if perhaps dully) refer to one's lowest emotional ebb, but an ebb is low by definition.

main protagonist
I don't hold with the notion that a story can have no more than one protagonist, but "main protagonist" grates.

merge *together*

might *possibly*

moment *in time*
Whitney Houston notwithstanding.

more superior

Mount Fujiyama
As we note that *yama* means "mountain," we also note that we can refer to Fujiyama or to Mount Fuji.

mutual cooperation

___ o'clock A.M. *in the morning*
Just plain unacceptable. Ditto "P.M. in the evening."
    While we're here, let's dispatch "twelve midnight" and "twelve noon"; "midnight" and "noon" are all you need to say.

orbit *around*

overexaggerate
Even spellcheck sneers at it.

passing fad
A fad is, by definition, of brief duration. A fancy may not be (though it's certainly superficial and usually capricious), so Ira Gershwin ("The radio and the telephone / and the movies that we know / may just be passing fancies and in time may go") and Cole Porter ("And it's not a passing fancy or a fancy pass") are in the clear.

past history

personal friend, *personal* opinion

"Personal," more often than not, begs to be deleted whenever or wherever it shows up.* And the only thing worse than "my personal opinion" is "my own personal opinion."

PIN *number*
PIN = personal identification number.

plan *ahead*

*pre*plan
Horrid.†

raise *up*

reason *why*
I include this here largely to disinclude it. You can usually do without the "why," but there's no particular reason you ought. Not "the reason is because," though. That's a bit much.

regular *routine*

return (or recall or revert or many other things beginning with "re-") *back*

rise *up*
If you think I'm going to pick a fight with Lin-Manuel Miranda, who uses the phrase "rise up" repeatedly in *Hamilton*'s "My Shot," you have another think coming.

---

* I'd like to be able to condemn "personal friend" as a product of our modern era of actual friends and virtual friends, but I can't, as I've found numerous uses of the phrase going back to the 1800s.

† An awful lot of "pre-" compounds work just fine without the prefix, so be on your guard. Some people quibble over "preorder," but it does carry a meaning that "order" doesn't quite: If I order something, I expect it to be delivered as close to immediately as is humanly possible. If I preorder something—a book, say—I recognize that it's not yet available and that I'm going to have to wait for it.

short *in length*

shuttle *back and forth*

sink *down*

skirt *around*

slightly ajar

sudden impulse

surrounded *on all sides*

swoop *down*
To be nitpickingly technical about it, swooping is a downward action, so "swoop down" is one more word than one needs. But everyone says it, so let's give it a pass. We're also very used to "swoop up," as in swooping up (or scooping up) a dropped ball or child.

sworn affidavit

undergraduate *student*
"Undergraduate" is an excellent noun. No need to use it as an adjective to modify itself.

unexpected surprise
Dreadful. And common, in both senses of the word.

unsolved mystery
Once it's solved, it's not a mystery anymore, is it.

*un*thaw
Come now.

usual custom

wall mural
No, really, I've seen this.

wall sconce

Same.

Copyediting FAQ

Q. What's the most redundant redundancy you've ever encountered?

A. I recall it as if it were yesterday:

"He implied without quite saying."

I was so filled with delight on encountering that, I scarcely had the heart to cross out "without quite saying" and to note in the margin, politely and succinctly, "BY DEF."

But I did it anyway.

CHAPTER 13

The Miscellany

Hᴇʀᴇ's ᴇᴠᴇʀʏᴛʜɪɴɢ I ᴄᴀɴ ᴛʜɪɴᴋ ᴏғ that I think is important—or at least interesting, or at least simply odd—
that I couldn't find a place for elsewhere.

1.

Strictly differentiating between "each other," in reference to
something occurring between two people,

> Johnny and I like each other.

and "one another," for three or more,

> "Everybody get together, try to love one another right
> now."

is yet another of those shakily justifiable rules invented by
some obscure grammarian of centuries past that, nonetheless,
I like to observe, particularly as many writers flip back and
forth between the two apparently at random, and randomness
in writing, unlike raindrops on roses and whiskers on kittens,
is not one of my favorite things. You cannot properly be criti-

cized if you don't follow the rule (or, let's say, "rule"), but nei-ther can you be criticized if you do.

2.

If you only see one movie this year . . .

Normal human beings frontload the word "only" at the beginning of a sentence. Copy editors will tend to pick up that "only" and drop it next to the thing that's being "only"d:

If you see only one movie this year . . .

Or, for instance:

NORMAL HUMAN BEING: You can only watch a movie ironically so many times before you're watching it earnestly.

COPY EDITOR: You can watch a movie ironically only so many times before you're watching it earnestly.

Does the latter perhaps sound a bit stilted? Perhaps it does, but to be perfectly honest, there's a certain tautness in slightly stilted prose that I find almost viscerally thrilling.

I also think that readers don't much notice when prose is wound up a bit too tight but may well, and not favorably, no-tice overloose prose.

Moreover, a loosely placed "only" can distort the meaning of a sentence entirely.

That said, in copyediting fiction, especially fiction with an informal narrative voice and, even more so, dialogue in fiction, I'm most likely to leave the "only" where the author set it.*

---

* This also applies to the temporal use of "just" and the difference between writing, say, "I almost just tripped on the stairs," which sounds perfectly natural, and "I just almost tripped on the stairs," which makes a bit more sense. If I've inspired you to give it an extra thought every time you're about to write or say the words "only" and "just," I feel I've done my job.

3.

Fifty-five years and counting after the assassination of John F. Kennedy and the conspiracy theories it gave birth to, I continue to caution writers against describing any other grassy knoll as a "grassy knoll." It remains, I think, a distractingly potent term.

4.

Here's a fun weird thing: The word "namesake" works in both directions. That is, if you were named after your grandfather, you are his namesake. He is also yours. Who knew.

5.

Back in the 1990s, it seemed as if I couldn't turn a manuscript page without running into the words "inchoate" and "limn," and I began to shudder at their every appearance. Oddly, I can't recall the last time I ran into either. So, by all means, please start using "inchoate" and "limn" again. I rather miss them.[*]

6.

Clichés should be avoided like the plague.

7.

There's a world of difference between going into the water (an action generally accompanied by flailing and shrieking and other merriment) and going in the water (an action generally accompanied by staring abstractedly into the distance, and, no, you're not fooling anyone), and it's a difference to be honored.

Into = movement.

In = presence.

The same applies to, say, "jumping into a lake" (transfer-

---

[*] Copy editor's addendum: "For me, it was candles 'guttering' and 'tang' used for smell; both were used so often in literary fiction, I'd begun to think they were handed out with the MFA."

ring from pier to water) and "jumping in a lake" (in the water already and propelling oneself vertically upward), but the vernacular being what it is, no one will object to the traditional dismissal "Aww go jump in a lake."

8.

There is a world of difference between turning in to a driveway, which is a natural thing to do with one's car, and turning into a driveway, which is a Merlyn trick.

9.

Of two brothers, one fifteen and one seventeen, the fifteen-year-old is the younger, not the youngest, and the seventeen-year-old is the older (or elder, if you like), not the oldest (or eldest).

It takes three to make an "-est."

Except, English being English, in the phrase "best foot forward."

10.

If you love something passionately and vigorously, you love it no end. To love something "to no end," as one often sees it rendered, would be to love it pointlessly. If that's what you mean, then OK.

11.

The habit of inauthentically attributing wisecracks, purported profundities, inspirational doggerel, and other bits of refrigerator-door wisdom to famous people is scarcely new—members of the press, particularly newspaper columnists, have been doing it for decades—but the Internet has grossly exacerbated the problem, with numerous quote-aggregation sites irresponsibly devoted to prettily packaging the fakery, thus encouraging the unwary (or uncaring) to snarf it up, then hork it up, ad nauseam.

To cite one majestically apposite instance: In July 2017, the writer Colin Dickey stumbled upon a 2013 tweet from the elder daughter of the person who would, eventually, assume the presidency of the United States:

> "If the facts don't fit the theory, change the facts."
> —ALBERT EINSTEIN

As Dickey then himself tweeted, "That Einstein never said any such thing only makes this tweet that much more perfect."

And indeed and in fact, and no matter the hundreds of Google hits suggesting otherwise, the quip had not ever emerged from the mouth or pen of Albert Einstein. It's simply a bit of unattributable pseudo-cleverness assigned, presumably to lend it weightiness and importance, to someone who, particularly in this case, would never have said it.

Einstein is only one of the pin-the-wisdom-on-the-maven targets. Five'll get you ten that a quote you find attributed, particularly without reference to a published source, to Abraham Lincoln is inauthentic; the same goes for Mark Twain, Oscar Wilde (and with the thousands of witticisms Wilde uttered, why would anyone put words into his mouth?), Winston Churchill, or Dorothy Parker (like Wilde, an industrial-strength generator of cleverness).*

There are any number of ways to verify or debunk quotes:

- Wikiquote, with individual entries for just about everyone who ever picked up a pen, not only lists a writer's greatest hits but helpfully links you to the published sources of said hits and, perhaps even more helpfully, includes reliable sections on disputed and misattributed quotes.
- If you want to explore on your own, make use of the highly searchable books.google.com. If you can't, with a modicum of effort, find a published source for

---

* Also, in no particular order, Ralph Waldo Emerson, Henry David Thoreau, Voltaire, Mahatma Gandhi, and (impudently and absurdly, given how easily traceable every word he ever wrote is) William Shakespeare.

a quote, the odds are at least reasonable that it's a sham.

• I also commend to you the work of the doggedly thorough Garson O'Toole, who runs the Quote Investigator website (access it via quoteinvestigator.com, to be sure) and tweets as @QuoteResearch, and who specializes in not only debunking fake or misattributed quotes but time-traveling backward through the archives to discern, if he can, how and when the fakeries and misattributions first occurred.

Now, what has any of this to do with writing?

Lazy writers, particularly of business and self-help books,[*] often litter their manuscripts with allegedly uplifting epigraphs they've plucked from either the Internet or the works of their equally lazy business and self-help predecessors, and thus the manure gets spread.

At Random House, copy editors are mandated to search for and either verify or call into question all such quotes. If some days this feels tantamount to warding off a plague of locusts with a fly swatter, well, one can do only what one can do.

In an era redolent to the high heavens with lies passed off as truths—often by career perjurers rabidly eager to condemn as fabrications facts they find inconvenient—I beg you not to continue to perpetrate and perpetuate these fortune-cookie hoaxes, which in their often insipid vapidity are as demeaning to the spirit as in their inauthenticity they are insulting to the history of the written word.

May I make a suggestion?

Build yourself, on either a virtual or a paper tablet, what's known as a commonplace book—someplace you can copy

---

[*] "The very existence of self-help books is all the evidence you need that they don't work," a former colleague of mine once quipped—perhaps more cleverly than truthfully, but the quip business is built more on rat-a-tat effectiveness than on strict accuracy.

down bits of writing you encounter and find clever and/or meaningful—and keep it handy for future use, even if that future use is simply your own edification. (Don't forget to make note of where you found the stuff.) Then at least, should you find yourself in a position to share with the world your own wisdom and want to periodically sprinkle it with others' smarts, you'll at least have something fresh and heartfelt to offer.

12.

Title case is the convention of capitalizing, in titles of works (books, book chapters, plays, movies—you get the idea) and, often though not always, in newspaper and magazine headlines, the first letter of all the important words.

Which are the important words of a title?

- the first word and the last word
- all nouns, pronouns, verbs, adjectives, and adverbs

Which are the words that don't make the capital cut?

- articles ("a," "an," "the")
- conjunctions ("and," "but," "if," "or," etc.)

Then clarity goes to heck.

What about prepositions?

If you say "prepositions are invariably to be lowercased," as some indeed say, you're going to be up against titles like *Seven against Thebes* or *I Served alongside Rommel,* and that certainly won't do. The cleverer people endorse lowercasing the shorter prepositions, of which there are many, including "at," "by," "but," "from," "into," "of," "to," and "with," and capping the longer ones, like "despite," "during," and "toward." I'll admit that the four-letter prepositions can cause puzzlement—I'd certainly never cap "with," but a lowercase "over" can look a little underrespected.

Which leads to the next confusion: Did you notice that,

above, I listed "but" as both a conjunction and a preposition? That's because, depending on how you use it, it can indeed be a conjunction or a preposition. Fine enough, as in either case it would be lowercased. But "but" can also be an adverb (in the sense of "merely," as in "he is but a stripling") or a noun (as in "no ifs, ands, or buts about it"), which means that if you were using the word in that capacity in a title it would require a cap. Similarly, the word "over" also serves as both preposition and adverb (and, in cricket, noun). I can assure you that the trip to the dictionary to discern whether that "off" or "near" you're contemplating capping is a preposition or an adverb (or an adjective or a verb) may well be unilluminating to the point of headache-inducing. (You'll also note that some dictionaries haul out terms like "particle" and "determiner," which doesn't make things easier.) Loath as I am to shrug and concede "When in doubt, do what your eye tells you to do," that's nevertheless what I'm saying. And when someone attempts to correct you, look that person square in the eye and say, "I'm using it as an adverb," then walk away quickly. Works every time.

Furthermore:

- Particularly don't forget that some terribly important words are terribly short. Make sure you've capped that "It" (to say nothing of that "He," that "She," that "His," and that "Hers"), and especially make sure you've capped those big leaguers "Is" and "Be," the lowercasing* of which is as close to a title-case capital crime as I can think of.

---

*Did You Know? Capital (majuscule) letters are called uppercase letters, and the smaller (minuscule) letters are called lowercase letters, because in the era of movable type (manual typesetting, that is) the capital letters, less frequently used, lived in the case set above the case that held the rest of the letters. "Uppercase" is not to be confused with "top-drawer," which derives from domestic furniture and is where you store your better things.

Oh, and:

- There's a thing called a phrasal verb, which is, perhaps unsurprisingly, a verb in the form of a phrase, often including a preposition and/or an adverb, and when one of these shows up in a title, both its bits get capped, as in, say:

  Hold On to Your Hats!

  (whereas the "on" in *The Mill on the Floss* is lowercased)

  or

  Stand By for Updates

  (whereas the "by" in *The House by the Lake* is lowercased).

Not to mention:

- Some people choose to capitalize each of the words in an off-the-cuff hyphenated compound but capitalize only the first word in a permanent compound, only that might lead to something like

  My Mother-in-law Enjoyed a Death-Defying Ride on a Merry-go-round

  which may strike you as a bit lumpy-looking. You will not be faulted if for the sake of visual euphony you choose, in this case, to cap "law," "go," and "round" (though not, to be sure, "in").

In conclusion:

- There's many a day I'm sympathetic to the title-case policy of capping every damn word and the hell with it, but then I see a headline like

The Fault Is Not In Our Stars But In Our Stars'
Salaries

and I cringe and change my mind.

13.

Q. What do you have to say about the increasing use of "woman" as an adjective, rather than "female," as in "woman candidate" instead of "female candidate"? It's not as if anyone ever says "man candidate."

A. People don't often say "male candidate," either; they just say "candidate." I suppose that brevity goes back to the peculiar notion that a default human being is a male.* Or a man. I, like you, do increasingly see "woman" used as an adjective; I wonder if it's because to some the word "female" looks particularly biological, as if a "female cashier," say, totes up your purchases with her uterus. That said, the use of "woman" as an adjective isn't particularly new. Even as I type this I'm looking at a reference to "your women guests" in Peg Bracken's wonderfully subversive 1960 *The I Hate to Cook Book*. You want to be especially careful, though, not to turn the tables and refer to a woman as "a female." "Female" as a noun is rarely meant as a compliment, and it's unlikely to be taken as one.

Here, from Clare Boothe Luce's play *The Women:*

SYLVIA: Why should I be jealous of Mary?
NANCY: Because she's contented. Contented to be what she is.
SYLVIA: Which is what?

---

* At the dawn of my career I frequently encountered in manuscripts the unspoken notion that a default human being was white. That is, only nonwhite characters would ever have their race specifically called out. One still often runs into the notion that the unmodified use of "man"—as in articles about what men do or don't like about women—inarguably means "heterosexual man." It doesn't.

NANCY: A woman.

EDITH: And what, in the name of my revolting
    condition,* am I?

NANCY: A female.†

And, I must emphasize: *Whether* you choose to characterize professionals by gender is not my business. *How* you do it is. Dammit, Jim, I'm a copy editor, not a sociologist.

14.

A button-down shirt is a shirt whose collar points fasten to buttons on the upper-chestal zone of the shirt. It is not any old shirt that buttons from neck to waist. Call that a dress shirt, if it happens to be one (there's no need, by the way, ever to refer to something as a "long-sleeve dress shirt," because there is no such thing as a "short-sleeve dress shirt"), or a button-front shirt, or a button-up shirt, I don't really care.

15.

You don't tow the line. You toe it.

16.

The approving ejaculation‡ is not "Here, here!" but "Hear, hear!"

17.

Streets lit by gaslight are gaslit.

The past tense of the verb "gaslight"—as in that which Charles Boyer does to Ingrid Bergman in the eponymous 1944 MGM thriller by undermining her belief in reality to the point she believes she's going mad—is "gaslighted."

---

* Pregnant, that is. Don't shoot the messenger.

† OK, let's balance that sourness with a little swinging, romantic Cole Porter, from *Silk Stockings:* "When the electromagnetic of the he-male / meets the electromagnetic of the female / If right away she should say 'This is *the* male' / it's a chemical reaction, that's all."

‡ Whatever.

18.

Something that is well established down to the marrow is not "deep-seeded," which may sound as if it makes sense but, I'm assured by people who know how plants work, doesn't. It is, rather, "deep-seated."

19.

In an emergency you call 911.

The similarly numbered day of catastrophe was 9/11. (In the rest of the world it's 11/9, but we Americans are alarmingly stubborn in our date styling.)

20.

They're not Brussel sprouts. They're Brussels sprouts.

21.

A reversal is a total 180.* If you do a total 360, you're facing the same direction as when you began.

22.

"Stupider" and "stupidest" are too words.

23.

I'm well aware that my job is not to copyedit your day-to-day speech, but I'd be grateful if in responding to, say:

"Do you mind if I sit beside you?"

you would answer not, as everyone seems to nowadays:

"Yes! Please do!"

but

"Of course not! Please do!"

---

* Is the term "full 180" tautological? Isn't it enough to say "I did a 180"? Sure, and sure. And yet.

24.

I once, in a U.K. manuscript, encountered this bit of dialogue:

"Oh, well, tomato, to-may-to."

I stared at it for a full thirty seconds before I understood what I was looking at.

For the record, though the Brits do indeed pronounce "tomato" with an "ah" in the middle, they pronounce "potato" the same way we do, with an "ay" in the middle. Ira Gershwin— "You like potato and I like po-tah-to / You like tomato and I like to-mah-to"—was being terribly clever, but also a cheat.

Also by the way, that old story about unwitting English singers commencing "Let's Call the Whole Thing Off" by singing, "You say eyether and I say eyether / You say nyther and I say nyther" is, at least according to Ira Gershwin in *Lyrics on Several Occasions,* true. Grain of salt.

25.

I note that, increasingly often, some people refer to other people referring to themselves as "we" as "speaking in the second person." Nope. Speaking of oneself as "we"—which unless you're Queen Victoria you oughtn't—is speaking in the first person plural. The second person is "you," as in, as a writer once wrote, "You are not the kind of guy who would be at a place like this at this time of morning."

26.

The line from *Hamlet* is not "Methinks the lady doth protest too much"; it's "The lady doth protest too much, methinks." Also, if you haven't been dead for four hundred years and are planning on using the word "methinks" in the spirit of roguish cleverness, please don't.

27.

"Pulchritudinous" is a not very attractive word for "beautiful." At some point when people like me weren't paying proper attention it attempted, with some success, to redefine itself as "buxom"—"zaftig," if you will, and even if you won't— which, I suppose, if you prefer your women on the plumply bosomy side, makes a sort of sense.* But lately I'm seeing it increasingly often used as a synonym, and a pejorative one at that, for "fat," and OK let's please stop with the redefining. There are any number of synonyms, some nicer than others, for "fat"—including "bovine," "stout," and (one of my favorites, since an art history professor applied it to a Renoir nude) "fubsy"—and we don't, I think, need another one.

* In Yiddish, *pulkes* are thighs, particularly as admired on a baby (or a chicken) for being plump. Perhaps some well-meaning Jewish linguist—don't look at me—got pulkes and pulchritude mixed up, and this is the result.

OUTRO

By Way of Conclusion

I think perhaps you don't finish writing a book. You stop writing it.

My favorite last line in all literature has long been this, from Virginia Woolf's *To the Lighthouse:*

> It was done; it was finished. Yes, she thought, laying down her brush in extreme fatigue, I have had my vision.

I lack, by far, Lily Briscoe's certainty, though I recognize her exhaustion.

An early title for this book was *The Last Word,* which was soon discarded for any number of excellent reasons, one of them being that there is no last word. There's no rule without an exception (well, mostly), there's no thought without an afterthought (at least for me), there's always something you meant to say but forgot to say.

There's no last word, only the next word.

THINGS I LIKE

Beyond the sources of information already mentioned throughout, I commend to you:

Theodore Bernstein's *Miss Thistlebottom's Hobgoblins,* one of the charmingest, smartest, most readable books on the subject of language I've ever read

and these exceptionally erudite, eminently bookmarkable sites, to which I return over and over:

Grammarist (grammarist.com)

Patricia T. O'Conner and Stewart Kellerman's Grammarphobia (grammarphobia.com)

Jonathan Owen's Arrant Pedantry (arrantpedantry.com)

Kory Stamper's Harmless Drudgery (korystamper .wordpress.com)

Online Etymology Dictionary (etymonline.com)

Mignon Fogarty's Quick and Dirty Tips (quickanddirtytips.com/grammar-girl)

Stan Carey's Sentence first (stancarey.wordpress.com)

John E. McIntyre's You Don't Say (baltimoresun.com/ news/language-blog)

ACKNOWLEDGMENTS

I have never before been so happily and gratefully in debt, and at long last it's time to pay up.

My teacher Gerry Pagliaro taught me how to play with words, and my professors Linda Jenkins and David Downs taught me how they work.

Meg Drislane, of St. Martin's Press, took a chance on me, sight unseen, and gave me not only my first proofreading and copyediting jobs but careful, kind instruction and bountiful encouragement.

Amy Edelman furthered my education, uttered the fateful words "If you want to be a full-time freelancer, I'll make sure there's always something on your desk," then upped the ante by inviting me to join the copyediting department of Random House. No fledgling production editor could have asked for a better, wiser, more supportive boss.

My early days in the house were blessed by the masterly professionalism of, particularly, Mitchell Ivers, Sono Rosenberg, Jean McNutt, Virginia Avery, the scintillating Jim Lambert, the once and future Bob Loomis, Kathy Rosenbloom, Deborah Aiges, and my eventual confidant, co-conspirator, and dear friend Kenn Russell. In due course of time I gained the acquaintance of Dan Menaker, who, though neither of us could have known it at the time, eventually flicked the switch that sparked the composition of this book. Lee Boudreaux, Sharon Delano, Laura Goldin, Libby McGuire, Timothy Mennel, Susan Mercandetti, Jennifer Smith, Benjamin Steinberg, Mark Tavani, Bruce Tracy, Jane von Mehren, and Amelia Zalcman have been as well quintessentially the right colleagues at the right moments, and also much more than that.

I have been honored to work hand in hand with scores of gifted authors, and as I did my best to offer them and their books support, attention, and care, they gave much to me as well. I bow particularly to Gail Buckley, Michael Chabon, E. L. Doctorow, David Ebershoff (who efficiently doubled as a superb colleague), Janet Evanovich, Brenda Fowler, Leonard Garment, Jesse Green, Gerald Gunther, Fred Hobson, Frances Kazan, Lauren Kessler, Tom King, Michael Korda, Elizabeth Lesser, Robert K. Massie, Patrick McGrath, Nancy Milford, David Mitchell, Edmund Morris, Angela Nissel, Whitney Otto, Suzan-Lori Parks, Thomas Perry, Michael Pollan, Peter Quinn, Frank Rich, Sam Roberts, Isabella Rossellini (it's a long story, and a good one), Nancy Rubin, Richard Russo, Lisa See, Nancy Silverton, Elizabeth Spencer, Peter Straub, and Calvin Trillin.

My voyage these last few years has been guided and safeguarded by myriad beacons of light. I can't possibly thank here everyone I'd like to and ought, so this improbably succinct (no, really) list must serve as synecdoche, with a pledge to convey further gratitude face-to-face as the opportunity presents itself:

Ryan Adams, Sam Adams, Robert Arbuckle, Kevin Ashton, Mark Athitakis, Nathalie Atkinson, Dan Barry, Roland Bates, John Baxindine, Tom Beer, Adam Begley, Matt Bell, Jolanta Benal, Brooks Benjamin, Melanie Benjamin, Eric

Berlin, Jesse Berney, Glenda Burgess, Allison Burnett, Isaac Butler, Rosanne Cash, Kashana Cauley, Alexander Chee, Nicole Chung, Sarah Churchwell, Donald Clarke, Meg Waite Clayton, Nicole Cliffe, Jon Clinch, Clare Conville, Isabel Costello, Nick Coveney, Gregory Crouch, Quinn Cummings, Anne Margaret Daniel, Kevin Daly, Sir William Davenant, Dexter Davenport, A. N. Devers, Colin Dickey, Nathan Dunbar, Rhian Ellis, Teressa Esposito, Stephen Farrow, William Fatzinger, Jr., Tim Federle, Adam Feldman, Charles Finch, Toby Finlay, D. Foy, Chris Geidner, Eve Gordon, Elon Green, Matt Greene, Elizabeth Hackett, Rahawa Haile, Alex Halpern, Josh Hanagarne, Liberty Hardy, Quentin Hardy, Benjamin Harnett, Mark Harris, Scott Jordan Harris, Jamey Hatley, Bill Hayes, Meredith Hindley, Elliott Holt, Alexander Huls, Brian Jay Jones, Molly Jong-Fast, Guy Gavriel Kay, Joe Keenan, April Kimble, Julie Klam, Brian Koppelman, Rick Kot, Kalen Landow, Victor LaValle, J. Robert Lennon, Kelly Link, Laura Lippman, Brian Lombardi, Laura Lorson, Lyle Lovett, Lisa Lucas, Kelly Luce, Sarah Lyall, Jon Maas, Susan Elia MacNeal, Ben Mankiewicz, Josh Mankiewicz, Lily Mars, Max Maven, Alicia Mayer, Walter Mayes, Theodore McCombs, John McDougall, Jenny McPhee, Jennifer Mendelsohn, Susan Scarf Merrell, Lincoln Michel, A. R. Moxon, Laurie Muchnick, Jennifer Mudge, Tomás Murray.

Breath.

Phyllis Nagy, Patrick Nathan, Farran Smith Nehme, Sally Nemeth, JD Nevesytrof, Sandra Newman, Maud Newton, Celeste Ng, Liz Nugent, Daniel José Older, Kerry O'Malley, Annette O'Toole, Pippin Parker, Bethanne Patrick, Nathaniel Penn, Sarah Perry, Lisa Jane Persky, Megan Phelps-Roper, Arthur Phillips, Andrew Pippos, Ivan Plis, Seth Pollins, Lily Potkin, Charlotte Prong, Paul Reid, Leela Rice, Mark Richard, Ben Rimalower, Michael Rizzo, Doug Robertson, Isabel Rogers, Helen Rosner, Gabriel Roth, Eric Ruben, Tim Sailer, Luc Sante, Mark Sarvas, Michael Schaub, Lucy Schaufer, Will

Scheffer, Amy Scheibe, J. Smith-Cameron, Justin St. Germain, Levi Stahl, Daniel Summers, Claudette Sutherland, Quinn Sutherland, Sam Thielman, Paul Tremblay, Peternelle van Arsdale, Eileen Vorbach, Ayelet Waldman, Tim Walker, Amanda Eyre Ward, Todd Waring, Katharine Weber, Sarah Weinman, Kate Williams, Shauna Wright, Simon Wroe, Stephanie Zacharek, Laura Zigman, Jess Zimmerman, Stefano Zocchi, and Renée Zuckerbrot.

Was it not the poet who said, "Wait, I'm just beginning"?

I salute the members of Wordsmith Twitter, that peculiar subset on whom I rely for so many things, including keeping me in line, among them Mark Allen, Colleen Barry, Ashley Bischoff, Emily Brewster, DeAnna Burghart, Jeremy Butterfield, Stan Carey, June Casagrande, Iva Cheung, Karen Conlin, Katy Cooper, Jon Danziger, Allan Fallow, Emmy Jo Favilla, Mignon Fogarty, James M. Fraleigh, Nancy Friedman, Joe Fruscione, Henry Fuhrmann, Peter Ginna, Jennifer Gracen, Jonathon Green, Sarah Grey, James Harbeck, Andy Hollandbeck, Ross Howard, Martyn Wendell Jones, Blake Leyers, Gretchen McCulloch, John McIntyre, Erin McKean, Lisa McLendon, Howard Mittelmark, Lynne Murphy, Lauren Naturale, Mary Norris, Jonathon Owen, Maria Petrova, Carol Fisher Saller, Heather E. Saunders, Laura Sewell, Jesse Sheidlower, Peter Sokolowski, Daniel Sosnoski, Dawn McIlvain Stahl, Kory Stamper, Eugenie Todd, Christian Wilkie, Karen Wise, and Ben Yagoda.

For keeping me alive and kicking when that seemed something other than an inevitability, I thank Keili Glynn and Jori Masef, and for ongoing maintenance I thank Christina Sekaer and Noa Phuntsok.

For invaluable guidance, I thank Catherine Boyle, Gregor Gardner, and Katharina Tornau.

Love of an ineffable sort to Alan Bowden, Hannah Bowden, Joe Chiplock, Kathleen Daly, Alison Fraser, Ron Goldberg, Ruth Hirshey, Rupert Holmes, Susan Kartzmer, Mark Leydorf, Paraic O'Donnell, Deanna Raybourn, Sabrina Wolfe, Jacob Yeagley, and Jeff Zentner.

To the memory of Kenn Hempel, Victor D'Altorio, and Martha Lavey.

For her boundless love, compassion, generosity of spirit, and wit, I continue to pledge my fealty to Her Grace Duchess Goldblatt. One could not ask for a truer fictitious friend.

Victory Matsui, Cal Morgan, and Cassie Jones Morgan were key and crucial readers of this work at key and crucial moments, and Jon Meacham makes his presence known in all the best ways.

Out of the goodness of his heart, Mathew Lyons bestowed on me a most precious gift: a title.

In a class by themselves are my muses Amy Bloom, Rachel Joyce, Yiyun Li, Elizabeth McCracken, and that one particular spirit who cloaks herself in shadow but every now and then lets me know she's there, paying attention.

A unique thank you to the unique Sanyu Dillon, who might not have known what a seemingly offhand remark one noontime would lead to, but probably, in that way she has, did.

I do not have anything like the proper words to thank Kate Medina, Connie Schultz, Elizabeth Strout, and Ann Wroe, but I will do my best to embody my devotion for the rest of my days.

I am grateful to my departmental colleagues, with whom I collaborate day after day to produce, all credit to them, excellent book after excellent book: Pam Alders, Ted Allen, Rebecca Berlant, Matt Burnett, Evan Camfield, Kelly Chian, Nancy Delia, Paul Gilbert, Penny Haynes, Laura Jensen, Dylan Julian, Vincent La Scala, Steve Messina, Loren Noveck, Beth Pearson, Jennifer Rodriguez, Leah Sims, and Janet Wygal. And particular gratitude to my brother in arms and this book's mighty production editor, Dennis Ambrose.

My dazzling agent, Jennifer Joel, has been my tireless champion from the day we first breakfasted—impossibly patient, affectionately imposing, eternally supportive. Through the great swaths of time when I was certain I couldn't and wouldn't ever complete this book, she made certain that I knew that I both could and would. And thus I did.

I have benefited immeasurably from the guidance of supernal editors Noah Eaker, Ben Greenberg, and Molly Turpin, who have, as necessary (and boy was it necessary), word-wrangled, nerve-soothed, whip-cracked, head-patted, and gone a terribly long time never quite knowing who was stalking them on any given day: the briskly efficient managing editor or the utterly rattled author.

Gina Centrello, Lisa Feuer, and Susan Kamil have been my generals, my guides, my encouragers, and my friends, and they have supported me in myriad ways, this book almost least among them. They have made and maintained a place for me, and that, as they say, has made all the difference.

Tom Perry and Andy Ward are two of the hardest-working men in show business, and surely the smartest. And kindest. And cleverest.

Carole Lowenstein designed this book's text so empathically that, as I first set eyes on her jubilantly brandished sheaf of sample pages, I knew that I was seeing precisely what I'd been hoping to see for years, which she rightfully presented as an exquisite inevitability.

The jacket is as well everything I could have dreamed of, and I hope that the insides of the book have lived up to the wit and elegance of that which is wrapped around them. For this I thank Jamie Keenan and Joe Perez.

Production manager Richard Elman knows how to turn a book into A Book: a tangible, palpable, corporeal thing, beautiful to look at and a pleasure to hold. I thank him for mine.

My publicist, Melanie DeNardo, has done a capital job of preparing me for the world and vice versa, and audio producer Kelly Gildea, director Scott Cresswell, and engineer Brian Ramcharan have given me voice.

Bonnie Thompson is (literally!) a copy editor's copy editor, and I'm happily beholden to her for cheering me on while kindly calling out all my worst habits, firmly disagreeing with me when I needed to be firmly disagreed with, bringing order to my endlessly digressive digressions, and every now and then oh just *suggesting* a bit of alternate text so astonishingly adept that I had no choice but to appropriate it and stuff it into the manuscript. As I trust she knew I would.

Further shout-out to proofreaders Kristin Jones, Kristen Strange, and Rachel Broderick, for scouring, scrubbing, crossing the i's, dotting the t's.

Thank you to Chris Carruth, for indexing above and beyond the call of duty.

In further and appropriate gratitude, I would, if I could, set here the full contents of the Random House divisional phone directory, but I must of necessity home in on this book's particular co-creators and express my appreciation to and for: Rachel Ake, Jennifer Backe, Janice Barcena, Maria Braeckel, Heather Brown, Porscha Burke, Jessica Cashman, Dan Christensen, Susan Corcoran, Denise Cronin, Andrea DeWerd, Toby Ernst, Barbara Fillon, Deborah Foley, Lisa Gonzalez, Michael Harney, Mika Kasuga, Cynthia Lasky, Leigh Marchant, Matthew Martin, Sally Marvin, Caitlin McCaskey, Catherine Mikula, Grant Neumann, Tom Nevins, Allyson Pearl, Paolo Pepe, Matt Schwartz, James Smith, Philip Stamper-Halpin, Bill Takes, Patsy Tucker, Katie Tull, Erin Valerio, Sophie Vershbow, Stacey Witcraft, Katie Zilberman, and Theresa Zoro.

I can't, I find, bring adjectives and adverbs to the subject of my family, because family is too big a concept, too brimming with content, to be neatly modified. Simply, then: To Diana and Stanley Dreyer, to Nancy Dreyer (and the late Joan Koffman), to Gabriel Dreyer, to Sam Hess, to Julie Toll, James MacLean, Emma MacLean, and Henry MacLean, to Diane Greenberg: Thank you for being on my side.

Her very own thank you to Sallie, because she is the dictionary definition of unconditional love and is, as well, a Very Good Girl.

And finally: Robert Schmehr is my traveling companion, my heart and my soul, my first thought every morning and my last thought every night. Robert, you have waited a long time for this book. Here it is.

INDEX

ABOUT THE AUTHOR

BENJAMIN DREYER is vice president, executive managing editor and copy chief, of Random House. He began his publishing career as a freelance proofreader and copy editor. In 1993, he became a production editor at Random House, where he oversaw books by writers including Michael Chabon, Edmund Morris, Suzan-Lori Parks, Michael Pollan, Peter Straub, and Calvin Trillin. He has copyedited books by authors including E. L. Doctorow, David Ebershoff, Frank Rich, and Elizabeth Strout, as well as *Let Me Tell You,* a volume of previously uncollected work by Shirley Jackson. A graduate of Northwestern University, he lives in New York City.

Twitter: @BCDreyer

ABOUT THE TYPE

This book was set in Sabon, a typeface designed by the well-known German typographer Jan Tschichold (1902–74). Sabon's design is based upon the original letter forms of sixteenth-century French type designer Claude Garamond and was created specifically to be used for three sources: foundry type for hand composition, Linotype, and Monotype. Tschichold named his typeface for the famous Frankfurt typefounder Jacques Sabon (c. 1520–80).